THE POLITICS OF
RESTORATIVE JUSTICE

THE POLITICS OF RESTORATIVE JUSTICE

A CRITICAL INTRODUCTION

ANDREW
WOOLFORD

Fernwood Publishing • Halifax & Winnipeg

Editing: Tara Seel
Cover Design: John van der Woude
Printed and bound in Canada by Hignell Book Printing
Printed on FSC Certified paper.

Mixed Sources
Product group from well-managed forests and other controlled sources
www.fsc.org Cert no. SW-COC-003438
© 1996 Forest Stewardship Council

Published in Canada by Fernwood Publishing
32 Oceanvista Lane
Black Point, Nova Scotia, B0J 1B0
and #8 - 222 Osborne Street, Winnipeg, Manitoba, R3L 1Z3
www.fernwoodpublishing.ca

Fernwood Publishing Company Limited gratefully acknowledges the financial support of the Government of Canada through the Book Publishing Industry Development Program (BPIDP), the Canada Council for the Arts and the Nova Scotia Department of Tourism and Culture for our publishing program.

 Canadian Heritage Patrimoine canadien The Canada Council for the Arts Le Conseil des Arts du Canada NOVA SCOTIA Tourism and Culture

Library and Archives Canada Cataloguing in Publication

Woolford, Andrew, 1971-
The politics of restorative justice : a critical introduction / Andrew Woolford.

Includes bibliographical references.
ISBN 978-1-55266-316-5

1. Restorative justice--Political aspects. 2. Restorative justice. I. Title.

HV8688.W65 2009   364.68   C2009-901070-0

Contents

Preface and Acknowledgments

This text derives from a space of ambivalence. On the one hand, I fashion myself a critical scholar, since in much of my academic work, I deploy insights drawn from critical social theory to interrogate and problematize dispute resolution claims. On the other hand, I spend a portion of my non-academic hours as chair of the board of directors of the John Howard Society of Manitoba, an agency that describes its principles and mission statement in the language of restorative justice. This ambivalence, I believe, is reflected in the make-up of this book, in which I attempt to challenge restorative justice, which emphasizes the involvement of offenders, victims, and community members in resolving the harms associated with crime, for all its potential faults, but also leave room for its improvement and advancement — for it to become something more than what it already is.

This book is also the product of having taught a course on restorative justice at the University of Manitoba for the past six years. When Wayne Antony approached me with the idea of writing a text on the topic, my first inclination was to decline. I had just then completed a manuscript with my co-author, R.S. Ratner, in which we compare restorative justice with civil mediation and reparations politics, and I was not sure that I had much more to say on this topic. I also was not convinced we needed yet another text on restorative justice. However, I eventually decided to give it a try, simply because I felt there was an absence of introductory-level texts that offer a critical sociological investigation of restorative justice concepts. My aforementioned manuscript, as well as George Pavlich's work, provide critical social theoretical insights into the conceptualization and practice of restorative justice, but are written for more advanced students. In contrast, this book aims to bring critical sociological awareness of restorative justice to students in their second or third year of university or college classes, as well as to practitioners and those in the general public interested in matters of restorative justice. This does not mean that this text is always an "easy" read. It is my firm pedagogical belief that students at all levels of learning must be pushed to expand their vocabularies and to contend with abstract and complicated ideas. While I try to clearly communicate theoretical concepts, I am loath to boil them down to the point where they become oversimplified and deprived of their full critical force.

I was also swayed to write this book because I felt insufficient thought had been directed toward what I term here "the politics of restorative justice." This is not to say that politics had not already factored into many previous studies of restorative justice — certainly, it had. However, these authors tended to work with a narrower conception of politics, locating restorative justice within a political world, but not questioning the ways in which restorative justice is itself complicit in certain forms of politics. In addition, there is a noted communicative divide between the theory and practice of restorative justice (Gavrielides 2007) whereby the insights of restorative justice theory find less traction within actually existing restorative justice programs. In my view, the bridge to cross this divide can be forged through a theoretical investigation of the political context and political meanings of restorative justice, which can then contribute to a strategic conceptualization of the way forward for restorative justice.

I offer these thoughts as a preface out of the belief that all projects should begin from a point of reflexivity. As an author presenting a description of what restorative justice is and a vision of what restorative justice could be, it is important to reflect upon my grounding assumptions that are the framework for my understanding of this phenomenon, since these factors certainly shade and influence the interpretations presented in this book. So let me reveal up front that, intuitively speaking, the values of restorative justice initially "felt right" to me when I first came upon them, in the sense that I have, since my early teens, been slow to anger and more one to reflect upon the elements of a conflict than to rush in and take sides. This is, in part, a product of a particular Christian upbringing, where the pastoral figure of Christ as wise, understanding, and forgiving served as an ideal role model. However, although elements of this upbringing certainly remain operative within my current sense of self, I lost this faith during my early university years when a Marxist atheism spoke more directly to my working-class roots and the sense of alienation I felt within what I perceived to be an upper-middle-class university milieu. Under this critical influence, I embraced more radical philosophies and longed for a praxis that would spark transformative social change.

Today, gone are the more feverish ideological attachments of my youth, although remnants are certainly still visible in the scholarly choices I make. But, out of both of these extremes come my more mature years, in which I hope to balance a desire for collaborative conflict resolution with an understanding of the need, at times, for direct and oppositional political action. This is the first guiding framework for this book. The second is a preference for viewing the world in flux rather than in fixity. Whereas some may be drawn to the parsimony and analytical clarity of an airtight typology, my goal is always to leave room in my conceptual models for process and change. In my view, although the world is consistently structured and sufficiently regular in a manner that allows us to navigate our day-to-day lives, it is also constantly in movement, requiring us to adapt and change our actions and thoughts, depending upon the circumstances. I seek to situate restorative justice within this world of flux — to demonstrate that the boundaries of this so-called justice alternative are not firmly set, and to leave room for the debates and discussions that create and re-create the universe of restorative justice.

This manuscript owes much to Wayne Antony, who convinced me to undertake this project. As well, I would like to acknowledge the excellent work of the Fernwood production team, especially Tara Seel (editing), Beverley Rach (design and layout), Debbie Mathers (pre-production), Brenda Conroy (proofreading), and John van der Woude (cover). Funding for the research that informs this book has come from the Social Sciences and Humanities research Council (SSHRC) of Canada and the University of Manitoba. The book has benefited from my conversations with Bob Ratner, Bryan Hogeveen, George Pavlich, Frank Cormier, Jens Meierhenrich, Rob Vallis, and the board of directors and staff of the John Howard Society of Manitoba. In addition, the constructive suggestions made by Kearney Healey and the two anonymous readers helped me refine and expand my initial manuscript. A great debt is also owed to Rene Durocher for generously allowing me to begin the manuscript with his amazing story. I look forward to his future memoir and the full telling of these events. Moreover, thanks are extended to Steve Brickey and Elizabeth Comack, who have offered me wise career advice and opportunities for intellectual growth.

Jessica and Ella Woolford have buoyed and supported me always, but especially as my manuscript deadline loomed. Finally, I owe a great debt to my 1994 Geo Metro in which I sat and wrote this manuscript, free from the distractions of home and office. I also thank the residents living near Stafford and Grant Avenues in Winnipeg for putting up with a strange fellow sitting in his beat-up car while typing away on his notebook computer.

Chapter 1

Introduction to the
Politics of Restorative Justice

R ene Durocher spent twenty-three years of his life as an inmate in seventeen different penitentiaries. He entered his first correctional institution at the age of seventeen for an act of armed robbery. At the time, the Crown decided to try Mr. Durocher as an adult to teach him a lesson — a lesson for which he was not yet ready. Raised in a large family by an abusive father, Mr. Durocher had learned to use his fearlessness and daring to get what he wanted. And although he never wanted to physically hurt anyone, he did not expend much thought on the emotional and financial harm he was exacting upon his victims.

Rene Durocher was released in 1963, but found himself back in prison within the year. He had walked into a store while firing a newly purchased shotgun into the air. Once again, he was arrested, and this time, he was sentenced to fourteen years. While in prison, he took lessons from the more experienced inmates and eagerly awaited parole to test his new criminal knowledge. However, when at last he was released on parole, this knowledge soon failed him, and he was re-arrested only four months later. In this instance, he and some associates had purchased machine guns and were using them to conduct bank robberies. One robbery went wrong, and a shoot-out transpired. Mr. Durocher exchanged fire with the police with little thought of the risk to himself and others. He was the only one of the bank robbers who was not shot that day.

In prison again, this time for twenty-two years (and only twenty-five years old), Mr. Durocher had earned the respect of his fellow inmates. He was the "crazy Frenchman" who had shot at the police. However, Mr. Durocher ignored his notoriety and sought to improve his formal education. While in prison, he also fell in love. Upon his third release from prison, he tried to lead a law-abiding life, but after several bad jobs and a failed business venture, Mr. Durocher found himself in debt to organized crime, with a wife and two children to support. To correct the situation, he returned to what he knew best — crime — and participated in what was, at that time, the biggest robbery in Canadian history. On July 8, 1985, Mr. Durocher and his partners robbed a Brinks truck. He used the money from the robbery to buy a house and pet store. He was arrested for a final time six months later.

It was only at this point in his life that Mr. Durocher began to try to change himself. He worked with the prison psychologist at Stony Mountain

Penitentiary in Manitoba and learned to take responsibility for his crimes and to recognize the harm he had done to others. Upon his final release from prison, he committed himself to helping others and has since worked with agencies, such as Lifeline, the John Howard Society of Manitoba, and the St. Leonard's Society, to assist inmates in turning their lives around.

The retributive mode of punishment, which seeks to be "tough" on offenders in order to deter future criminal activity, clearly did not help reform Mr. Durocher. For Rene Durocher, prison often felt like "home," and it was not until he was prepared to change himself that he was able to shake his criminal career. This raises the questions: might another approach to justice have helped lead Mr. Durocher to this realization sooner? If so, are we as a society ready to think differently about justice and to provide offenders meaningful opportunities to reform themselves? And are we ready and willing to reform society in the process?

Introducing Restorative Justice

To answer these questions, we must first look at our justice impulses because when we hear about crimes like those committed by Mr. Durocher, our first instinct is, typically, to call for punishment, no matter how counter-productive this punishment may be. Indeed, the punitive conceptualization of justice is deeply ingrained. From early in our lives, we are inculcated with notions of right and wrong, and of just and unjust punishment. This conditioning is further reinforced by a cultural mythology of criminal justice. A common motif of our culture is the good (eventually) receive the rewards and the bad are punished. Thus, justice is culturally constructed as an either/or dichotomy and is assumed to have winners and losers. Imagine the difficulty, then, of trying to encourage a different notion of justice, one designed to care for the different needs of those who commit harms and those who are harmed. Such a project would require more than just platitudes and good ideas; it would require a politics — a strategic plan for countering the current arrangements of social power — to challenge entrenched and dominant notions of justice. This book is intended to contribute to such a project. Through an introduction to the basic themes, theories, and practices of restorative justice, I hope to demonstrate that restorative justice is an idea that needs to achieve traction and resonance within a distinctly political environment. Moreover, I will propose that restorative justice must develop an enabling politics so it may more effectively spread its messages among the general public and contribute to social transformation. However, before we can approach the issue of the politics of restorative justice, we must first contend with the question of what restorative justice is.

Restorative justice is a term deployed with great frequency within contemporary criminal justice systems. More and more, criminal justice programs aimed at diverse goals, such as reintegrating offenders, healing victims, and dealing with crime in communities, describe their principles and their mission statements in the language of restorative justice. As well, restorative justice is receiving greater recognition in formal law. The 1999 *Youth Justice and Criminal Evidence Act* in England and Wales and the 2003 Canadian *Youth Criminal Justice Act* both make room for restorative practices within their respective youth justice systems (Crawford and Newburn 2002; Charbonneau 2004). In 2002, the United Nations released its guidelines for applying restorative justice to criminal matters, touting restorative justice as a legitimate and beneficial means for dealing with criminal harms (United Nations Economic and Social Council 2000; see also United Nations 2007). Thus, restorative justice has achieved a great deal of political recognition over recent years and has come to be viewed in many quarters as a viable alternative within the criminal justice system. This trend is evident in the numerous restorative justice programs sprouting up worldwide.

Despite its growing popularity, restorative justice does not lend itself to easy definition. For example, it is often described as a participatory practice that involves the victim, offender, and community in resolving the harm caused by a specific crime. More directly, according to Tony Marshall's (1999: 5) definition, it

> is a process whereby all the parties with a stake in a particular offence come together to resolve collectively how to deal with the aftermath of the offence and its implications for the future.

An image that immediately springs to mind is of a rural community hall where neighbours gather to discuss a criminal event, such as a break and enter. The offenders are present with heads bowed to demonstrate the deep shame they feel as they stand before their community. The victims are there as well and are surrounded by their supporters. And what unfolds is a conversation that results in a novel solution: the offenders, sincerely apologetic, offer to help the victims clean the mess and recover their losses; the community unites around victim and offender, offering their collective support; the victims forgive and move forward with neither hatred nor fear nesting in their hearts. This romantic narrative is a potential reality, but it does not reflect the typical practice or outcomes of restorative justice (Daly 2003). In many cases, offenders are slow to repent, victims refuse to participate, and communities are largely indifferent to or unaware of the entire business. In response to these and other challenges, restorative justice programs will often adapt their practices while, at the same time, seek to remain located within a more general restorative justice conceptual framework. For example, they may choose to work with an offender who appears ready to take responsibility and change his behaviour, even without direct victim and community involvement.

The absence of these key stakeholders may perhaps be addressed through the involvement of proxy victims (i.e., victims of similar crimes who communicate to the offender what one may experience when one is a victim of this sort of incident) or through a written statement made by the victim, and the program workers may themselves stand-in for the community, articulating the fear and distrust crime breeds. However, with these adaptations, the restorative justice program strays from Marshall's definition of restorative justice: that is, it is a stretch to say the offence is being collectively resolved when such changes are put into effect.

Perhaps, then, a more flexible and accurate definition of restorative justice would be along the following lines: "Restorative justice attempts to address the harm(s) caused by crime in a manner that meets the specific needs of the involved parties while using the resources available." This definition communicates the adaptability of restorative justice. However, it is unsatisfactory in that it lacks precision. What is there in this definition to differentiate restorative justice from other criminal justice practices? Do not criminal courts, at times, also fit this description? Imagine, for example, two individuals awaiting a court hearing. One, the accused, sits nervously with his lawyer, wondering about his fate. The other, the victim, is ready to serve as a witness and has prepared a victim impact statement to express the harm he suffered at the hands of the accused. The act of writing this statement has afforded him some relief, allowing him to name the confusing emotions he felt in the aftermath of the event. Then, immediately before the trial, the Crown attorney approaches the victim to inform him they are considering a plea bargain. She reports that the accused has taken responsibility for his actions, has begun alcohol and anger management treatment, and is not perceived to pose a threat to the community. The victim, relieved to see the accused is making positive efforts to change his life, as well as happy to avoid the stress of the courtroom, gives his blessing to the plea bargain (although the Crown could move forward with the plea bargain without this blessing) and subsequently leaves the courthouse feeling the matter is resolved. Is this restorative justice? If so, how is it that a restorative moment arises within the alleged adversarial environment of the criminal justice system?

One may assume that, if restorative justice amounts to anything at all, there must be something at its core that would allow us to differentiate it analytically from adversarial approaches to justice. It is not enough to say it is "informal," "healing," and "participatory," since all of these aspects were present in the plea bargain example offered above. In this example, the lawyers for each party informally negotiated the plea bargain, the offender was set on a path of healing, and the victim was offered a modicum of participation. Therefore, for the sake of conceptual clarity, we must seek to identify some of restorative justice's *ideal traits*. Restorative justice is:

1. *Open and Actively Participatory*: Restorative justice is open to the participation of all interested parties, although it does not mandate their participation. Moreover, this participation is *active* in the sense that it allows participants more than just a consultative role; indeed, they have an actual say in the process and outcomes. In the plea bargain example used above, the victim was set to act as a witness, and was later consulted on the plea bargain, but his role could hardly be described as "active" participation in the sense that he would be able to offer suggestions or information that would sway or alter the course of the justice process.

2. *Empowering*: This active role for participants is intended to offer participants in restorative justice a significant degree of ownership over the process. They play a part in determining how the process will unfold and in the decision-making that is the crux of restorative justice practice. This offers them an investment in the resolution, which ideally results in them becoming the principal agents of its implementation. Returning to the plea bargain example, the victim left the courtroom more with a feeling of relief than empowerment. He held no personal investment in the resolution, but rather merely experienced some ease of mind that his assailant was now set upon a more positive path and unlikely to re-offend in the near future. However, he has received nothing from this experience that will allow him to better manage future conflicts.

3. *Satisfying and Offers a Relational Healing Process*: Restorative justice derives its legitimacy not from state support or by achieving state-designed outcomes; instead, its primary objectives are to satisfy participants with respect to their collectively negotiated resolution and to start them on a process toward healing the harms associated with the wrongful event (Llewllyn and House 1998). In short, it seeks to give participants an opportunity to fashion something positive out of a negative event. Certainly, the plea bargain described above brought the parties a degree of satisfaction, but much of this occurred through the independent actions of the parties (e.g., the accused took it upon himself to seek help with anger and alcohol issues), rather than through a "relational" process, which refers to an interactive process that engages existing relationships, but also helps create new ones.

These ideal traits provide a basic framework with which we might assess the restorative-ness of any given program, but we still must be prepared to find anomalies. In any specific application of restorative justice, moments may arise when these ideals are unreachable or temporarily bracketed. Take the case of Don and Mary Struefert, who in 1991 lost their eighteen-year-old daughter, Carin, at the hands of Guy Sullivan and Jim Swanson in Minnesota. Guy Sullivan and Jim Swanson forced Carin at gunpoint into their van before taking her to a wooded area where they raped and murdered her. The arrest and prosecution of the two culprits left the Strueferts feeling unfulfilled, thus leading Don to consider restorative justice as a post-sentencing reconciliation option. This means the restorative justice meetings would have no bearing on Sullivan's and Swanson's sentences, which had already been determined by a judge. Rather, the restorative justice program, in this case, was intended largely to allow the victims to ask questions of the offenders as a step on their personal journey of recovery. Sullivan agreed to meet with the Strueferts, resulting in some very emotional and oftentimes frustrating sessions (see the National Film Board of Canada documentary, *Glimmer of Hope*).

Returning to the ideal traits listed above, while Don maintained a largely positive attitude toward the restorative justice process throughout its course, Mary experienced moments when she felt neither empowered nor satisfied. For example, when Sullivan told the Strueferts that Carin's last words amounted to a plea for him to help her, Mary was overwhelmed at the thought that Sullivan just stood there and did nothing, and she felt intense anger toward him. Yet, a decade after first meeting with Guy Sullivan, Mary told a crowd in Winnipeg she had forgiven Sullivan. She had only realized this when she learned Sullivan had overcome his illiteracy, and she discovered that she was, at that moment, very proud of him.

When examining *actually existing restorative justice*, one is confronted with the limits of such lists of ideal traits. The Strueferts experience of restorative justice can be described as open, participatory, empowering, satisfying, and healing, but not consistently throughout its application. There were moments of deep hurt before healing eventually occurred. There were times when empowerment was frustrated by conversations characterized by problematic communication, and satisfaction was not an immediate or guaranteed outcome of the Strueferts interactions with Sullivan. Of course, analytical categories, like the ideal traits listed above, are only intended as a guide to our thinking and should not be taken to be perfect realizations of the actual world, since concepts are rarely able to fully contain the complexity of social reality. Thus, to complement this list of ideal traits, and to add an important reminder of its limits while also capturing inconsistencies within actual restorative justice practice, let us try to establish some of the basic *morphological properties* of restorative justice. Morphological properties are so called because they alert us to the malleability and uncertain shape of restorative justice.

1. *Restorative justice is contextually specific*: it must adapt its practice to specific harm contexts rather than applying a "one size fits all" approach. "Crime" is a term with varying meanings that is used to describe a diversity of events, ranging from minor offences against property and person to massive scale destruction, such as genocide. It would be naïve

to expect we could develop a concept of restorative justice that would definitively prescribe the processes used and outcomes to be achieved in response to such a broad range of events. This is even more true, as we will see in the next chapter, for those restorative programs that want to deal with harms beyond those that are designated as "crime" (such as regulatory offences like those related to the spread of pollutants). Thus, whatever restorative justice *is*, it will change as it is applied in multiple and complex circumstances. Restorative justice will also adapt to specific cultural contexts with respect to both its practice and outcomes. For example, whereas certain cultural communities employing restorative justice may reject all forms of punishment (e.g., prison) as inappropriate, others may find cultural practices of punishment (e.g., banishment from the community) as a reasonable outcome for a restorative meeting.

2. *Restorative justice is a process*: it does not follow a pre-set linear course; instead, it is a process through which the parties arc offered an opportunity to create new positive meanings out of a situation that they, in most cases, experienced as negative. Given this processual character, it is impossible to impose specific desired outcomes on restorative justice. Facilitators of restorative justice may enter restorative meetings with an ideal script in mind of how they would like the meeting to transpire — e.g., that the parties will move from describing and emoting about the events toward problem-solving — but they still must be prepared to allow this process to unfold in a winding manner, with fits and starts, progress and fallbacks.

3. *Restorative justice is negotiated and can be the subject of heated debate and disagreement*: it is not guaranteed that participants will simply embrace one another in a desire to resolve their conflict. Restorative outcomes are difficult to reach and often require heated negotiations to arrive at a point of resolution. This point can also be used to help us better accept the debates and disagreements that exist over the definition of restorative justice. Restorative justice, as a social movement (see below), is in a constant process of negotiating its meaning, or identity, and therefore, it is perfectly understandable that there exists no one master definition of the concept.

4. *Restorative justice is a living model*: it is not any unitary "thing" but, rather, a continuously evolving body of ideas intended to articulate a method of justice built upon the active participation of stakeholders. Ideally, what we understand restorative justice to be today will not be the same as what it is in the future. Preferable would be a restorative justice that has developed, reformed, and/or revised itself to meet future challenges.

A final morphological property that is true of my own ideal, but one I cannot claim to be true for all forms of restorative justice, is that restorative justice is *transformative* (Morris 1994; Sullivan and Tifft 2001). By transformative, I mean restorative justice creates conditions for pursuing forms of personal and, perhaps more importantly, social change. Indeed, restorative justice should be concerned with more than just the crime or conflict that triggered the restorative justice meeting. It must be about fostering opportunities for individuals and collectives to evaluate their lives and their worlds, and to initiate attempts to bring change into these arenas: to address injustice and to improve the lives of the many. We saw in the example of the Strueferts and Guy Sullivan that the participants were able to take what was a very negative event and to fashion something positive out of it. This is not to say the positive can ever outweigh something as negative as the loss of a loved one; however, we can take a negative experience and learn from it in hopes of individual and societal improvement. Thus, restorative justice should be mobilized for purposes of transformation, whether in the form of everyday transformations, such as a commitment to greater personal literacy, or societal transformation, such as what is hoped will follow when restorative justice is employed in the aftermath of mass violence, or when people use a restorative justice meeting to discuss more broadly the social problems that affect their lives and to devise strategies for addressing these challenges. As will become increasingly evident throughout this book, my preference is toward a transformative restorative justice that reaches toward social change.

Let's examine another example to further illustrate the transformative potential of restorative justice, but also the role of politics in transformation. The South African Truth and Reconciliation Commission (SATRC) was intended to create public awareness about the harms committed under the racial system of apartheid and to initiate a society-wide conversation toward collective healing. For years, the apartheid government had used violence and torture to suppress black South African demands for equal rights and freedom, but when victims sought justice for acts of state violence, their claims were denied. Authorities told people who lost family members, or who had themselves been seriously scarred by apartheid violence, that their complaints were unfounded. In the aftermath of such circumstances, it was believed revelation of the truth of apartheid would have a transformative effect, and the South African Truth and Reconciliation Commission was to be the primary vehicle for this transformation. It should also be noted that the SATRC was, in part, a product of a political compromise. When the apartheid government fell, and Nelson Mandela's African National Congress was elected to power in 1994, this new government faced a tricky challenge: how could they deliver justice for past misdeeds when the people who committed these misdeeds still held a great deal of power in South African society? The civil service, the judiciary, and the military, for example, still rested in the hands of the whites, and there was a risk civil war would erupt if the new government sought to drag too many of these people before a tribunal. Thus, although the SATRC does possess transformative potential, it, nonetheless, owes its existence to favourable political circumstances that made its brand of justice appear more palatable (Adam 2001).

In this case, we see the transformative potential of a restorative process narrowed by prevailing political conditions. This brings us to the major theme of this book: the politics of restorative justice. For restorative justice to live up to its transformative potential, there needs to be a deeper understanding of the political contexts in which restorative justice is situated and through which it operates so restorative justice may be more effectively strategized as a form of transformative politics.

The Politics of Restorative Justice

This book begins with the observation that restorative justice is a *political* process. Restorative justice is political in at least three senses:

1. Restorative justice exists in a political context that is, at different times, favourable, unfavourable, or indifferent to its practice, and which influences its conceptual development. Dominant political discourses and ideologies (i.e., the way the criminal justice system "thinks"), as well as institutional arrangements (i.e., the way the criminal justice system "works"), have an impact on how alternative policies, such as restorative justice, are received and implemented (if at all).

2. Restorative justice is itself a form of governance in that it aspires to change offender behaviour, heal victims, and revitalize communities (Pavlich 2005). These efforts complement governmental goals, such as ensuring social peace and minimizing costly forms of conflict. Following from this, because restorative justice can assist in the project of social control, it faces the constant danger that it may be co-opted and set to the task of reproducing dominant social relations.

3. Restorative justice needs to mobilize a politics in order to realize its broader social justice and transformative goals. Restorative justice advocates, or "restorativists," need to become politically savvy actors who are capable of navigating the political world. As mentioned in the previous point, one danger of failing to mobilize a politics of restorative justice is that other political actors will appropriate restorative justice and employ it toward their own instrumental ends. This has been the fate of other ethically-charged notions, such as "human rights," which, although promoted as being somehow apolitical in a pure conceptual sense, are still used by political powers to launch wars for strategic gain, such as the belated human rights justifications used to legitimize the most recent U.S. invasion of Iraq.

The purpose of this book is to move beyond outlining the justice ideals that inform the principles and practices of restorative justice and to initiate consideration of the challenges faced in implementing a transformative restorative justice under difficult political conditions. However, I should note up front that I employ a very broad notion of the political, by which I mean not just the narrow world of party politics and government, but also the politicized forces of economy, society, and culture that shape contemporary governance, as well as everyday life. The notion of the "political," then, is here used to reference the ever-present forces of power and domination, which work to maintain and entrench the current state of affairs in which economic and cultural control are predominantly in the hands of powerful actors, such as the political, economic, and state/military elites. Moreover, I do not merely wish to address restorative justice as an "object" of politics, in the sense that it is debated by political actors looking to tackle crime or gain popular support; rather, it is my intention to treat restorative justice as a political project — as a social movement working toward important forms of social and political change.

To refer to restorative justice as a social movement (Daly and Immarigeon 1998; Sullivan and Tifft 2001; Johnstone and Van Ness 2007), is not to say that restorative justice programs comprise a unified body of actors or that restorative justice philosophies form an undifferentiated body of ideas. As was suggested above, this is clearly not the case for restorative justice, but this is also not true for most, if any, social movements. Social movements are networks in which actors with varying interpretations of what the movement is about, and different levels of commitment to the movement, negotiate the meaning of a linked set of "big ideas" as well as their ideal application in everyday life. According to Mario Diani (1992: 1), social movements are

> Networks of informal interactions between a plurality of individuals, groups and/or organizations, engaged in political or cultural conflicts, on the basis of shared collective identities.

Thus, a social movement is not a single group or organization but rather a host of individual and collective agents engaged in a process of movement definition, issue or grievance articulation, activism, and program implementation. For example, within the environmental social movement, we see a number of agencies and individuals engaged in a project of articulating the dangers posed by environmental neglect and damage and proposing recommendations as to how we might rectify these problems. However, among this movement's supporters, we are likely to find a wide range of perspectives on environmental issues. The groups under the environmental movement umbrella range from those that are quite radical, such as Paul Watson's Earth First, to those that often seek to work in partnership with government, such as the David Suzuki Foundation. Efforts may be initiated to create conversations across these diverse groups, but the conversations are always ongoing and never fully resolved, other than, perhaps, in the form of occasional policy or protest statements framed around a single pressing issue (e.g., the harmful effects of clear-cut logging).

Such diversity is also true of the restorative justice movement, where heated debates occur among practitioners, theorists, and agencies with respect to questions like: can restorative justice work in cooperation with the formal criminal justice system, or does it require a completely separate institutional framework? How important is the involvement of offenders, victims, and community members in restorative justice processes? Should restorative justice be defined based on outcomes or processes? Is restorative justice a set of values or practices? What sort of practices can be considered "true" forms of restorative justice? (See Gavrielides 2007: 36–43 and Daly 2006:135 for a list of restorative justice "faultlines.") Rather than any particular answer to one of these questions being definitive of the restorative justice movement, it is the case that the process of negotiating possible answers to such questions is what constitutes the movement.

As a social movement, the meaning of restorative justice is negotiated by a group of actors that includes:

1. *Governing Authorities*: Even though they would not necessarily be considered part of the restorative justice social movement, state agencies and other governing bodies have an obvious influence on the restorative justice movement since they provide the resources (e.g., money and referrals) that make the practices of restorative justice possible. Much economic and administrative support for restorative justice programs comes from federal, provincial (or state), and/or municipal governments, each motivated by a specific set of goals, but also potentially wary of the bad "optics" that might arise from this support (e.g., if an offender who is processed through a restorative justice program recidivates by committing a high profile offence). Therefore, restorative justice agencies cannot rely on unconditional governmental support and often need to turn to non-governmental funding agencies, such as the United Way or private investors, to ensure their continued and unfettered operation.

2. *Restorative Justice Agencies*: These are the groups (both state-based and not-for-profit) that deliver actually existing restorative justice programs. Through their implementation of restorative justice, they play a significant role in defining what restorative justice is. They also face the difficult task of negotiating demands placed upon them by the governing authorities while still trying to remain faithful to the principles of restorative justice, as laid out by various restorative justice visionaries.

3. *Restorative Justice Visionaries*: This is the group of often charismatic practitioners, academic theorists, and other restorative justice advocates who contribute to the discussion about the collective definition of the restorative justice movement (e.g., what are its essential values and practices? What outcomes are truly restorative?). These are the people who are seen attending restorative justice conferences and writing books on the topic, trying to convince a broader public of the benefits of the restorative approach.

4. *Third Party Interests*: Restorative justice is not an isolated field of justice activity. The application of restorative justice has a significant bearing on the work performed by activists and practitioners in connected areas of concern, such as victim rights, prisoner rights, family violence, and abolitionism, to name but a few. Therefore, it is no surprise that critical and/or supportive contributions from these individuals are part of the restorative justice social movement. For example, Susan Herman (2004) of the National Centre for Victims of Crime has offered support to the idea of restorative justice but also expresses reservations that it still appears to be a very offender-centred process, much like the criminal justice system. Such criticisms have contributed to debates within restorative justice about the lack of attention to victim's needs and the overemphasis in some programs on offender reintegration, leading to attempts to define a more victim-centred model of restorative justice.

5. *Stakeholders*: Too often, the victims, offenders, and community members who are the primary subjects of the restorative justice movement, in that they are the ones who participate in restorative justice programs, are ignored voices within the larger movement. This should not be the case. Any appreciation for or dissatisfaction with restorative justice issuing from these stakeholders should become part of the broader discussions about what restorative justice is and should be.

It must be noted that an individual could move between categories, or find that he or she fits within multiple categories. However, despite this potential for fluidity and overlap, there are tensions existing between the categories that make it unlikely there will ever be complete agreement across the entire field of restorative justice. For example, whereas the governing authorities often seek to have restorative justice implemented in a manner that meets state goals of lowering recidivism and reducing the cost of justice, the visionaries tend to view the values and desired outcomes of restorative justice in a more holistic light, emphasizing goals such as individual and community healing. As mentioned above, restorative justice agencies must therefore navigate these perspectives, while also taking input from third parties and stakeholders.

To become a transformative social movement, restorative justice must resist conservative tendencies within this broader dynamic. Typically, for example, governing authorities are not seeking to foment social change through their (often limited) support of restorative justice; they are invested in the status quo and see restorative justice as a means to preserve it or to modestly improve it. Thus, it is with respect to the goal of transformation that a politics of restorative justice becomes most crucial. Returning to the three senses of the political upon which this book draws, a transformative politics of restorative justice would mean:

1. *Assessing the political context in which restorative justice operates.* What are the policy rationales that guide current government and donor thinking? In this book, emphasis will be placed on neoliberal politics and the influence it has had on criminal justice thinking in contemporary societies. Like restorative justice, neoliberalism is a flexible and context-specific form of governance, but one that attempts to shape local contexts in a manner that favours the profit and mobility demands of transnational corporations and investors. Neoliberals often support competing justice strategies rather than putting all of their eggs in the basket of one justice form. For minor crimes, they turn to informal, more cost-effective measures (such as restorative justice) as a way of making offenders more responsible for their actions and therefore less prone to re-offending. However, for repeat or major offenders, neoliberals often seek to bring to bear on the offender the full might of the state, using instruments such as minimum sentences, zero tolerance measures, and other forms of "tough on crime" punishment. Under such conditions, restorative justice advocates must be sensitive to the perpetual threat of co-optation. In other words, there is concern restorative justice will be adopted and supported by state actors so they can direct it toward acting as an accompaniment to the punitive criminal justice system, dealing with only the "small fish" (Hogeveen and Woolford 2006).

2. *This leads into the second form of politics, which concerns the fact that restorative justice constitutes a form of governance.* As an approach to "criminal" justice, restorative justice offers a means for dealing with actors who violate state-defined normative standards. Thus, restorative justice is inevitably immersed in the task of governing such "unruly" individuals. For this reason, it needs to find ways to think and apply its governance in a manner that goes beyond the dictates of the state, or, once again, it faces the threat of co-optation. Resistance to co-optation involves a reflexive assessment of restorative justice theories and practices to try to establish for restorative justice a foundation that does not depend solely on governmental definitions of wrongdoing, or import government assumptions about crime and criminals into its practice.

3. *Social movements articulate grievances in the hopes of seeing them register with the general public, as well as to foster or prevent social change.* To shift society from retributive and toward restorative justice standards requires strategic political engagement in order to spread the message of restorative justice and to have it resonate with the broader public. The Italian Marxist, Antonio Gramsci (1971), famously spoke of the need to launch both a "war of movement" and a "war of position." Whereas the war of movement consisted of the deployment of troops to achieve military control, the war of position aspires to win the battle for the people's hearts and minds. In Gramsci's view, society is entrenched by the *hegemony* of the ruling class, a dominant worldview that shades the way we see and act within the world. Through fostering their hegemony, the ruling class is able to transform its interests into a general "common sense," and thereby make ruling class goals and objectives seem natural and inevitable. According to this perspective, social change requires more than just the overthrow of the ruling powers — it necessitates an effort to transform the ways in which people think about the world around them. Simply put, a restorative justice war of position entails overcoming assumptions that punishment is the natural response to wrongdoing.

Politics and Justice

Much of the writing about restorative justice focuses upon what it means to be "restorative." This book also engages this question. However, its more pressing concern is that of "justice." On what grounds does restorative justice claim to be "justice?" What does it mean to be "just?" Without in-depth discussion of such questions, restorative justice risks operating based upon unacknowledged or disguised presuppositions, and therefore, it is more likely to solidify rather than transform existing relations of governance. That is to say, it fails to be honest (with others, but also with itself) about the basis for its principles and practice; this failure can result in notions of restorative justice that are grounded upon naïve and overly idealistic foundations.

The question of justice will receive more attention in the chapters that follow. To begin, a basic definition of justice is that it is a means to solving a problem by offering "a way out of a morass of conflicting claims" (Fisk 1993: 1). Justice can solve such conflicts in two basic ways. First, substantive theories of justice provide us a moral framework for deciding upon justice. In other words, the theory of justice guides us in deciding what the "substance" or content of justice should be. In contrast, procedural theories of justice offer no prescription for the substance of justice. Instead, they define a procedure through which fair and agreed-upon decisions might be made. Examples of such theories will be discussed in the next chapter. Although restorative justice is often described as a "process" or "procedure" (see Marshall's definition above), there are substantive qualities embedded within its practice (Pavlich 2007). This hidden substance will be addressed in later chapters, particularly Chapters 3 and 4.

Whether one's approach to justice is substantive or procedural, however, there still might be an expectation that just decisions will somehow be beyond politics. For example, in the tradition of justice inspired by the philosopher Emmanual Kant, the just individual is expected to separate himself or herself from the everyday world and to assume a reflective position that allows him or her to make a moral decision. In such a process, the mundane world of politics would simply be noise that would distract the individual decision-maker and therefore must be blocked out. However, such an ideal of justice is often far moved from reality. As Jürgen Habermas (1990) has argued, philosophers and judges can no longer assume themselves above or outside of the social world and therefore in a position to cast judgment on the requirements of justice. We are always already immersed in the social world and cannot simply bracket away its influences. Instead, we are left with the world of communicative engagement, where justice must be negotiated among individuals whose lives are deeply political.

Thus, justice is inseparable from the political, and, moreover, its pursuit requires a politics. Justice is inseparable from the political in the sense that it involves processes of negotiating the competing claims of politically situated actors, who each bring their own socially constructed worldviews to the negotiation table. Justice requires a politics because, in order to advance an alternative vision of justice or to institute new justice procedures, we must engage in political debates and discussions. Thus, justice is both a critical and a communicative project in that it involves assessing current political conditions and strategizing ways to advance a different vision of the world.

Chapter 2

What Events Trigger
a Restorative Response?

How does a restorative justice process begin? In a typical example, a criminal offence is committed, a suspect is apprehended, and something about the suspect makes him or her seem suited to restorative justice. Perhaps the accused takes immediate responsibility for his or her actions, or maybe she or he comes from a strong family and has good community supports to draw upon (although such criteria could result in class-biases in restorative justice, since "good families" are often assumed to be middle- and upper-class families). For some such reason, this person is considered a promising candidate for an alternative justice option, and they are typically referred to a restorative justice program by a police officer, judge, lawyer, counsellor, or other criminal justice gatekeeper — that is, someone who has sufficient authority or decision-making power to facilitate another person's progress through the criminal justice system.

Victims, however, can also initiate restorative justice processes, as was the case for Don and Mary Struefert (see Chapter 1). In this example, Don felt unsatisfied with the criminal justice system response and turned instead to a restorative justice program, arranging for a post-sentencing meeting with Guy Sullivan. Thus, there are a number of persons who are able to initiate a restorative justice intervention.

There are also a variety of times when an offender may be referred to a restorative justice program. Therefore, we should take some care to discuss the *stages* at which restorative justice may be introduced. These are:

- *Pre-sentencing*: restorative justice encounters may be held prior to sentencing, perhaps to clarify the matters of the dispute or so the meeting-derived recommendations can be passed along to the deciding judge. Such a process is more common, however, in civil (non-criminal) cases, where in some jurisdictions, defendants and complainants are mandated to take their case before a mediator before they can proceed to trial.
- *Sentencing*: restorative justice encounters may take place for purposes of sentencing. Here, the participants are empowered to decide upon an appropriate sanction and strategy for the offender to earn redemption. In many instances, participants will receive guidance from various justice professionals as to what sort of programs are available within the community to help the offender (e.g., addiction or anger management

programs). It is also quite often the case that a judge may need to approve the recommended outcomes to ensure the agreed upon sanction meets formal legal standards.

- *Post-sentencing*: victim and offender may meet in a mediated session after a judge has delivered the sentence. The offender may be held within a correctional institution or living within the community, but the restorative justice meeting has no bearing upon his or her sentence (other than potentially demonstrating the offender's commitment to taking responsibility and making positive changes, which could potentially be admissible to the proceedings of a parole hearing). Most importantly, such meetings are intended to address unanswered questions for the concerned parties.

The different stages at which restorative justice might take place are a further testament to the flexibility of the restorative justice process, as programs must adapt their practices according to the stage at which they enter the conflict. A pre-sentencing session designed to inform the judge and counsel about various issues related to the case is much different than a post-sentencing meeting intended to answer victim questions and to move the parties toward reconciliation.

Trigger Events

The discussion thus far has touched only upon the individual initiators or "gatekeepers" for restorative justice. In other words, it looks at how restorative justice processes are begun under most contemporary criminal justice systems. However, let us take a step back from this discussion and address a more fundamental question: What sort of events *should* trigger a restorative response? This is a question of what sort of crimes, conflicts, harms, normative violations, wrongdoings, or injustices are the basis for launching a restorative justice response, for it would be problematic to assume restorative justice is restricted only to the harms prohibited under various national criminal justice codes. To base restorative justice on such a limitation would be to burden it with existing presuppositions about what justice is (i.e., it would suggest justice is only what the law says it is) without asking exactly what is meant by the "justice" of restorative justice. Simply put, restorative justice needs to identify its object or target independent of the criminal justice system, since, as critical criminologists have long alerted us, the criminal law is not reflective of an overarching collective consciousness or consensus, but rather the product of specific political circumstances. For example, while some events are defined as crimes (marijuana usage) under our criminal code, other comparably harmful behaviours are not (alcohol consumption). A restorative justice program that focuses its energies on the ounce of marijuana in the pocket of an individual who followed and intimidated an elderly pedestrian would certainly be ignoring the primary source of harm. As well, not all crimes are necessarily well-suited to a restorative response. A casual marijuana smoker may violate the law, but it is not necessary to hold a restorative justice conference to discuss this "crime" and its effects on the community, unless we know for certain that someone else feels harmed by this behaviour. To avoid the ethical confusion that comes with an over-reliance on a politically charged criminal code, restorative justice needs to strike out on its own and to define its own terms.

In addition, if one aspires toward a transformative approach to restorative justice, then harmful events that are not recognized under criminal codes must be taken into consideration. The structural harms of gendered inequality, racist misrecognition, or unfair economic distribution, for example, are often at root in the everyday social conflicts that are the fodder of restorative justice. Therefore, any concept of restorative justice that does not open restorative meetings to discuss these and other such issues is unlikely to inspire much in the way of social transformation.

What follows is a more detailed examination of some of the possible "trigger events" for restorative justice, i.e., the events that could or should require a restorative response.

Crime

The event that triggers restorative justice, in most cases, is a "crime." By crime, we typically refer to an act that has been designated criminal by the state and that is codified within domestic or international criminal law. However, this is an odd starting point for a justice "paradigm" that claims to be alternative (Zehr 1990 and 1995) or even oppositional (Sullivan and Tifft 2001) to the formal criminal justice system (see Pavlich 2005). By accepting the laws of formal criminal justice as its starting point, restorative justice does much to reproduce criminal justice ways of thinking that

1. privilege some harms (e.g., property crime) over others (e.g., the spread of pollutants). As mentioned above, criminal codes are rarely neutral and apolitical. The process of establishing something as "crime" often involves an intensive political lobbying effort to place a certain form of wrong within the criminal code;
2. construct the reductive identities of victim and offender, even though there may be multiple and overlapping levels of victimization and offence. In other words, the labels of "victim" and "offender" are sometimes too simplistic to describe the dynamics of conflict situations. For example, crimes are at times (if not most often) committed by individuals who have themselves experienced a great deal of victimization. As an illustration,

the story of Yvonne Johnson demonstrates the breadth of suffering that lies behind a single criminal act (see Wiebe and Johnson 1999). Yvonne Johnson was sentenced to twenty-five years for first degree murder for the September 14, 1989, killing of a man she believed to be a child molester, but antecedent to this incident were years of poverty, addiction, and abuse, including sexual assaults at the hands of her grandfather, father, brother, and a stranger. Restorative justice, if true to its principles, requires a language that allows it to be sensitive to cases such as this, where there exists many levels and layers of victimization and wrongdoing;

3. increase the power and status of governing criminal justice institutions and actors by making them the key decision-makers about crime and its appropriate sanctions. Because police personnel, judges, and lawyers are the primary gatekeepers who determine which individuals will be referred to restorative justice, they amass new powers through the introduction of restorative programs; and

4. foster non-disruptive behaviour that allows for the maintenance of the political and social status quo. Although we often place high value on peaceful and conciliatory behaviour, in its extreme form, such behaviour can be viewed as passive and subservient, and therefore in danger of lessening motivation for social change (these points are adapted from Pavlich 2005: 11–15)

For restorative justice programs that seek social transformation in the form of equal social participation in justice decisions and expanded community input into determining social norms, the affirmation of existing criminal justice laws through restorative justice processes presents acute problems. How can restorative justice transform a criminal justice system when it takes the presuppositions of this system for granted? The problem is one of placing limits on the potential of restorative justice by restricting it from the outset to a narrow criminal justice focus. When crime is the primary trigger event for restorative justice, it becomes harnessed to the criminal justice system in a way that discourages a broader rethinking of what we consider to be right and what we consider to be wrong. For instance, should restorative justice not concern itself with interethnic tensions in a neighbourhood when they have not yet spiralled into criminal actions? It would seem most practical and preventative for restorative justice to involve itself at an early stage in such matters, rather than waiting for a "crime" to occur.

Harm

Some have proposed that the ideal trigger event for restorative justice is "harm" not crime (Mika and Zehr 2003). Following in the footsteps of peacemaking criminology (Pepinsky and Quinney 1990), which turned criminological attention toward the broader issue of "suffering" instead of crime, some restorative justice advocates have suggested their true concern is for all forms of harm, criminal or non-criminal, experienced by human beings. However, whereas "crime" is too narrow a trigger event for restorative justice, "harm" is too broad. There are many things that cause harm that may not be well suited to a restorative approach. When a natural disaster strikes, such as an earthquake that destroys an apartment complex, an individual may have cause for a facilitated restorative justice meeting with her landlord to discuss the unstable construction of the building that contributed to its demise. This individual will not, however, be able to hold a mediated session with the earthquake. To suggest that restorative justice might nonetheless play a role in healing this individual from the trauma caused by the earthquake is to conflate restorative justice with victim counselling and other individual-based approaches to healing. Restorative justice is a *relational* approach to justice that depends on real or potential relationships between people. In other words, restorative justice responds specifically to interpersonal harms — that is, it addresses harms caused through interaction between two or more individuals.

Conflict

Others have argued that crime is a form of "conflict" and therefore place restorative justice under the broader rubric of conflict resolution. This approach begins with the seminal work of Nils Christie (1977), who suggested that conflict is a form of property that is "stolen" from communities. When communities are deprived of this resource, they lose the ability to creatively address their problems and to build something new and hopeful out of a troubling event (see Chapter 3). Later theorists have continued within this tradition of thought, offering arguments that most criminal harms are simply forms of conflict that are officially prohibited. Under this logic, a property offence, such as shoplifting a pair of basketball shoes from a store, is really just a conflict between the store's owner, who wants to charge high prices and earn a profit from the shoes, and the young offender, who desires the shoes and cannot afford the high prices. Similarly, a drug offence is a conflict between the drug user, who wishes to feel the effects of a prohibited substance, and the state, which has forbidden its use.

Based on these examples, one might note that this understanding of conflict as a restorative justice trigger event bears a resemblance with Austin Turk's (1969) non-partisan conflict theory of crime, whereby it was suggested that crime is a mode of conflict between "Authorities" who define, interpret, and enforce the law, and "Subjects," who obey or resist the same laws. However, in the case of "crime as conflict," the notion of "conflict" is extended well beyond Turk's understanding of the term to encompass a very broad array of behaviours. In fact, it becomes difficult to discern between which conflicts deserve restorative attention and which do not. In other words, this approach can make it seem as though conflict is necessarily a problem that needs to be resolved. However, as is often noted within the broader conflict resolution literature (see Kriesberg 2008), some conflicts need to be played out and should not be forced toward an early resolution, since new or intensified hostilities would potentially arise, or entrenched injustices may persist. This speaks to the issue of the "ripeness" of the conflict and the "timing" of conflict resolution, since conflicts are "ripe" for peacemaking interventions when certain political, historical, cultural, and social conditions are present (Aggestam 1995; McEvoy and Newburn 2003). For example, a victimized group may be too disempowered to achieve a fair settlement with a wrongdoer, making conflict resolution premature. Along these lines, many of the still surviving "comfort women," who hail from Korea, China, and other nations subjugated by the Japanese in the 1930s and 1940s, have refused privately funded reparations and an unofficial apology from Japan. Their insistence is that a dialogue be initiated within Japanese society about the injustices imposed upon them, bringing an end to the nationalist denial that has branded these women as willing "prostitutes." In this case, the conflict has not yet reached the point where a viable and acceptable resolution can be achieved, and the remaining "comfort women" and their supporters have little choice but to continue their struggle for a more meaningful outcome.

Conflict resolution specialists also draw a distinction between constructive and destructive conflicts (Deutsch 1973; Kriesberg 2008), with the former leading toward maximal benefits and minimal harm between adversaries, while the latter produces suffering on all sides. Taking this point even further, one could argue conflicts sometimes have a purpose. When the black inhabitants of South African "homelands" took to the streets to protest the indignities of apartheid, many would suggest this conflict was indeed justified and that it would have been irresponsible to try to impose upon it an early resolution. Instead, the governors of the apartheid system had to feel the sting of local and international protests for many years before they were ready to come to the table and negotiate a peaceful resolution to their conflict.

Normative Violation

Given the interpersonal dimension of restorative justice, one could suggest that restorative justice is truly concerned with *normative violations*. "Norms" are group-established behavioural codes that guide the activities of individuals belonging to the group. These norms, and the sanctions that arise in response to their violation, can be formal or informal; that is, they may be recorded in a legal code, such as the criminal law, or simply known through socialization into the group in question, such as standards of politeness. For example, if a young person riding a bus vandalizes the seat in front of him by tagging it using a black felt marker, he has violated a formal norm, one that is contained within the criminal code and could possibly result in a formal sanction; however, if he does not rise to offer his seat to an elderly person or pregnant woman who boards the bus, he has broken an informal norm. Such a violation will not result in a formal punishment, but could lead to informal sanctions, such as the disapproving stares of fellow passengers (see distinctions between norm and law as found in the work of Weber 1946; Simmel 1908; Durkheim 1984 c. 1933).

Using norm violation as a trigger event, restorative justice might respond to any number of breaches of the normative order. Property crime or inter-personal violence would certainly constitute formal normative breaches, but so might the careless spread of pollutants or even the hurt caused by name-calling. In the latter case, a Facebook group dedicated to insulting one's classmate may not constitute a formal normative violation (unless it is a violation of the school's formal rules — or if "cyber-bullying" has been criminalized by the time of this book's publication), but it certainly could cause a great deal of hurt to the person targeted by this page. In such a case, the school might opt to use a restorative justice approach to bring together the individuals who started and contributed to the webpage with the individual victimized by it (as well as some of her supporters) to discuss how this public humiliation made her feel and the deep impact it has had on her life (see Morrison 2007 for further discussion of the school-based use of restorative justice).

For many conventional practitioners of restorative justice, this definition would be sufficient. For them, the goal is to maintain social order and to return affairs to the status quo. However, for those adhering to a transformative no-tion of restorative justice, this definition is problematic. In fact, one criticism of the notion of normative violation as a trigger event for restorative justice is much the same as that offered with respect to the notion of conflict. In particular, basing restorative justice upon normative violations assumes the value of the normative social order, ignoring that breaches of this order might be fully justified or even necessary. An example can be used to further illus-trate this point: Rosa Parks, the African-American seamstress from Tuskegee, Alabama, who on December 1, 1955, refused to relinquish her seat on the bus to a white passenger. At this time, racial segregation was normative, as was deference by those of African ancestry to those of European heritage. By violating these norms, Rosa Parks sparked the Montgomery Bus Boycott, which was one of the influential events that inspired Martin Luther King Jr. and the U.S. Civil Rights Movement. Therefore, if a "normative viola-tion" is assumed to be something that must be corrected (and the status quo thereby "restored"), restorative justice would fail to acknowledge that Rosa Parks' actions were a legitimate response to an unjust situation. In this sense, this conceptualization of the trigger event for restorative justice potentially possesses a conservative bias.

Norms are socially and politically constituted codes and therefore must be left open to criticism. Although in some cases norms may reflect the considered agreement of a community or other social grouping, it is just as likely they reflect the current confluence of power relations. For this reason, restorative justice cannot simply accept existing "norms," "conflict," or "crime" as its object, since this would serve only to reproduce dominant societal codes, for good and for ill. Instead, restorative justice requires guidelines that will allow it to actively and critically assess the norms and harms it takes under consideration.

Injustice

It seems we have reached something of an impasse. On one hand, "crime" is too narrow a trigger event, potentially limiting restorative justice to matters officially defined as "criminal." However, on the other hand, alternate concepts like "conflict," "harm," and "normative violation" are too broad to serve as triggers, potentially lending themselves to what we will later in the book refer to as "net-widening" (the extension of the net of social control to previously non-criminalized behaviours).

Based on the analysis above, "injustice" offers a preferable frame for identifying restorative justice trigger events (see also Sharpe 2004). In the introduction to this book, I offered a very basic definition of justice, but such a notion requires more in-depth investigation. In particular, the idea of justice presupposes a specific form of wrong, an "injustice," that calls forth the need for justice. To elucidate what an injustice is, and thereby to give clarity to the idea of what a restorative justice response to injustice should be, let us briefly review some prominent figures in the philosophy of justice.

Under liberal principles of justice, such as those espoused by John Stuart Mill, Immanuel Kant, or John Rawls, injustice is often viewed as a violation of the public good or of universally afforded rights. For example, according to John Stuart Mill's (1993 [c1861]) theory of utilitarianism, what morally is considered good is that which is of the most utility to society. Injustices are therefore those events that violate the social order and which represent a disutility. To commit a crime like a bank robbery or a mugging is to act selfishly and in a manner that harms the public good. Thus, there would be a utilitarian interest in punishing these crimes to deter further such acts.

For Kant and Rawls, their efforts are directed less toward prescribing the content (or "substance" — see Chapter 1) of justice (and thereby defining injustice) and more toward outlining the ideal procedures for arriving at just decisions. With Kant, this involves the "categorical imperative," which is a principle that strikes invalid any norm that cannot be assented to by all who might be affected by it (Kant 1873; see also Habermas 1990). This does not require that these individuals actually meet and discuss the norms that govern their society, but rather that decision-makers reflect on these various interests and consider the potential for collective assent to their decisions. Such an approach, however, assumes a shared (or universal) understanding of what is an injustice and what sort of justice is needed to remedy it. But do we all share similar notions of injustice? Think for a moment about what causes you offence, and compare that to what might offend someone from another generation or culture. Are these sensibilities always universally shared? For some, marrying outside of one's religious or cultural group could cause great offence, while for others, intermarriage is an accepted practice of modern, pluralistic societies. For this reason, it is highly questionable that one person could alone reflect upon all the hurts and harms that might possibly constitute an injustice and separate him or herself sufficiently from his or her private beliefs in order to ably reach a broadly agreeable resolution.

Rawls recognizes that belief systems differ among various cultures and subcultures, and thus claims his "political" model of justice is only appropriate to modern constitutional democracies (Rawls 1993). This is because the rights-based nature of a constitutional democracy presupposes that individuals are to be provided political equality and liberty. Indeed, for Rawls, these principles are ingrained within our understanding of "society as a system of fair cooperation between free and equal persons" (Rawls 1993: 52). Thus, Rawls limits his focus to a particular form of injustice — violations of the rights of equality and liberty. As noted, Rawls does not discount that individuals and groups of individuals possess divergent and sometimes intractable visions of the "good"; however, the conditions of a constitutional democracy direct us toward a "reflective equilibrium," whereby any strictly political conception of justice must be in accordance with our convictions about the inherent importance of equality and liberty within a democratic society (Rawls 1971). Under these conditions, Rawls suggests that when conflicts arise, those engaged in the conflict must step away from their privately held or culturally specific conceptions of the good, and think in terms of the underlying political values of their society. In this vein, individuals are directed to resolve conflict by referring to the "original position," that is, by seeking a position outside of their own particular lives from which they can decide what is fair, based on the requirements of the political system. An integral feature of the "original position" is what Rawls (1971) describes as the "veil of ignorance," which refers to a self-imposed ignorance that allows individuals to abstract from the immediate conditions of the social world so they can avoid being influenced by the power imbalances that are inevitably part of the institutional context of the conflict and that threaten the 'fairness' of any instance of conflict resolution.

In more concrete terms, we could understand Rawls's theory of justice as offering an ideal model for a judge in a democratic society. For example, Justice Beverly McLachlin of the Supreme Court of Canada describes the judge's role as follows:

> The judge's role is the human role of resolving the legal disputes our society throws up as impartially as is humanly possible. This function is basic, not only to justice but to democracy.... In a democracy, citizens are entitled to bring their disputes and claims before an impartial arbiter with full confidence; the judge will decide the issue impartially, without fear or favour. (McLachlin 2004)

Here, the judge is not presented as a robotic dispenser of a justice that is fully prescribed by the legal code. Instead, the legal code is indeterminate, and the judge must do her best to make fair decisions that are free from undue bias or error. By seeking to take a neutral stance, the judge helps ensure citizens of fair and impartial conflict resolution, and of the protection of their rights.

This appears, on the surface, a fair way to determine the nature of injustice and justice in our liberal democratic societies. Since we are all assumed to have consented to live in such societies, one would think we could unite around these common values. However, this position rests too heavily upon the capacity of a lone individual to step back from his social situation and to reflect fairly upon what is in the best interests of all persons. Yet, we know from the world of law that adjudication is a "human process" (see Hogarth 1971), subject to the cultural and social assumptions of those in positions of power. Asking such individuals to remove themselves from what are deeply socialized, embodied, and intuitive beliefs about the social world is bound to lead to bias. Along these lines, keep in mind that it took feminist activists many years to convince judges and lawmakers their masculine and patriarchal biases influenced the justice they sought to define and deliver, and still these activists work to point out masculine assumptions in the world of law. For instance, in the case of Murdoch v. Murdoch, which reached the Supreme Court in 1973, Irene Murdoch petitioned the court for rights to a portion of the property she had helped her former husband to acquire and sustain. But, in denying her claim and awarding her former husband sole ownership of the property, the Supreme Court agreed with a lower Alberta court, which had ruled the work Irene Murdoch had done in "sewing, cooking, cleaning, mowing, driving trucks, haying, dehorning, branding, and quieting horses" was "only a normal contribution as wife, to the matrimonial regime" (Heritage Community Foundation 2002).

It is also worth noting that Rawls' model of justice and injustice is a poor guide for restorative justice, since it emulates the traditional justice system by asking decision-makers to take on a role very similar to that occupied by a judge when reflecting on matters of justice. Restorative justice, as a communicative process, requires a theoretical framework that can support its emphasis on dialogue. Moreover, as will be argued below, it is through dialogue and communication that we are more likely to challenge our existing worldviews and open our minds to transformative change.

The challenge that arises with liberal philosophies of justice is that they offer what is primarily a political definition of injustice. Although scholars such as Rawls admit as much up front, we increasingly face the perplexing challenge of dealing with injustices within competing polities and intercultural settings, where such shared agreement about norms and what constitutes their violation does not yet exist. How do we claim such broad agreement in nations such as Canada, where the unity of the nation itself is called into question by competing self-determination claims from Aboriginal peoples and Québécois? For this reason, we turn instead to theories that suggest an open notion of justice (and injustice) that must be subject to ongoing negotiation.

The work of Jürgen Habermas (1984 and 1990) offers a strong statement of the negotiated nature of norms and justice. For Habermas, reason and argumentation are necessary components of our world. When communicating, even if we intend to argue our faculties of reason are flawed or inherently problematic, we are required to use these very same faculties to convince others of our position. Therefore, when one tries to deny the power of reason, one is immediately caught in a "performative contradiction" — the expression of reasonable arguments against the power of reason exposes the very power of reason. Thus, Habermas views reasoned argumentation as a universal practice upon which a system of ethical communication can be built.

Habermas contends it is the active participation of agents taking part in a reasonable discussion about what is right and wrong (or what is just and unjust) that is the ideal basis for norm validity; that is, for reaching agreement about shared norms. In this manner, Habermas differentiates his theory of communicative ethics from the theories of justice offered by Kant and Rawls when he identifies his approach as "dialogical" (i.e., based on dialogue) rather than "monological" (i.e., based on an individual monologue, as was the case for Kant and Rawls). For a communicative dialogue to act as a vehicle for fostering normative agreement, however, Habermas argues certain conditions must be in place. Habermas lists these communicative requirements as follows:

1. Every subject with the competence to speak and act is allowed to take part in discourse.
2. a) Everyone is allowed to question any assertion whatever, b)

everyone is allowed to introduce any assertion whatever into the discourse, c) everyone is allowed to express his attitudes, desires and needs.

3. No speaker may be prevented by internal or external coercion from expressing his rights as laid down in (1) and (2). (1990: 89)

When these procedural conditions are met, the discourse that follows allows for the development of a normative consensus — or agreement about right and wrong. Following from this, Habermas states a norm is valid when "all affected can accept the consequences and side effects its general observance can be anticipated to have for the satisfaction of everyone's interests (and the consequences are preferred to those of known alternative possibilities for recognition)" (1990: 65). Discourse or communicative ethics, then, rests upon the process through which norms are validated, whereby "only those norms can claim to be valid that meet (or could meet) with the approval of all affected in their capacity as participants in a practical discourse" (Habermas 1990: 66). Thus, unlike the models put forward by Kant and Rawls, an actual public discourse is necessary to define what is just and what is unjust. However, it is important to note Habermas is here speaking of a "practical discourse," and acknowledges it is unlikely all interested parties will be involved in the actual discussion. What is necessary is they, or their representatives, receive opportunity to participate in the actual discussion.

Injustice, under this framework, can be understood as a matter to be negotiated rather than something that is pre-set. In this manner, although a particular event — a mugging, a violent assault, or parental emotional violence — may spark a restorative justice meeting, the meaning and boundaries of such an event should remain open to discussion within the actual meeting. In other words, restorative processes would ideally facilitate dialogue on what injustices occurred, as well as on other related injustices, so the group can reach a deeper sense of the forms of suffering that exist within their social world and reflect on a specific problem from this light. As well, restorative justice encounters are an opportunity for public discussion of community normative standards rather than for the unquestioning defence of these standards. Based on such a principle, a restorative justice meeting would not simply work to try to convince Rosa Parks to obey Alabama's racial laws but would make possible a broader collective questioning of these unjust standards.

In this sense, Habermas's theory of discourse ethics appears to offer a vision of justice and injustice that is suitable to flexible restorative justice processes. However, the theory also presents some difficulties for the restorative approach. For example, in Habermas's theorizing, individuals are expected to bracket their particular life views when they enter into communicative situations. The primary goal, for Habermas, is one of establishing consensus, and such consensus is impossible if we are too immersed in the specific struggles of our day-to-day lives and not thinking of the more general good. Such a perspective, then, is imperfect for a restorative philosophy that prides itself on opening processes to the specific "needs" of participants, since our particular needs are shaped by our everyday lives, not solely by an abstract notion of the general good. However, other theorists have developed Habermas's theory of discourse ethics so the "particular other" — that is, an individual with all his or her specific experiences and identifications — can engage in normative discussion (Benhabib 1992). Under this refinement of Habermas's approach, less emphasis is placed on achieving consensus, and more on using the discussion as a means for expanding our justice horizons and learning about the specific needs of others.

A very different conceptualization of justice and injustice can be found in the work of Jacques Derrida (1992). Derrida points to deconstruction and the role it might play in exposing law's "mystical" foundations, as well as the force that brings law into existence. Often, within its ideological framework, law hides the fact it is a reflection of the economic and political interests of dominant forces in society. These interests have been codified as law in society through a moment of force. To say law arises from a moment of force does not necessarily mean powerful people employed physical violence in order to subject others to their law and rules, although this is possible. Force also arises through everyday acts of interpretation (or interpretive violence) through which one particular interpretation of justice is disseminated amongst a larger public. For example, consider how we commonly employ terms such as "offender" or "property crime" in our everyday language. We too often take these things as givens, as matters of common sense, and ignore that certain acts or individuals are being interpreted through a specific cultural lens. In this regard, when Will Goodon shot a ringneck duck near Turtle Mountain in October 2004, the state charged him with hunting out of season. Goodon, however, disagreed with the state's interpretation of his action. Goodon argued his Métis Harvester Card was sufficient to demonstrate he had an Aboriginal right to hunt in this area. In his case before the Supreme Court of Canada, Goodon questioned the state's power to define such laws, and, more generally, he challenged the state's power to define what it means to "illegally" hunt or fish (see CBC News 2009). Should a history of Aboriginal rights be ignored because of the imposition of colonial law and the existence of often-violated treaties? What about the rights of Aboriginal people to continue their traditional activities?

Deconstruction exposes the mythical foundations of law not merely out of some spirit of academic sport, but in hopes of bringing about change; that is, to intervene in the construction of law or norms in a responsible manner.

However, it does not claim for itself a standpoint from which it can say the force that constructs these mythical foundations is unjust, since this would imply deconstruction itself possessed some direct knowledge of justice, which Derrida sees as being impossible. For Derrida, law, authority, and most other supposed absolute concepts are deconstructable — we can examine how they are founded or constructed through historically and socially contingent interpretations. None of our concepts has a "natural" origin; they have all arisen through human actions and carry with them the taken-for-granted assumptions that are characteristic of specific times and places. However, for Derrida, what is important about justice is it cannot be deconstructed. Justice is an "experience of the impossible," by which he means justice, in its idealized sense, represents something that is always "to come" rather than realizable in any immediate form.

In a more concrete sense, for Derrida, justice represents a concern with the singularity of the Other. This means addressing oneself to the Other in the language of the Other. Although it is impossible for one to fully under-stand what another person means (you can never see entirely into the head or be "in the shoes" of another person), we must nonetheless try to place ourselves in their position and seek to comprehend the very specific qualities of their life experiences. Unfortunately, we too often fail to truly hear what others are saying and instead translate their words from the perspective of our own specific experiences of the world. In my research on treaty nego-tiations in British Columbia, for example, I frequently witnessed this failure to communicate. On occasions when Aboriginal groups spoke about their territory and its centrality to what it means to be an Aboriginal person, and thereby told of the deep injustice of colonial land appropriation, the gov-ernment negotiators often heard these statements as demands for resources and territory. They were understood to want control over property rather than stewardship over land, which was part of their Aboriginal identity, and the capitalist notion of property ownership framed much of the subsequent discussion (Woolford 2005).

Derrida's conceptualization of justice clearly opposes Habermas's notion that there exists a universal reason that allows for the possibility of unproblematic speech under certain conditions. In contrast, Derrida sug-gests communication is always and inevitably problematic. For this reason, he argues deconstruction *is* justice. It is a form of responsibility to the Other in the sense that it seeks to uncover points in any conversation where certain worldviews or culturally based understandings are imposed. Furthermore, Derrida's perspective requires us to always accept any consent or common understanding that we reach as tenuous and uncertain. Perhaps put too sim-ply, deconstruction is justice because it never allows us to settle upon taken-for-granted assumptions; we are always required to question, to probe, to interrogate common-sense meanings so we become aware of their arbitrary foundations. In this way, deconstruction is always ready to denounce injustice because it vigilantly watches out for the forceful imposition of meaning on any situation.

Derrida concludes it is beyond our ability to completely reflect justice in our laws, to calculate its requirements. However, we cannot simply use this as an excuse for staying out of conflict or for allowing conflicts to rage on. Justice requires that we attempt to calculate the just, but that we do so in a way that we are always reflecting on these calculations (laws) and re-negotiating their boundaries. Although Derrida places great emphasis on the work of deconstruction in taking apart our common-sense views, this does not mean we can simply stand back and criticize without taking any forward-looking action. Injustice is immediate, it is there in our presence, and demands our response, but we must be willing to critique, re-examine, and potentially alter any specific remedy or response.

The works of Habermas and Derrida are, to a great degree, incompatible, since the former proposes a realm of uncoerced communication whereas the latter refuses the notion that uncoerced communication is possible. However, Derrida's deconstruction does offer guidance that can help restorative justice practitioners to foster transformative communication in a more open, reflexive, and critical fashion. Habermas provides a vision of communication as a way to work toward normative agreement, even to the point of allowing us to decide what is and what is not unjust in any particular situation. But Derrida's model of deconstruction demands that, once reached, we probe these agreements even further, to look for the traces of power — the unspoken presuppositions that are at work in such agreements — and be willing to turn a critical eye toward these conversations.

What does this all mean in the concrete world of restorative justice practice? It means that if we take "injustice" to be the trigger event that sparks a restorative justice, we do so with some reservations. The "injustice" that sparks the restorative encounter is not the full extent of the injustices that might be discussed in such a meeting; it is just an immediate need to which we must respond, but may also be a symptom of or signal to larger harms. Therefore, a break-and-enter may be the trigger event that leads us to restorative justice, but the restorative meeting has the potential to raise issues of ageism (if, say, an elderly person was victimized), neighbourhood poverty or economic disparities, youth disempowerment, or any number of issues. Unfortunately, it is too often the case that restorative justice programs fail to meet the standard that C. Wright Mills proposed for sociology; that is, they do not draw the link between "private troubles" of crime commission and victimization and "public issues" of structural disadvantage and inequality (Mills 1959).

To illustrate this point with an example, in the case of a seventeen-year-old male, who admitted responsibility for a serious act of arson in Renfrew, Ontario, the restorative justice conference was directed primarily toward exposing the young person to the harmful consequences of his actions. He had been careless while smoking and drinking behind a local school, which had resulted in a wooden trash container catching fire, and the fire subsequently spread, causing $14,000 damage to the building. The principal, vice-principal, teaching aid worker, as well as the youth's parents, all impressed upon this young man their deep upset and the many challenges the school faced as a result of his actions. However, the report from this conference offers no details of discussion concerning the situation faced by youth in this community — e.g., their sense of boredom, disconnection, alienation, or whatever other factors that might attract them to this behaviour (see Hunt 2000).

The crucial issue here is that restorative justice can aspire to a form of discourse ethics around an injustice, but if the restorative justice program is to have any transformative potential, the discourse must be open to other possibilities — to new potential problems or understandings of a specific problem. It must be more than the collective imposition of shame for what is presumed to be an isolated act. This is something many restorative justice practitioners intuitively know: that a crime or other single injustice that triggers restorative justice is only an initial pathway of what may be, in fact, a complex network of injustices.

This self-corrective capacity of a restorative justice guided by discourse ethics is not enough, however. The practices of restorative justice cannot simply be taken as a foundational means for uncovering injustice and finding its remedy. Instead, restorative justice must continually reflect upon its practice to see where new injustices might arise: Does restorative justice tend to get assigned to individuals in a particular age, ethnic, or class bracket? Is restorative conflict resolution being used, in a particular case, to placate and dampen a necessary and righteous dispute? The practice of deconstruction reminds us we must not allow restorative justice practices to become sedimented — to become unquestioned and frozen, and therefore no longer open to critical questioning. In addition to fostering open dialogue amongst various parties who have experienced a common harmful event, restorative justice must continue to foster dialogue about its own practices and grounding assumptions, never allowing itself to become an unchanging orthodoxy.

Chapter 3

Delineating the Restorative Justice Ethos
History, Theory, and Restorative Justice

Restorative justice theorizing has gone through some major developments in recent years. While some thinkers and practitioners have tried to create a consolidated or universal restorative justice "theory" — that is, a theory of restorative justice that would apply in all times and places, and to all restorative justice programs — it is more useful to identify a restorative justice *ethos* or, in other words, the dispositions or guiding beliefs of the restorative justice movement. The restorative ethos is built upon a common set of assumptions that links together even the most conservative and radical restorative justice programs. The notion of a restorative justice ethos, in this sense, allows one to include the debate and contention that characterizes the restorative justice movement (see Chapter 1), without forcing closure onto this debate by declaring a full and final theorization of the principles of restorative justice. As well, the act of delineating a restorative justice ethos allows for a more fundamental critique of the tendencies within the restorative justice movement that inhibit rather than foster transformative change.

Before we begin, however, it is worth noting that some would contend that restorative justice was first a practice, and it has only subsequently been theorized. For this reason, attempts to theoretically grapple with restorative justice can seem somewhat "after the fact" in that they try to add conceptual flesh to what has been an intuitively rational and culturally salient approach to communal conflict. To address this claim, as well as to explore the roots of the restorative justice ethos, the theoretical overview will begin with a brief examination of historical claims about restorative justice.

Traditions of Dispute Resolution

To suggest restorative justice is a natural historical approach to justice is to ignore that the histories we carve out to support this claim are themselves politicized in the sense that the "truth" they purport to uncover has implications for how things are perceived in the present. This scepticism about the motivation behind historical truth claims should not, however, be taken to mean there is no "real" history. Certainly, there are uncontested historical events, such as the fact that there were multiple fronts of battle during an era we refer to as World War II, and during this period the Nazi regime worked to eliminate European Jewry and other targeted groups through a variety of kill-ing methods. Denial of such events is, without doubt, "revisionist." However, there is nonetheless a large degree of contestation over the interpretation of such events. As well, there is even, at times, contestation over the historical details that comprise these events. For example, although only the revisionist fringe disputes the occurrence of the Holocaust, there is much argument over what we consider the Holocaust to be. Along these lines, historians have long debated the question of when precisely the Holocaust began. Did Hitler plan the extermination of European Jews prior to his rise to power, but wait until international war provided him a cover for carrying out his deadly ambi-tions? Or did the Holocaust emerge gradually as the Nazi regime radicalized and other plans for "dealing" with Jews, such as a proposal to ship them to Madagascar, failed (see, for example, Browning 2004)? Debates such as this are seldom simply contestations of fact; they also reflect specific political leanings. With the former, the Holocaust is the product of a calculated and long held hatred, and this is a perspective that suits a liberal viewpoint that prioritizes the thinking agent as the source for historical change. With the latter, the Holocaust is still an intended horror, but it arises haphazardly out of a very specific social and political context, and therefore appeals to those who view social structures to be, at least partially, responsible for the way events unfold. In each case, history cannot escape politicization because it has implications for how we view and understand the crime of genocide in the present — is it necessarily the product of consciously premeditated and deadly animus? Or can it also or instead result from immediate and extreme radical response to perceived problems? Therefore, because historical claims are often subject to competing socio-political interpretations, we must ap-proach any claim to "true" historical representation with a critical eye and great caution so we can assess the assumptions that are built into whatever act of historical representation we are witnessing.

This is undoubtedly the case in most attempts to represent the history of dispute resolution, where one confronts many uses and abuses of history that are committed in order to serve a contemporary agenda. For example, an author approaching this history from the perspective of the state is likely to present the historical narrative as one of civilizational progress. According to this perspective, prior to the twelfth century, the world (usually meaning Europe) was a dark and violent place. During this period, with little systematic dispute regulation in place, there was always the potential that any wrong committed would spark a bloody cycle of vengeance, which, in the worst-case scenario, would take the form of a blood feud between kinship groups. Into this chaos entered the state, which declared certain forms of wrong to be public harms, thereby making itself solely responsible for the adjudication of justice. An example given by those who espouse the progress narrative is the system of *composition*, as defined by the Laws of Ethelbert of Kent (approximately 600 A.D.), which enforced a practice whereby wrongdoers would pay *bot* for injuries that did not cause death and *wite* to the state to offset the costs of administering justice for the case (Weitekamp 2003). This system of dispute resolution is often viewed as an early stage in the gradual rationalization of justice. However, this story of state progress and the humanization of law tends to ignore or minimize the injustices that accompanied newer, more "rational" approaches. The system of composition, for example, often led to further injustices, since the rich could easily pay their debts, while the poor, at times, had little choice but to sell themselves into slavery to cover their debts. As power became more concentrated in the hands of leaders such as paramount chiefs, feudal lords, and kings, it became more brutal, as these leaders sought to display their might through the administration of punitive violence (Kueneman 2008). Thus, in its early incarnation, the criminal justice state was still unfair and brutal in its dispensation of justice, offering cruel punishments. However, proponents of a historical narrative of progress would argue that gradually the state became more humane and enlightened in response to wrongdoing, thus producing due process rights and other procedural protections to prevent abuses of state power (for further discussion, see Johnstone 2002).

Michel Foucault (1977), in *Discipline and Punish*, has done much to expose the mythic nature of this progressive rendition of criminal justice history. Foucault begins his book with the story of the regicide Damiens, who attempted to kill King Louis XV. Damiens, according to the ritualistic regulations of eighteenth-century punishment, was to be tortured, drawn, and quartered, but the performance of his death was compromised when the horses failed to pull him apart, and the executioner had to intervene to try to facilitate the process. In a spectacle such as this, which is designed to illustrate the unchallengeable power of the king, performance disruptions can be highly problematic. For instance, the crowd's animosity toward the offender may turn into sympathy, and then there is the potential for a public protest or riot to erupt. In short, the spectacle fails when the crowd begins to identify with the punished rather than fear and respect the might of the punisher. According to Foucault, this is part of the reason that punishment began to change course during the eighteenth century. Following the lead of various disciplinary institutions, such as the monastery, the military, and the school, governments sought to retrain criminals rather than brand upon them the power of the sovereign. Foucault, however, portrays this shift as an uneven and elliptical development, and not as the product of a linear and increasingly enlightened progress.

In contrast to Foucault's complex history of punishment, restorative justice advocates have too often offered their own simplified historical narratives to compete with those that suggest the progressive triumph of an enlightened criminal justice. In what Johnstone (2002) describes as a story in which informal justice responses are lost, we see prior to the twelfth century not a period of widespread violence, but, rather, a world where restitution and negotiation are the primary features of dispute resolution. It is only when the state "steals" crime (Christie 1977) from communities that things begin to unravel. In closely interconnected and interdependent small-scale societies of the sort that populated most of the globe for much of human history, there was a definite interest in resolving conflict amicably so as to preserve the harmony of the community, but once the state declared certain wrongs to be public wrongs, then victims and communities were shut out of dispute resolution processes, depriving these groups of an important opportunity to participate in public deliberation and creative problem-solving (Braithwaite 1999). In this sense, the story of the rise of the state and the concentration of political power is one in which our primordial restorative tendencies are displaced in favour of retributive, state-centred justice.

Although this is a simplified story, there is a truth that lies within the restorative justice historical narrative that is central to the arguments presented in this book, and it is that justice becomes more distinctly political after the twelfth century. It is in this period that justice is appropriated to serve state purposes and is more strategically crafted as a technology for regulating broad and diverse populations. But the "story of loss" cannot be taken uncritically, since the increased politicization of justice does not necessarily mean we have linearly descended from a paradise of informal justice into our present retributive criminal justice reality.

It is not just European history that has been oversimplified in the restorative justice literature. One can, for example, be equally critical of the ways in which some restorativists employ the traditions and histories of indigenous peoples when advancing their claims. To begin, it is an error of presentism — of interpreting the events of the past through the ideas of the present — to suggest that past indigenous justice practices were restorative justice. Yet, this is what many restorativists do when they review the past and claim indigenous justice as part of their lineage. This is not to suggest these practices do not exhibit elements of what we might today view as restorative justice; however, it is important to recognize they were developed in distinct cultural contexts. Take, for example, the traditional justice practices of the Aboriginal peoples who reside in what is now Canada. One of the primary forms of dispute resolution employed by some of these Aboriginal groups, especially those in the Prairie regions, was the use of community meetings, or "circles" (see Chapter 4), to determine a resolution to the harm caused. Contemporary restorative justice practitioners have since adopted circles as a means to bring a variety of stakeholder voices to bear on a particular case of wrongdoing, but there is not a straightforward and unbroken line between traditional Aboriginal circles and those used today. Nor is there a single, unitary practice of circling that was used across the diversity of Aboriginal groups that populated Canada prior to colonization.

For these reasons, we must trace the lineage of restorative justice carefully. Beginning with the traditional justice practices of Canadian Aboriginal peoples, it would be disingenuous to suggest all Aboriginal cultural groups used a justice that was predominantly restorative (Laroque 1997). Much depends upon factors such as cultural region, historical period, and the conflict to be addressed. In some cases, such as when a male combatant was caught by a competing war party, punishment could involve a sentence as retributive as death or slavery, but, typically, given that Aboriginal societies were more tightly knit, with strong interdependencies and shared cultural norms, there was a clear interest in conciliatory forms of dispute resolution. Given the reliance of one group member upon the other, Aboriginal groups often could not allow conflict to continue in a never-ending spiral, since such conflict could seriously disrupt group life. Therefore, compromise and mediated settlement were widely practised to ensure group harmony. However, the compromises viewed as culturally appropriate in these communities, at times, diverge radically from contemporary restorative sanctions. In some west coast Aboriginal communities, for example, wrongdoing by a member could result in a community recommendation of banishment; that is, the wrongdoer would be asked to leave the community, perhaps to live alone on an uninhabited island for a period of time.

One might still argue that at the core of such practices was a desire to restore community harmony, and, therefore, the link to today's restorative justice can be found in this common goal, but this ignores the historical processes of colonialism. After a period (approximately sixteenth to early seventeenth century) of relative cooperation between Aboriginal peoples and the traders and explorers who ventured to what is now Canada (namely through the fur trade), colonial settlement (beginning in earnest in the mid-seventeenth century) brought deep disruptions to Aboriginal communities. Suffering first from the European diseases that came with the explorers, Aboriginal peoples subsequently felt the force of European law as it stretched across the continent. Legal documents were signed to remove Aboriginal lands, acts of parliament such as the *Indian Act* (1876) defined all Aboriginal peoples legally as "Indians," with a determinate set of rights and obligations, and eventually, the Canadian police and judicial systems included even the most remote Aboriginal community within their regulatory domain. The world of Aboriginal dispute resolution was not simply forgotten or lost; instead, it was colonized. It was forcibly replaced through the imperial march of Canadian law. Therefore, to simply claim to be renewing Aboriginal justice traditions, without serious consideration of the colonial acts that disrupted the social conditions that made these traditions possible, is to risk performing new acts of colonial appropriation and erasure. The authenticity of an imagined "noble savage" justice is drawn upon to lend credence to modern practices, but without any real historical continuity existing between the two justices. Even worse, as restorative justice is reintroduced into Aboriginal communities, but now at the discretion of a Canadian criminal justice system, there is a fear that Aboriginal justice is being appropriated in an act of neo-colonialism. Indeed, whereas Aboriginal traditional justice practices once achieved their saliency from being culturally embedded in self-determining Aboriginal cultures, contemporary circle sentencing achieves legitimacy through state sanction (for discussion of Australian indigenous peoples see Cunneen 1997, 2002, and 2007). Renewals of Aboriginal justice traditions, therefore, could be argued to strengthen the colonial state as much as they do Aboriginal communities.

This is not to suggest that we cannot learn anything from the past, nor is the caution expressed here to be taken as evidence of an underling radical historical relativism that suggests the past and present are so incommensurate that knowledge cannot travel through the ages. In contrast, the argument is that indigenous knowledge is itself a resource belonging to specific communities that have experienced the onslaught of colonialism. Restorativists must therefore be very careful not to simply appropriate or wrongfully borrow that knowledge without proper recognition of its source and a commitment to "decolonizing" the social conditions that contributed to the removal and repression of indigenous justice traditions.

Based upon these challenges of historical claims-making, one cannot avoid theoretical engagement with the topic of restorative justice. There is no natural or inevitable tendency toward restorative justice; therefore, we must explore theoretical questions about why restorativists believe what they believe, as well as questions about the assumptions that are built into restorative justice practice.

Theories of Restorative Justice

The use of the term "theory" to describe the conceptualization of restorative justice may seem overly ambitious to some. What we find in restorative justice writings are not typically systematic theorizations of the epistemological (that is, an inquiry into how restorative justice knows what it claims to know) and ontological (that is, an exploration of the assumed nature of the social and political world that restorative justice inhabits) (see Hay 2006) foundations of restorative justice. More often, we find instead clusters of ideas that represent a rethinking of contemporary criminal justice and conflict resolution practices. In particular, much restorative justice theorization represents an attempt to construct a theory of the practice of restorative justice; that is, it offers an explanation as to why restorative justice is effective in what it seeks to accomplish, and of how it might be even more effective in the future. In contrast, the emphasis in this chapter is upon the "social theory" of restorative justice, which focuses less upon the everyday practice of restorative justice and more upon its grounding assumptions: How does restorative justice know what it claims to know? What assumptions does restorative justice make about the nature of the social world? What is the restorative vision for society? The answers offered to these sorts of questions provide insight into the underlying restorative justice ethos that shapes restorative thought and practice.

The last section touched briefly on the historical lineage of restorative-like ideas, tracing them primarily through traditional indigenous justice practices. However, the modern variant of restorative justice emerged in the 1970s, as a confluence of forces made possible a re-evaluation of our responses to crime. These forces include the following:

1. An earlier effort to reform criminal justice, rehabilitation, had been dismissed by advocates of the notion that "nothing works" (Martinson 1974; see also Duguid 2000), who suggested society is unable to change the behaviour of offenders and has little option but to incarcerate and warehouse them. The hopelessness of the "nothing works" mantra led more idealistic criminologists, justice workers, and prisoner advocates to search for a new alternative.

2. Radicalism of the 1960s spearheaded an era of identity politics in which individuals began to organize around cultural and symbolic identifications, such as gender, race, ethnicity, and sexual orientation rather than their class positions. These efforts contributed to demands for greater community autonomy and control over local matters, as identity-based communities sought greater participation in the decisions affecting their day-to-day lives.

3. A move toward "deinstitutionalization" (removing power and control over social life from the hands of bureaucratic organizations) and "deprofessionalization" (removing power and control over social life from the hands of professionals) accompanied the era of identity politics, leading to demands to scale back the power of institutions, such as the prison, the asylum, or even the hospital, and to re-empower communities to deal with local concerns (e.g., see Illich 1977 and Illich et al. 1977).

4. Spiritual groups and reformist criminal justice agencies began to experiment with alternatives to incarceration, using conciliatory and negotiative approaches to encourage social harmony through reconciliation.

5. Underlying these developments was an economic shift from welfarism toward the neoliberal policies of Margaret Thatcher, Ronald Reagan, and

Brian Mulroney. Under welfarism, the state established a social safety net to ensure the well-being of all citizens and to protect citizens against social harms, such as unemployment and poverty. However, the maintenance of the social safety net was perceived by some economic and political elites to be too costly and difficult for government. This perception produced a call to "roll back" the welfare state and to impose policies designed to make individuals responsible for their own well-being, rather than tasking the state with this objective. Under these political conditions, one can anticipate the appeal of alternative justice strategies like restorative justice, which promise to ease the burden on our criminal justice system by asking communities and offenders to become more responsible and accountable for repairing criminal harms (see Chapter 6).

Amid these and other conditions, reformist scholars emerged to capture and theorize a new vision of criminal justice (e.g., Barnett 1977; Zehr 1990; Wright 1991; Van Ness 1993; Galaway and Hudson 1996; Kurki 2000). Although the contributions were many, there are a few key moments in the development of the restorative justice ethos, and there is no better person to start with than Nils Christie.

A Norwegian criminologist and anti-prison activist, Nils Christie published in 1977 a paper titled "Conflicts as Property" in the *British Journal of Criminology* (Christie 1977). Here, Christie argued that crime, as a form of conflict, is a valuable resource or "property." In particular, possession of this property allows communities to participate in key forms of decision-making and creative problem-solving, as well as to contribute to local processes of norm development and clarification. However, when the state, through the work of state professionals, "steal" these conflicts and make them cases for the criminal justice system to deal with, a great community loss is suffered. Criminal issues become removed from the everyday life of communities, and community members are therefore not required to confront these problems with creative solutions. In addition, the distance of the courts from the community contributes to the dehumanization of offenders, who are no longer perceived as community members, but rather as excluded parties removed from the realm of community life. For Christie, this system required replacement by community-based and victim-oriented courts that would provide citizens greater input into justice outcomes.

In the early 1990s, restorative justice would receive clearer formulation in the work of Howard Zehr, a Mennonite scholar who had become familiar with the idea through his involvement in a victim-offender reconciliation program. Zehr called for a "paradigm shift" away from a criminal justice system that had failed victims by not meeting their needs or empowering them, and that had failed offenders by not holding them to a standard of

Table 3.1 Paradigms of Justice — Old and New

Retributive	Restorative
Crime defined as violation of the state	Crime defined as violation of one person by another
Focus on establishing blame, on guilt, on past (did he/she do it?)	Focus on problem-solving, on liabilities, obligations, on future (what should be done?)
Adversarial relationship and process normative	Dialogue and negotiation normative
Imposition of pain to punish and deter/prevent	Restitution as a means of restoring both parties; goal of reconciliation/restoration
Justice defined by intent and process: right rules	Justice defined as right relationship; judged by outcome
Interpersonal, conflictual nature of crime obscured, repressed; conflict seen as individual versus the state	Crime recognized as interpersonal conflict; value of conflict is recognized
One social injury replaced by another	Focus on repair of social injury
Community on sideline, represented abstractly by state	Community as facilitator in restorative process
Encouragement of competitive, individualistic values	Encouragement of mutuality
Action directed from state to offender -victim ignored -offender passive	Victim and offender roles recognized in problem/solution -victim rights/needs recognized -offender encouraged to take responsibility
Offender accountability defined as taking punishment	Offender accountability defined as understanding impact of action and helping decide how to make things right
Offence defined in purely legal terms, devoid of moral, social, economic, or political dimensions	Offence understood in whole context — moral, economic, and political
"Debt" owed to state and society in the abstract	Debt/liability to victim recognized
Response focused on offender's past behaviour	Response focused on harmful consequences of offender's behaviour
Stigma of crime unremoveable	Stigma of crime removable through restorative action
No encouragement for repentance and forgiveness	Possibilities for repentance and forgiveness
Dependence upon proxy professionals	Direct involvement by participants

"real" accountability whereby they would need to face those who they had harmed (Zehr 1995). By a "paradigm shift," Zehr means we require a new way of seeing the world — a new lens that will allow us to surpass all of our notions of criminal justice that are entrenched within a punitive worldview. Zehr argues this punitive worldview is the dominant interpretive lens in contemporary societies, leading us to automatically expect retribution to be the response to any harm, even if retribution proves to be a counterproductive means in the sense that it neither deters potential offenders nor does it rehabilitate those who are apprehended. Zehr begins the project of encouraging such a shift from this punitive worldview by drawing a series of oppositions between "restorative" and "retributive" justice (see Table 3.1).

Zehr has since been criticized for creating too stark an opposition between "restorative" and "retributive" justice, and it has been argued the two justice forms overlap more than Zehr admitted (see Chapter 7). It is also the case that such an exercise defines restorative justice predominantly in terms of what it is not. Such an act of definition by negation has a way of anchoring restorative justice to criminal justice by making the two ideas conceptually dependent on one another. As Pavlich (2005) points out, this binding of the two ideas makes it very difficult to establish a truly alternative justice, since restorative justice ends up using "retributive" justice as its eternal reference point, and thus allows formal criminal justice to set the terms of debate and development. Due to this dependency, restorative justice often ends up reacting to criminal justice policy and practice rather than creating an approach to justice that is truly "new."

In the late 1980s, John Braithwaite was at work on a similar set of ideas that would eventually merge with the notion of restorative justice. A particular benefit of this merger is that Braithwaite's thinking helps insert restorative justice more firmly within existing criminological theory. Specifically, Braithwaite's work helps address the related conundrums of labelling and stigmatization. Simply put, when an individual commits an initial act of deviance, she or he may, as of yet, be uncommitted to a criminal identity. Indeed, it is common for young people to "drift" in and out of criminal behaviour (Matza 1990). However, the way in which we process people through the criminal justice system may have the effect of committing them to a criminal lifestyle. Courts, for example, represent what Harold Garfinkel (1956) once referred to as "degradation ceremonies" in that they serve to publicly lower the status of the offender, marking him or her as a devalued person. This change in status is most clearly illustrated by the criminal record, as is evident in the troubles experienced by the young man in Box 3.1, even after he has paid his "debt to society." Here, "Rocky1982" uses an online forum to express his frustration at the difficulty he is having finding a job with his criminal record for a first-time offence.

Box 3.1 Canadians Who Are
First Time Offenders and Looking for Jobs

I just wanna see how many people out there in Canada have a criminal record and are looking for jobs and having a hard time. This is strictly for first time offenders and I'll explain why later. It seems like every company and business are starting to do criminal record check and most likely if you have a record your not gonna get the job.

I have talked to so many people where I live who have a criminal record, their first one and they all say that its hard to get a job and the only other option they have to do is illegal stuff to make money. I have also talked to people who had a first offense and then ended up getting themselves charged again because they went the wrong way to start to make money.

Now we all know that you can pay a x-amount of dollars to get your record erased or sealed after so many years and that's only if you have been keeping out of trouble. First how are you to get a job if you have a criminal record, secondly how are you to pay that fee if you can't get a job, and thirdly to not be able to find a job and have no money ends you up getting into trouble because your gonna do what it takes to make money even if its to break the law.

Now alot of you reading this are probably saying well you shouldn't have gotton yourself into trouble in the first place. Well first there's reason why people do certain things that got them into trouble in the first place, secondly just in the wrong place at the wrong time.

As a first time offender myself, I have had a hard time finding a job where I live now, I did my dues, I paid for my crime and it seems that having a criminal record, your punished for life. I have been crime free for years now it opened my eyes up, but it was a mistake when I did the crime and I apologized for it. I was going through tough times at the time of the crime that I committed.

But as I walk down the streets everyday, I see a new sign saying they are hiring, and businesses/companies are starting to feel the pain as they can't find people to fill positions and I'm sure there are tons of people out there who are qualified to do the job but can't because of their criminal record. As years go by I believe its only gonna get worst, more and more companies/businesses are gonna require a criminal record check.. I like to hear some other stories out there who have a criminal record

So the reason why I wanted only first time offenders is because I like to see the law changed and that is if its your first offense and depending on the charge its erased or sealed as they call it, and that's only if you have done your dues and have been crime free for 5 years, your still on record but when a criminal record is done it doesn't show and its as if you haven't done anything wrong.

Source: Comment by Rocky1982, posted to //forum.kijiji.ca/about6774494.html, November 06, 2008 1:47 pm.

In addition to the practical consequences of public stigmatization — e.g., the difficulty an offender may experience finding a job or suitable housing — degradation ceremonies contribute to the further alienation of offenders from law-abiding society. Through processes of labelling and stigmatization, the offender may feel he or she has little choice but to embrace a criminal identity, since he or she senses the rejection of the mainstream world. Thus, a criminal subculture or gang may become a more appealing form of group identification, and/or the person may accept "offender" or "criminal" as his or her "master status" — i.e., the primary identity that defines who he or she is.

In contrast to this self-defeating and self-perpetuating criminal stigmatization process, Braithwaite (1989; see also Braithwaite and Mugford 1994) recommends we fashion instead "reintegration ceremonies" for offenders. The underlying principle of such ceremonies would be that they shame the act and not the actor. This modification of the Christian tenet of "hating the sin and not the sinner" reflects Braithwaite's concern that we not simply do away with shame. For him, correcting the problems of criminal justice is not as simple as reversing the labelling process so there is no more shame. Instead, Braihwaite differentiates between good shame and bad shame. Bad shame stigmatizes individuals and leads to their disconnection from their networks of support, but good shame would aim to reintegrate them. Indeed, in his study of societies that effectively prevent offenders from committing new crimes (e.g., Japan), Braithwaite (1989) identified the productive use of shame as the most important factor. Therefore, rather than treating the act as fully representative of the character of the offender, Braithwaite suggests that although we must be tough in admonishing wrongful actions, we must also seek to re-affirm the admirable qualities of those who have done wrong. A young offender, then, should not be subjected to endless tirades about their misbehaviour in a restorative justice session. Time must also be given to discussing what is good in that person — his or her more noble traits — to accentuate a positive identity and to make room for his or her re-immersion in community life (Braithwaite 1989).

In following up his work on reintegrative shaming, Braithwaite has also contributed to the development of a more systematic theorization of restorative justice (in this case, theory with a capital "T"). Indeed, Braithwaite's work with Phillip Petit (Braithwaite and Petit 1990) on a "republican theory of criminal justice" (see also Braithwaite 2002; Braithwaite and Daly 1994; Walgrave 2002) does more than most theories of restorative justice in the sense that it seeks to formulate a more general vision of ethical and political life. This perspective centres on the notion of "dominion," which refers to the rights and freedoms assured to citizens of democratic societies. "Domination," in contrast, according to Braithwaite and Petit, refers to incursions upon these rights and therefore represents the primary form of social harm that is to be minimized within justice contexts. It is the state's role to create opportunities for dominion and to minimize the likelihood of domination. With respect to restorative justice, this entails the state acting to maintain space for community-based restorative justice programs to freely arrive at their own justice sanctions, while simultaneously ensuring general principles of human rights are maintained. For example, restorative justice might provide citizens the chance to interact and address harms within their community, but this is done within legal limits enforced by the state, which ensures the rights of each party to the restorative justice encounter are respected, and intervention occurs when they are not.

Braithwaite and Petit's republican theory of criminal justice intersects with a more recent area of restorative justice theorizing that borrows heavily from complementary work being done on the issue of deliberative democracy (see Chapters 6 and 7 for further discussion). Like the ideas of Habermas discussed in Chapter 2, deliberative democracy emphasizes open public participation in decision-making processes (Habermas 1999; Benhabib 1996; Fishkin 1991; Dryzek 2000). Thus, the deliberative democratic vision of society is one in which ordinary citizens have a voice in their governance. As Dzur and Olson (2004: 99) note, there are "close resemblances between restorative justice ideals and deliberative democratic ideals of public participation and reasoned value-oriented debate in political forums." Dzur and Olson contend that restorative justice could follow deliberative democracy in the establishment of basic guidelines or norms, similar to Habermas's communicative presuppositions discussed in Chapter 2, which direct participants in deliberative settings toward rational, respectful, and consistent discussion. Moreover, they argue such guidelines provide a means for assessing the communicative potential of restorative justice by identifying the places where it fails to live up to the ideals of deliberative democracy. In this regard, they point to coercive and unequal moments within restorative justice encounters, where offenders are intimidated into participation through the threat of formal judicial action, or victim's voices and accounts are privileged over those of offenders. If an offender is strongly encouraged (or, some would say, coerced) by court or police authorities, or even by restorative justice practitioners, to take responsibility and proceed through a restorative process rather than face a potentially punitive judge, his or her participation in restorative justice can no longer be described as free and uncoerced. Likewise, if the victim's version of the events that transpired is automatically accepted as truth, and the offender's counterclaims disregarded as exculpatory rationalizations, then the communication in that meeting can hardly be described as open and democratic. For Dzur and Olson, it is necessary that "progressive" restorative justice advocates seek to improve the communicative potential of restorative justice by measuring restorative justice encounters up against the ideals of deliberative democracy so they can better ensure open and fair participation.

The Restorative Justice Ethos

Through this brief conceptual overview, we can begin to piece together the elements of a restorative justice ethos. At base, the following assumptions appear operative in the restorative justice ethos:

1. Conflicts are knowable: The idea that conflicts are intractable, or that they present an impossibly complex array of disputes is anathema to restorative justice thinking. For restorativists, there always exists the possibility that one can understand the parameters and antipathies of a given dispute, and therefore make a deliberate intervention toward resolving the conflict.

2. We can get to know conflicts through the act of communication: The means to understanding a conflict is through effective communication. When people gather together to discuss openly and freely their understandings of a given situation, a clearer sense of the conflict is developed.

3. Conditions can be established in which communication is unproblematic: With the right processes or conditions in place, people are able to communicate with one another in a non-coercive manner. According to this way of thinking, people may enter the restorative justice meeting with various advantages and disadvantages, but it is possible to level these inequalities through careful preparations and interventions conducted by the facilitator.

4. Human behaviour can be changed: Our behaviour is not set in stone or predetermined. Various social forces have assembled to influence and shape our current behavioural patterns, and it is possible to replace these influences with a new set of influences, such as reintegrative shaming and positive social networks, that will place us on a more caring course.

5. Humans possess the capacity for communication, and therefore for creative problem-solving: Due to our capacities for communication and behavioural change, we are also able to arrive at creative solutions for changing the conditions that led to conflict and for re-fashioning the world around us.

6. A society built upon effective communication will be more peacable and progressive: For all of the reasons listed above, effective communication provides the foundation for a society where people are able to live peacefully with one another, as well as to make changes and adapt to the social world when new problems arise.

Within this ethos, we see the primary components of a restorative justice *epistemology* and restorative justice *ontology*. With respect to *epistemology* (how we know), we glean a sense that the social world — in particular, the world of conflict — is knowable through our efforts to speak to one another. Derrida's (see Chapter 2) concern that we are never fully able to hear the voice of the Other, and that we are always engaging in an act of translation when we communicate, would be ignored or dismissed by most restorativists. With respect to *ontology* (assumptions about the nature of the social world), we see a social world where, despite multiple potential obstacles to communication, we are nonetheless able to speak with one another (assuming the right conditions are in place) and to change ourselves and the world around us. Thus, it is a malleable world in which we live. This leads us to what we might refer to as the restorative justice *teleology* — the end state to which restorative justice hopes to lead us — which is a vision of a world where communication is liberated so humans can collectively recreate society for the betterment of each and every one of us.

These underlying presuppositions appear common to most restorativists and are therefore presented here as constitutive of the restorative justice ethos. However, these presuppositions are not unproblematic when examined in light of actual conflicts.

The Canadian Truth and Reconciliation Commission for Residential School Survivors

In an attempt to place this ethos in more concrete terms, let us consider these issues in relation to the currently ongoing development of the Canadian Truth and Reconciliation Commission for Residential School Survivors.

Residential schools began operating in the late nineteenth century, drawing on an existing network of Protestant and Catholic schools. These were initially day schools, but their administrators felt it was problematic that the children returned to their parents at the end of each day, thus allegedly undoing their lessons in the proper conduct of "civilized" persons. In response, the schools began to hold students in residence for most of the year, providing the children only a month in the summer to visit their families. By 1920, these schools were made mandatory for all Aboriginal children. At many of the schools, conditions were so inadequate that large numbers of children died from ill health, exposure to the elements, and poor nutrition (Milloy 1999). Others suffered physical and sexual abuse, as well as a constant verbal assault upon their cultures, traditions, communities, and families. Upon completing their education, many no longer felt at home or welcome in their communities, and became distanced from their cultural traditions. Moreover, deprived of the experience of being parented, they later found it a great struggle to raise their own children (Haig-Brown 1988;

Monture-Angus 1999). Continuing cycles of emotional, physical, and sexual abuse, as well as addiction, suicide, and other markers of intergenerational trauma within Aboriginal communities are often cited as residual effects of the residential schooling experience.

In developing a truth and reconciliation commission, which, as will be noted in the next chapter, involves creating opportunities for victims to tell their stories so as to foster greater social understanding of their plight, restorativists would operate on the assumption that the world of residential schooling and the trauma it has caused is, to a certain degree, knowable and communicable. This means the residential schooling experience can be distilled into a story that communicates this complex experience to a general public that did not live through its reality. Furthermore, through this understanding, the general public should achieve a better sense of the plight of residential school survivors and a hint of the sorts of trauma they faced in the aftermath of these "schools." It should be noted the claim here is not that the non-Aboriginal general public is likely to fully understand the residential school experience in the way those who lived through this era (and its aftermath) understand it. Instead, non-Aboriginal persons will simply receive a picture of what it may have been like, and on the basis of this, might become more sympathetic to the current challenges facing Aboriginal peoples in Canada. Thus, the restorative justice ethos would presume that through such an understanding, a public discussion could then take place toward improving Aboriginal and non-Aboriginal relations in Canada.

The restorative justice epistemology and ontology are therefore geared toward providing us a way forward, whether from a troubled period or a distinct traumatic event. This is the basis for an ethos that it is resolutely optimistic that most, if not all, human problems can be fixed. However, this ethos requires a critical political sensibility to avoid charges of naïve hopefulness. In the everyday world of conflict resolution, barriers to communication arise and threaten to disrupt even the best-intentioned efforts at repairing harm. Restorative projects, such as truth and reconciliation commissions, are devised and implemented by political actors who possess clear interests and pre-formed assumptions about the social world.

Remaining with the example of the Canadian Truth and Reconciliation Commission for Residential School Survivors, one must begin by examining the fears of government liability for civil suits stemming from the abuses of residential schools that helped motivate government participation. Such lawsuits present the risk of untold costs to the government. In contrast, the symbolism of a truth commission, accompanied by a public apology and lump sum payments, offers a calculable pathway to resolving what has been a seemingly intractable and potentially expensive social problem. However, for this to be the case, great care must be taken to manage these reparation processes to ensure compensation is not too widely distributed and the symbolic acts of atonement do not compromise government legitimacy and authority by admitting too much (e.g., the government is unlikely to admit their contribution to widespread genocidal destruction through colonial policies such as residential schooling). In a situation such as this one, where the aging survivors of residential schools live in conditions of dire poverty and are in grave need of whatever compensation monies they can achieve, a degree of power is in the government's hands to shape the restorative process in its favour. Therefore, it will mobilize this power to place limits upon the degree of justice offered to residential school survivors.

This example illustrates the hopefulness of the restorative justice ethos often comes up against the crass political realities of conflict. As the rest of this book seeks to demonstrate, this ethos needs therefore to be strengthened by a political sensibility that allows it to better navigate the troubled waters of conflict resolution. As well, one must approach the restorative ethos, as it is described above, with a degree of caution. The ethics of communication and understanding that is contained within its principles needs to be examined within the power dynamics of both the actual practices of restorative justice (Chapter 4), as well as in the broader collective and social-structural circumstances in which restorative justice is implemented (Chapters 5 and 6).

Chapter 4

Restorative Justice Styles

There are several primary forms of restorative justice, most of which are still in use today. We need to know what these practices are, but, more importantly, we need to delve deeply and critically into the topic of restorative justice practices so we may explore their embodied politics, for actions do not simply reflect a straightforward enactment of our ideas and beliefs: they also derive from habituated dispositions that guide our day-to-day behaviour (Bourdieu 1990). Put in simpler terms, our everyday actions often reflect deeply ingrained sensibilities of which we are often unaware. Think, for instance, of practising a sport, such as hockey. The drills you run in practice are designed to habituate you to certain actions, so when the moment arises in a game, you can react in an almost automatic, but also somewhat creative fashion. For example, if you have practised breakaway after breakaway, a game-time opportunity to break free from the defence and approach the goalie unchallenged may play out almost instinctively. Instead of "overthinking" your move, you may instead rely on your training to guide you, as you move to the backhand, knowing (although not necessarily consciously thinking) from experience the goalie will not be able to move backward to stop the shot you lift into the top of the net. When put into practice, restorative justice seeks to guide us in the development of new conflict resolution dispositions based upon the restorative justice ethos that lead us toward improved communication and creativity. Discussed below are some examples of the types of retraining programs restorative justice has to offer.

Mediation and Community Mediation

Paul McCold (2006) notes the shared origins of mediation and restorative justice. Although most scholars are careful to differentiate between the two practices, they do have significant overlaps, and therefore, it is worthwhile to take some time to discuss this antecedent to restorative justice (see Woolford and Ratner 2008a for further discussion).

As mentioned in the previous chapter, the 1970s was a time when many people experienced disenchantment with the formal law. The courts were viewed to be inaccessible, as much of the business of law was carried out in esoteric and jargon-laden legal discourses, and legal decisions were most favourable to those who could afford the services of lawyers. The courts were also viewed to be unnecessarily adversarial. Courtrooms were perceived as spaces of combat, where there could be only winners and losers and nothing in between. For these and other reasons, many began to wonder if it might be possible to return to an earlier form of justice in which communities and local actors were empowered to creatively resolve the problems in their midst (Burger 1979).

This turn toward the community led to the development of community justice centres, community credit unions, neighbourhood-based health and food cooperatives, and other local experiments that were established under this new influence (Coy and Hedeen 2005). Most relevant to the rise of restorative justice are the community justice centres, where lay mediators volunteered to facilitate the resolution of neighbourhood-based disputes. These lay mediators were expected to use their status in the community to help persuade disputants to resolve their differences, all the while not seeking to advantage their own personal power. At the onset of these justice experiments, it was assumed these mediators would facilitate both civil and minor criminal conflicts; however, over time, community justice centres came to concentrate their efforts on civil disputes (Olson and Dzur 2004).

The San Francisco Community Boards (SFCB) is one of the most studied examples of community justice (see, for example, Fitzpatrick 1995; Pavlich 1996a). The aim of the SFCB was to build community harmony by addressing conflicts before they grew into more disruptive struggles, reduce fear of crime within the community, and provide residents with conflict resolution skills so they could apply them in their daily lives (Shonholtz 1984). During SFCB meetings, disputants would present their conflict to members of a volunteer-based panel that would attempt to facilitate an agreed-upon resolution. The members of this panel would be selected based on characteristics shared with the disputants rather than solely upon credentials such as social status or power. Presumably, these shared characteristics would allow the disputants to better identify with and feel understood by the panel. They also helped give the impression of equality amongst all participants in the SFCB process, so the disputants would trust their own authority within the process rather than look toward panel members for decisive interventions.

Community justice boards like this one offered many the hope that a deprofessionalized and deinstitutionalized local justice was, indeed, possible. However, community justice soon came under criticism for failing to live up to its promise. Instead of a local and autonomous justice, critics saw a justice process that served as a means for extending and entrenching state power at the local level, allowing social workers and community volunteers to take the place of state officials in ensuring community conflicts did not become socially disruptive (Abel 1982; Hofrichter 1982; Matthews 1988). Community justice boards were also accused of providing the formal justice system with a means to preserve its legitimacy by allowing it to overcome the many crises it faced, such as overloaded court dockets and citizen alienation from the justice process (e.g., Abel 1982; Selva and Böhm 1987). Other critics argued community justice served to pacify the workforce, resolving conflicts that might otherwise threaten capitalist means of production (Hofrichter 1987). For example, conflicts such as marital disputes or neighbourhood conflicts over property lines do not only disrupt the everyday lives of workers, they also threaten to spill over into their working lives, as they distract working people and effect their potential productivity. In addition, when these squabbles are brought to the courts, they risk draining legal resources that are viewed to be the privilege of the middle and upper classes. For reasons such as these, scholars such as Hofrichter argued the capitalist system had a direct interest in supporting gentle means of social control, such as those promoted through community mediation.

Victim Offender Reconciliation and Victim Offender Mediation Programs

The community justice ideal, however, did eventually find expression in the field of criminal justice. For instance, in 1974, an early victim offender reconciliation program was developed in Elmira, Ontario, not far from Kitchener-Waterloo (Peachey 2003). At this time, Mark Yantzi, a probation officer, was assigned the task of working with two teenagers who had gone on a vandalism spree in the small town. Yantzi felt it would be in the interests of all parties concerned if an effort was made to reconcile the teenagers with their fellow community members. He thus approached the judge for the case and proposed that, as part of their sentence, the young offenders be required to approach their victims and offer to make restitution for the damages done. The judge agreed, and Yantzi, together with David Worth, who worked for the Mennonite Central Committee, soon found himself escorting the teenagers as they visited the houses of those whom they had harmed. The teenagers met with their victims and agreed to make reparations to them, but also gained a clearer sense of the harm they had done. The success of this endeavour led the two men to create a post-sentencing reconciliation program (Peachey 2003).

The terms victim offender reconciliation (VOR) and victim offender mediation (VOM) are used almost interchangeably to refer to programs that follow this model. According to Mark Umbreit et al. (2006), the core elements of VOR and VOM are:

- establishing a safe environment;
- preparation;
- voluntary participation;
- a face-to-face encounter; and
- follow up.

Based on these criteria, it is important to note the encounter between the victim and offender is but one small, albeit crucial, part of the VOR and VOM processes. The activities that precede this encounter are central to the encounter's success, since this is how stakeholders are readied to meet one another. To begin, all parties must feel safe, develop a sense of trust in the mediator, and be reassured they will not experience any further harm through the VOR or VOM process. Once this is established, preparation can begin, as the mediator works with the parties to give them an idea of what to expect from the encounter and to help them understand the ground rules for the meeting (e.g., listen and do not interrupt others when they are speaking). The preparation stage can take as long as is necessary for the participants to feel ready to meet, since the mediator does not want to rush the parties toward an encounter. Moreover, throughout this preparation, and, indeed, throughout the entire restorative process, it is important the parties understand their participation is voluntary and they can withdraw at any time. If they feel in anyway coerced into participation, it is possible the parties may come to feel (re)victimized and resentful, and these are not conditions that lend themselves to effective communication or restoration. Finally, once preparations are complete, the parties are ready for the meeting, and it is here, with the assistance of the mediator, they will receive the opportunity to ask questions and work toward a resolution of the conflict.

In a VOR or VOM designed for purposes of sentencing, the initial discussion of the harmful event(s) that are the basis for the encounter will eventually need to transition into discussion of an agreement. An agreement of a sort may also be the goal of a post-sentencing VOR or VOM, although it functions less as an alternative sanction and more as a personal understanding between the participants. In either case, there are specific interventions the mediator might make to help the parties reach a mutual understanding of the event and a plan for its aftermath (these will be discussed later in the chapter). Even when an agreement is achieved, however, this does not spell the end of the VOR or VOM. Instead, a period of follow-up is required to ensure the parties are living up to their agreement, as well as to check to ensure their needs have been met and no renewed or new trauma has occurred. Within some versions of VOR and VOM, it may be necessary to hold a second meeting if the parties are not living up to the agreement, or if new issues have arisen that were not dealt with in the first meeting.

Family Group Conferencing

The traditional justice practices of the Maori people of New Zealand are often credited as the inspiration for family group conferencing, although this overstates the case. The 1989 *Children, Young Persons and Their Families Act* was instituted, in part, as an attempt to respond to concerns about the overrepresentation of Maori youth in New Zealand correctional institutions and to adapt justice processes to allow for the involvement of families (see Daly 2003). Through this legislation, family group conferences (FGCs) were designated the normal response for most youth crime violations, thereby bringing together victims and offenders, as well as their families and supporters, to resolve criminal incidents (see Consedine 1995 and 2003). In the 1990s, the small Australian city of Wagga Wagga followed New Zealand's lead with the introduction of a police-cautioning scheme that combined the framework of New Zealand's FGCs with John Braithwaite's concept of reintegrative shaming (see Chapter 3). This resulted in the establishment of police-led conferences to deal with young offenders (see Moore and O'Connell, 2003). The Wagga Wagga program further inspired similar projects in the mid-1990s, such as the one implemented by the Thames Valley Police (Pollard 2001).

Although these programs differ to various degrees, they all serve to bring the families of the victim and offender together to resolve the conflict. This occurs with the assistance of a state-appointed facilitator, in some cases a police officer, who is charged with the task of helping the families reach a consensual agreement (Raye and Warner Roberts 2007).

A more controversial variation of the FGC process is the family group decision-making (FGDM) program designed specifically for use in cases of family violence. According to the designers of this program, Joan Pennell and Gayle Burford (2002), FGDM employs a "feminist praxis" that attempts to "interrupt" gendered assumptions about male dominance and the roles of women and children within families, while also creating "links" between families and the resources they require to lead healthy and peaceful lives. The goal of FGDM is to give families (immediate and extended) ownership of their problems, but also to provide them with assistance to ensure family violence ceases. Indeed, unlike other restorative justice programs, where there is a need to balance offender and victim needs, FGDM must place priority upon the victims' need for safety, given the dangerous stakes involved when re-offending occurs. So, when a case is referred to a FGDM program, a wide spectrum of family members are invited, although attention is given to ensure these family members do not in any way condone family violence. After this selection process, emphasis is placed on safety concerns, ensuring all family members feel protected within the FGDM meeting and are prepared to participate respectfully. At the onset of the meeting, a family ritual, such as a reading or a prayer, is used to symbolize the bond between family members. A statement from a protective authority, such as a police officer or caseworker, is then provided to relay the history of family violence events. Next, local or regional service providers are invited to speak and make the family aware of the resources available to them within the community. With this knowledge, the family is then left on its own to devise a plan. The facilitator and protective authorities are never too far removed from this meeting, but they give the family space to work through these matters. This is the most controversial component of this model, as there are obvious concerns about leaving a family struggling with abuse and violence unsupervised. Once the family has arrived at a plan, protective authorities review it to ensure that it meets safety requirements, and, if it does, the family is then responsible for carrying out its components. If, however, the plan fails, or elements of the plan are not being met, a meeting is convened.

Circles

As noted in the previous chapter, contemporary restorative justice is often traced back to the traditional justice practices of indigenous peoples. In particular, circles are regularly cited as a method used by several Aboriginal groups who live in what is now North America. In the most basic terms, a circle is an occasion where a community is assembled to discuss matters related to and a possible resolution for an injustice that took place in their midst. All participants are given opportunities to speak, and their right to be heard is signified by the passing of a sacred object, such as an eagle feather, which, when held, communicates that all attention should be paid to that person.

Like VOR and VOM, there are several stages to circles. According to Stuart and Pranis (2006), these are:

- suitability;
- preparation;
- a full circle gathering; and
- follow up.

The first step is to ensure the case is suitable to the circle process. Has the offender taken ownership of his or her actions? Is the community in a position to provide the support needed by the victim and offender? Does the circle present any danger to the community? Once these and other issues are addressed, it becomes possible to begin preparing the parties for participation in the circle. Here, a facilitator will want to encourage the practices of respectful listening and dialogue, as was the case for VOR and VOM, but also to ready the parties for what those in attendance might have to say to them. Certainly, it is not in the interests of the circle to have an offender or victim go into a defensive shell if they feel the community assessment of their behaviour is too harsh. Only after these and other preparations have been made is it possible to initiate the circle. With so many potential participants present, these circles can be time-consuming affairs. Therefore, they require commitment from all parties so the circles are not rushed or pushed forward in a quest for judicial expediency. Finally, once the community has arrived at an appropriate sanction, and it has been implemented, the circle facilitator needs to follow up with the victim and offender to ensure the agreement is being lived up to. This may also involve a ceremonial feast or other activity to symbolize the offender's progress through the terms of the agreement and to mark his or her full return to the community (see Ross 1996; Stuart 1996).

Contemporary circles take many forms. A style familiar to many Canadians is the "sentencing circle," where a case may be diverted from the formal criminal justice system to be addressed within a (often Aboriginal) community. The circle will be convened by a facilitating party or group, and will be comprised of the victim and offender, their support people (e.g., family and friends), elders, a judge, defence and Crown attorneys, in addition to community members who have chosen to attend. Despite the presence of the judge and Crown attorney as representatives of the state, these individuals do not occupy a privileged position within the circle meeting. They do not wear ceremonial attire or sit on a raised platform as they might in a regular courtroom, and they are not entitled to speak any more than other members of the circle. Their presence primarily serves to ensure the circle process, and the sanction achieved through the circle, meet the standards of Canadian law. In this sense, the judge's power over the proceedings is still evident in the fact that he or she must approve the community sanction arrived at through the circle process.

A recent and controversial example of a sentencing circle can be found in the case of Christopher Pauchay, an Aboriginal man from the Yellow Quill reserve in Saskatchewan, who, on January 29, 2008, after drinking heavily, left his two daughters out in -30° C weather (see Box 4.1). While some, such as *National Post* columnist Jonathon Kay, bristle at the idea that Pauchay should receive a "traditional" justice response, such as a sentencing circle, former Crown prosecutor Pierre Rousseau rightly points out that the sentencing circle process does not attempt to fully revive "traditional" Aboriginal justice practices. Indeed, this process would better be described as a hybrid combination of Aboriginal healing circles with the Canadian criminal justice system, with the latter system still possessing the final authority over the sentencing decision. Along these lines, the judge in this case ruled in the end that Pauchay should serve a three-year prison term for his "reckless behaviour," despite the circle's recommendation Pauchay be given a conditional sentence to serve in his community.

The Navajo in the United States use peacemaking circles as a primary means of conflict resolution. According to Navajo tradition, a person who has been harmed is permitted to demand reparative action from the offending party. A *naat'aanii*, or respected community leader, then assists the disputing

Box 4.1 The Debate Over Sentencing Circles

The facts surrounding Christopher Pauchay's crime were so memorably awful that even now, a year later, unbidden images of it still occasionally dart through my brain whenever I am dressing my own children in their winter clothing.

Pauchay was a father living on Saskatchewan's Yellow Quill reserve. On the night of Jan. 29, 2008, after a hard bout of drinking, he staggered out into a blizzard with his two girls — aged three and one — and blacked out. Pauchay survived. But his children, facing -30°C weather in diapers and T-shirts, did not. In November, Pauchay pled guilty to criminal negligence causing death.

…Even in the very shadow of Yellow Quill's signature tragedy, our society's fixation on aboriginal cultural authenticity persists: This month, a judge declared that preliminary recommendations on Pauchay's punishment will be made by an aboriginal sentencing circle, a council led by "elders" in the Yellow Quill community.

…In 1996, the federal government began funding sentencing circles as part of its newly announced Aboriginal Justice Strategy, and amended the sentencing provisions of the Criminal Code to provide special treatment for aboriginals — later justified by the Supreme Court of Canada on the dubious basis that "many traditional aboriginal conceptions of sentence emphasize the notions of community-based sanction and restorative justice."

…The idea of applying a "traditional" model of native justice in Christopher Pauchay's case is particularly ridiculous…. "Traditional" aboriginal teachings, it is… worth noting, are equally useless in respect to the sex crime epidemic that afflicts many native reserves — since patriarchal hunter-gatherer societies generally assign no sexual autonomy to women. When sentencing circles have been used in cases involving aboriginal rapists, the practice often has proven humiliating, and even dangerous, for the victims…. The last place a native rape victim should want to find herself is in a room full of tribal grandees circling the wagons around her rapist.

There is a certain sort of perverse symmetry at play here: We encourage natives to live in Third World hellholes under the theory that cultural empowerment trumps the need to integrate them into mainstream society. Then, when they start killing and abusing one another, our legal system follows the same "traditional" playbook. How many more children must die before we realize that the fairy tales we tell ourselves about native culture always come with a tragic ending?

Source: Jonathan Kay, "The Folly of Native Sentencing Circles," *National Post*, January 20, 2009 <www.nationalpost.com/news/story.html?id=1196256>

Box 4.2 Pierre Rousseau: "The Truth about Sentencing Circles"

Posted: February 02, 2009, 10:30 AM by NP Editor

After reading Jonathan Kay's article about Christopher Pauchay's criminal negligence on Saskatchewan's Yellow Quill reserve ("The Folly of Native Sentencing Circles," Jan. 20), I realized that there is confusion about sentencing circles and aboriginal justice. I am a retired Crown prosecutor and spent many of my professional years working in aboriginal communities in northern Canada. I experienced first-hand the deficiencies of the criminal court system in those communities.

There is a misconception about sentencing circles. This is not an aboriginal process, but rather a process that was designed by judges who were concerned they had very little information about the communities they were sitting in and the people they were dealing with. A typical sentencing circle is composed of a judge, lawyers, the offender and, usually, the victim and members of the community that have an interest in the matter.

The purpose is to provide information to the court about the offender, the victims and the community, and to make recommendations about community resources to assist the court where there are possibilities of rehabilitation for the offender. The judge still decides on the sentence and has full latitude to impose a lengthy jail term. These circles, therefore, have no real impact on the suffering in the communities — they are only a consultation process used by the courts.

...Going back to Christopher Pauchay: His crimes are extremely serious and impacted his community in a way that is hard to imagine. Children are important in First Nations communities, and the Yellow Quill community was devastated by this awful crime.

The court got involved because this is how the government has decided justice should be rendered in these communities. The community did not request for the courts to get involved. But now the court wants to consult the community through a sentencing circle.

Once the court is informed of the impact of this crime on the community, and the circumstance of the offender, the victims and their families, then the judge will have the responsibility to apply the law to sentence this individual.

This is the judge's responsibility. Whatever the punishment handed to Christopher Pauchay, it will not be based on the decision of a sentencing circle.

Source: Pierre Rousseau: "The Truth About Sentencing Circles," *National Post, Full Comment*, February 2, 2009, <network.nationalpost.com/np/blogs/fullcomment/archive/2009/02/02/pierre-rousseau-the-truth-about-sentencing-circles.aspx> Pierre Rousseau lives in Sooke, B.C.

parties, along with their families and other affected clan members, as they meet to discuss the harm. A prayer begins the meeting to focus all participants on the issues at hand, and subsequently, each party details their version of the events that transpired. Next, everyone present is given the opportunity to speak about their thoughts and feelings with respect to the conflict and how it should be resolved (Yazzie and Zion 2003).

Healing circles follow a similar path to those practised in predominantly indigenous settings, although they are typically more directed at establishing dialogue and fostering recovery than "sentencing." As in the above two types of circles, healing circles are opportunities for the parties to come together in an inclusive environment and to hold an open discussion about a specific harmful event or series of harmful events. They can, in some cases, lead to subsequent sentencing circles if it is felt the discussion is positive enough to allow the parties to move toward cooperative settlement of the issue. However, they can also be used simply for the purpose of healing or reintegrating particular stakeholders. For example, in some cases, "circles of support" may be formed around a victim or offender to help that person recover from his or her pain and reintegrate into their community. This is a practice that is, on occasion, used for offenders who have committed child molestation and are returned to the community upon completing their sentence. Such individuals, because they are perceived to still represent a threat, have great difficulty forming social networks, so "circles of support" are formed in lieu of such networks to ensure these ex-offenders have the assistance they need to avoid recidivism.

In all circle types, a premium is placed upon the act of storytelling. The circle is an opportunity for multiple parties to present their own narratives of the events, but also to tell stories about the past that might offer some insight into current troubles (Pranis 2005). Through the sharing of stories, the parties can move toward an understanding of one another that has the potential to allow for either healing or consensual agreement, or both.

Truth and Reconciliation Commissions

During periods of authoritarian rule and mass violence, the power of the state often allows it to disguise or deny the existence of human rights abuses. Families who lose loved ones, or individuals who experience torture, may find themselves up against a justice system that denies the harm, or even their existence. For this reason, "truth" is often seen as a vital commodity in a post-authoritarian era. Once the authoritarian government is ousted, and democratic rule has been established, these new regimes often establish truth commissions to sort through the lies of the past and to facilitate the "transition" toward the future (see Kritz 1995; Teitel 2000; Offe 1997; Osiel, 1999; Marchak 2008).

Truth commissions have long been used in such situations (see Hayner 2002), but it is the South African Truth and Reconciliation Commission (SATRC) that has inspired the clearest association between Truth Commissions and restorative justice (Minow 1999; Llewellyn 2007). The negotiated demise of the apartheid system in South Africa raised the question of what is to be done with the former perpetrators of violence. Many would have liked to have seen these people punished within a court of law, or subject to vigilante retribution (Wilson 2001), but both of these responses raised the threat of civil war. The white minority that had long held power in South Africa still controlled many of the nation's vital institutions, such as the justice system and the military. It was deemed unlikely that they would just gracefully release power if they were faced with the threat of retribution. The truth commission was thus proposed as an alternative option. However, several of those who had been victimized under the previous regime were uncomfortable with the amnesty provisions that had typically accompanied truth commissions in Latin America. In Chile and Argentina, for example, blanket amnesties had been issued to release former perpetrators from all forms of civil and criminal prosecution, thus attempting to institute a complete letting-go of the past. The South African compromise offered that instead of a blanket amnesty, perpetrators would need to earn their amnesty. In short, they would need to stand before their fellow citizens and past victims and declare openly and honestly all that they had done. If they failed to tell the truth, their amnesty would be rejected, and they could potentially be subject to a civil suit or criminal charges.

This modified form of amnesty was still a difficult sell to South Africans who had been long oppressed by apartheid. To make it palatable, Bishop Desmond Tutu, who had been an outspoken critic of the apartheid system and was now chair of the truth and reconciliation commission, made the link between the truth commission and restorative justice. Tutu (1999) argued South Africa was heading toward a different type of justice, restorative justice, and, for the sake of individual and national healing, people needed to let go of their desires for retribution. For Tutu, South Africa had *No Future Without Forgiveness*, which is the title of his 1997 book about the SATRC, and in his view, it was only by forgiving past enemies that the country could make a relatively smooth transition from an apartheid regime into a modern democratic state. Furthermore, Tutu singled out the Bantu notion of *ubuntu* to demonstrate a long-standing African culture of forgiveness. Roughly translated as "a person is a person through other people," *ubuntu* suggests we are all interconnected and, therefore, whatever hurts one of us, hurts all of us. This sense of human relationality means we all have an interest in repairing rifts and healing harms, since any scar left unattended will affect the humanity of each and every one of us.

But in what sense was this truth commission a form of restorative justice? In its entirety, the SATRC consisted of three committees. First, there were the Human Rights Committees that travelled the country so select victims and victims' family members could recount their suffering and request reparation. To be eligible for a Human Rights Committee, one had to be the victim of a gross violation of human rights, meaning that only the most serious offences were considered by the SATRC. At the hearings, the commissioners would encourage the victims to offer their stories and would acknowledge the bravery and strength of each speaker. Counsellors were also on hand to speak with the victims and to discuss their needs for healing. However, the Human Rights Committee did not involve a face-to-face meeting with the perpetrators of apartheid violence. Instead, this opportunity would come at the Amnesty Hearings, the second committee of the SATRC. It was at these hearings that perpetrators of political crimes (and one had to prove that the crime had a political rather than criminal motivation) could reveal the full details of their actions in exchange for amnesty. These testimonies would then be vetted against the information gathered at the human rights committee hearings, as well as against the SATRC's own research into these past events. Victims were invited to attend the amnesty hearings and could, at times, be heard making sounds of admonishment when they felt a perpetrator was dissimulating or being less than truthful. However, an intensive discussion between perpetrators and victims was not facilitated by the SATRC. Indeed, the roles of "perpetrator" and "victim" were not always sufficiently clear to allow one to imagine a discussion occurring between distinct actors. For example, it was not just members of the apartheid state who were called to task for gross human rights violations. Members of black South African anti-apartheid groups were also complicit in these crimes. This included members of parties like the African National Congress or Inkatha Freedom, who used violence to eliminate or intimidate people suspected as informants, or who were members of competing organizations (see Wilson 2001; Krog 1998).

Box 4.2 offers a sample of testimony from the amnesty hearings. Here, Dirk Johannes Coetzee, a former South African hit squad commander, is questioned by his counsel, Mr. C. R. Jansen, and discusses the murder of human rights lawyer, Griffiths Mxenge. The family of Griffiths Mxenge were upset that Coetzee and his co-conspirators were provided amnesty by the SATRC because they felt, for one thing, it was not clearly demonstrated that Coetzee had a political motive for the murder, and it was not simply a matter of individual discretion on the part of the killers.

The dissatisfaction expressed by the Mxenge family illustrates the intense challenges of dealing with such a brutal past. We also see that in the very law-like proceedings of the amnesty hearings, there was no clear-cut con-

Box 4.2 Selections from the SATRC Amnesty Hearing of Dirk Johannes Coetzee (Griffiths Mxenge killing)

Mr Jansen: Can you relate to the Committee your involvement in this Mxenge matter? I think if you'd start with your presence in Durban at the time.

DJC: Mr Chairman, during November, early November — from early November onwards we were operating as a whole Vlakplaas [this is a farm that served as the headquarters of the South African Police counterinsurgency unit C10] team. All four teams were operating in the Durban area on instructions, and as usual I reported to Brigadier van Hoven's office as officer commanding every morning at half past seven, and every afternoon at 4 o'clock for debriefing and briefing. A few days before the 19th of November, on a morning briefing, he asked me to make a plan with Mr Mxenge. He then in very short terms briefed me that he was an ex Robben Island convict, that he was an attorney, that they were trying to build up a case against him, because he was an acting instructing attorney in all ANC cadres cases who were caught in the country, and that an amount something R200 000,00 went through his bank account. He then took me over to the office of then Captain Andy Taylor.

Mr De Jager: Did he add — sorry to interrupt. Did he add anything to the words, "You must make a plan with Mr Mxenge"?

DJC: He did, Mr Chairman, in the sense that he said we must not use guns or make him disappear, we must make it look like a robbery.

Mr Jansen: Can you continue. What happened thereafter?

DJC: He then took me across the passage to Captain Andy Taylor's office, the officer who handled the Mxenge case, who was on his specific case dealing with his surveillance, his phone tapping, etcetera, who then gave me a short description of his office and his house, of how many dogs he had on the premises. If I recall correctly he said it was four…. He then also went with us to show Mr Mxenge's house, and the information was also given to us that he usually works late at night, and his wife usually leaves before him. I requested Brigadier van der Hoven at the time to arrange with Brigadier Skoon for him to send Joe Mamasela [Mamsala is an *askari* or former resistance member who now works for the apartheid government] down for me as I would pick him as one of my team members. At the time Joe Mamasela was actually working with West Rand Security, Captain Jan Coetzee, who succeeded me on the 31st of December 1981 as commander at Vlakplaas, but whenever Captain Jan Coetzee didn't have work for him he would work with us, or when I needed him it would be arrange with Captain Jan Coetzee. So Brigadier van der Hoven arranged and, according to my recollection, Sergeant Schutte brought Joe Mamasela down on the 17th of November during the night which the dogs were poisoned. He brought down with him from Vlakplaas a hunting knife and two Okapi knives. Four pieces of meat we got from the police single quarters kitchen, and I had a bottle of strychnine in the back of my car, green crystals which the farmers used in the earlier days for jackal, to kill jackal that caught their sheep. Small slits — I made four pieces of meat, small chunks of meat with four slits in it, and put knife point — only a small knife point of strychnine in each piece of meat. This was not for the dog to taste the strychnine, and if you put in too much the dog would vomit it out. We then, on the night of the 17th, gave the pieces of meat — went to Mr Mxenge's house. Myself, and if I recollect, if my memory doesn't let me down, Captain Koos Vermeulen, Paul van Dyk, Almond Nofomela and Joe Mamasela drove to Mr Mxenge's house, where Almond and Joe got out of the car and the meat was distributed in the yard of Mr Mxenge. The next day some of the dogs got killed, I don't know exactly how many, and the idea was to leave it open for them to decide where they want to commit the murder, either at his place of work coming out, or on the road, or, if the situation might fall into their discretion as the right moment, at his house without being hampered by the dogs. Almond and Joe observed Mr Mxenge's office and his movements. The murder took place a day or two, if not three, after the poisoning of the dogs, and in fact on the night of the 19th of November. I had an arrangement with them that I would meet them....

Mr Jansen: If I may interrupt at that stage. Did you give the members of the team any instructions as far as the way in which the murder had to be committed?

DJC: Yes, I did, Mr Chairman. I said they should specifically not use guns, and must make it look like a robbery, and it was decided on knives, that Mr Mxenge will be killed with knives.

Mr Jansen: Did you give them any instructions as to how they should go about to conceal their involvement, or possible police involvement?

DJC: Well, they should not leave any tracks at all at the scene...

Mr Jansen: What is your present attitude towards what you did to the Mxenge family?

DJC: An extreme mixed emotions of /anger, for allowing me to get involved with this, all this nonsense — humiliation, embarrassment, and a helplessness of a pathetic, "I am sorry for what I've done," and I can do nothing else to them. What else can I offer them? A pathetic nothing, so in all honesty I don't expect the Mxenge family to forgive me, because I don't know how I ever in my life would be able to forgive a man like Dirk Coetzee if he's done to me what I've done to them. But I will hope that this will be the beginning of a new era in my life. I can just turn my back on it and walk on....

Source: Department of Justice and Constitutional Development, Government of South Africa. Proceedings held at Durban on November 5, 1996. <www.doj.gov.za/trc/amntrans/durban/coetzee1.htm>.

versation between perpetrators and victims of apartheid era harms. What was instead generated was a national discussion of the past. Daily reporting on the human rights violations exposed white South Africans more fully to the atrocities that had been committed in their name. This did not result in automatic societal reconciliation or consensus on the future, but it at least allowed black, white, and coloured South Africans to begin a discussion of their common future, albeit a future that has proceeded in the presence of severe social problems, such as extremely high crime rates.

The final committee is the Reparations and Rehabilitation Committee, which was charged with the task of recommending forms of material and symbolic redress for the victims of apartheid era violence. This committee possessed no formal governmental power and was therefore only able to suggest certain responses in the hope the government would implement them. Unfortunately, even the meagre compensation payments recommended by this committee were more than the South African government felt it could afford, and the government eventually only made 571.5 million rand (approximately $71.7 million Canadian) available to victims of apartheid, in contrast to the 3 billion rand (approximately $376 million Canadian) recommended by the Reparations and Rehabilitation Committee. The government also refused to implement a business tax on those companies that had profited from apartheid controls — a measure the Reparations and Rehabilitation Committee had recommended to redistribute wealth. In this sense, the outcomes of the SATRC have been, in many ways, less than restorative, but it is likely asking too much of any restorative justice process to achieve reconciliation so soon after a history of intense societal violence.

Restorative Justice and Reparations for Crimes of Mass Violence

The discussion of reparations brings us to another practice that is occasionally associated with restorative justice. With respect to crimes of mass violence, the term "reparations" is often used to refer to a wide variety of responses to an unsavoury past. Included within its ambit are truth commissions, but also compensation payments, restitution of stolen property, days of commemoration, memorial museums, lustration (i.e., the removal of members of a former regime from positions of power), and even tribunals (see Torpey 2001, 2003, and 2006).

Prior to World War II, such reparations were more commonly associated with warring parties rather than with the victims of state violence. In the aftermath of war, a victor nation would typically demand war reparations from the defeated party. However, the scale and scope of Nazi atrocities during World War II changed this arrangement. During the war, Jewish groups began organizing for victim reparations. These groups were engaged in the process of resettling refugees from continental Europe in the U.K., U.S., and what would become the nation of Israel, and they noted these individuals, who had been forced either to flee Europe to avoid Nazi death camps or massacres, had also left behind them a great deal of wealth (see, for example, Goldschmidt 1945; Moses 1944; Robinson 1944). Indeed, the Nazi-orchestrated Holocaust was not only an operation of massive killing; it was also one of large-scale theft. Every piece of property their victims left behind was appropriated by the Nazi regime or stolen by Nazi soldiers and guards. As well, Jewish slave labour had been used to manufacture arms and other goods for Germany. For example, the car manufacturer Volkswagen was a key supplier of armaments and vehicles for the Nazis and used Jewish slave labour in its wartime efforts. Even in death, the victims were robbed, as everything from their clothes, to gold fillings, hair, and prosthetic limbs were appropriated and recycled by the Nazis. Under these circumstances, it is not surprising Jewish survivors of the Holocaust felt they had a stake in reparations if and when the Allies won the war, especially considering the costs of Jewish resettlement they had to bear.

The lobbying efforts and negotiations engaged in by the Jewish groups that were soon under the Conference on Jewish Claims Against Germany (or Claims Conference) eventually achieved Allied support for Jewish reparations claims. Then, once the war ended, the American occupied zone of West Germany instituted a restitution policy (American Military Law no. 59) that was later adopted by the other Allied occupied zones. Efforts to achieve a broader reparations policy began in March 1952, in the Dutch town of Wassenaar, and culminated on September 10, 1952, in the Luxembourg Agreement, which featured a lump sum payment of DM3 billion (approximately $2.5 billion in current day Canadian dollars) to the fledgling nation of Israel (much of this in the form of goods), and also contained two settlements with respect to the Claims Conference: the first required West Germany to improve existing compensation and restitution legislation to make it more readily available to a wider group of claimants, and the second provided a payment of DM450 million to the Claims Conference (Goschler 2004).

This reparations agreement did not end Jewish reparations claims once and for all. Despite the agreement's requirements that West Germany improve its reparations policy, new demands continued to arise with respect to its limitations. For example, the 1956 revised Federal Compensation Law improved on the narrow framework of American Military Law no. 59, moving West German reparations beyond merely returning stolen items, but still presented several problems for claimants. First, it restricted claims to those based upon racial, religious, or political persecutions, which raised challenges for Roma and Sinti (formerly "Gypsies") claimants who had allegedly been persecuted as "criminals" because the Nazis associated their nomadic lifestyle with innate criminality (Puxon 1981). Second, only those who lived within the German borders as of December 1, 1937, or who moved to the Federal Republic within certain time limits, were permitted to apply, thus restricting reparations largely to those "who currently were German nationals or who had been German nationals at the time of their persecution by the Nazis" (Goschler 2004: 391). Finally, reparation was only available to claimants who lived in countries that held diplomatic relations with West Germany, thus excluding those victims from Eastern European nations or who had fled to them (Goschler 2004; Schrafstetter 2003). The continued efforts of the Claims Conference resulted in the 1965 "Final Law," a law that was final only in name as victims excluded from this law pressed for further legislation that would recognise their claims. More recently, Germany has attempted to forge a "legal peace" with respect to reparations claims through the establishment of the "Remembrance, Responsibility and Future" foundation (2000), which is intended, in particular, to bring an end to U.S.-based lawsuits against German corporations and the German government.

Alongside paying individual and collective compensation, Germany has made efforts to encourage remembrance and historical understanding of the Nazi past. This has involved several efforts at commemoration, through memorials, museum, school curricula, and other vehicles (see Niven 2002). In addition, monies paid to the Claims Conference contributed to the spread of "Holocaust consciousness" (Novick 1999) worldwide, as funds were used to educate people internationally about the horrors of the Holocaust and the need to prevent similar events from ever happening again. This is not to suggest German responses to the past have always been accepted without criticism — this is certainly not the case. However, it does illustrate a family resemblance between the philosophy of restorative justice and the practice of reparations. Reparations are typically negotiated between representatives from both the perpetrating and surviving parties. The goal is to arrive at an agreement that will satisfy the claimants (to the extent that this is possible after such terrible events) and will foster a degree of social healing. In this manner, one could argue reparations are a victim-centred process focused upon the needs and suffering of victims, both as individuals and as part of a collective (Cunneen 2006). As well, as in the case of Germany, the offending nation or party may even be seeking reintegration within the international community, as it was often said that German reparations were directed toward bringing Germany back into the "family of nations" (Jelinek 1990). It was also an opportunity for German "national self-interrogation" (Maier 1988) through which Germans eventually came to reflect upon what it was about their national identity that allowed them to become perpetrators of such vile crimes.

It should be noted the term "reparations" is also often used for monetary disbursements in the aftermath of other collectively harmful events, such as the sale of unsafe products or environmental damage caused by corporate negligence. However, such compensatory agreements are of a different category than the reparations described here. In particular, these disbursements are better described as "settlements," since they typically lack a significant symbolic component in the form of commemoration, public atonement, or apology (see Brooks 2003). Instead, they are more often than not monetary settlements designed to prevent more damaging civil lawsuits.

Grey Areas of Restorative Justice

In each of the "styles" discussed above, there exist shades of grey in terms of the degree to which its actual practice lives up to the principles of restorative justice. For example, many of these practices are unable to realize the ideal of local empowerment propounded by many restorative advocates (Christie 1977; Zehr 1990). As much as many practitioners would like to see a restorative justice that is largely administered within local community settings (and therefore "informal" as opposed to being part of the "formal" criminal justice system), state resources and agents are often necessary to the functioning of a restorative justice program. We saw in circle sentencing, for example, the involvement of criminal justice figures (e.g., judges and lawyers) at crucial stages of the process, such as the judge's role in determining whether or not the community's sanction meets the standards of Canadian law. One can also see at work within the South African Truth and Reconciliation Commission a great deal of formal law. The SATRC tended toward legal interpretations of key events, such as in deciding what is a "gross human rights violation" or "crime against humanity." As well, it employed legalistic rules of evidence, it used subpoenas to demand witness testimony, and followed a juridical rationale for determining whether or not perpetrators deserved amnesties (Christodoulidis 2000; see also Wilson 2001 and Meierhenrich 2008). Likewise, reparations often involve state-level negotiations rather than facilitated victim and perpetrator interactions.

But there exist other programs that borrow the label of restorative justice that are, perhaps, even more problematically situated within this category. For example, when conducting research on the practice of restorative justice in British Columbia, my co-investigator and I came across several programs that used a technique they referred to as "community accountability panels," which they described as a form of restorative justice. These panels were locally operated and, in most cases, were run by a group comprised largely of volunteer practitioners. They took referrals for cases of minor youth crimes that were diverted to them for sanctioning. Upon receiving a case, the program would assemble a panel of prominent members of the community with which the young offender would meet to discuss the crime. In rare instances, the victim may have also been present at the panel hearing, but this was hardly the norm. Instead, the youth would stand before the panel to listen to their advice and would be provided some limited opportunity for input into the sanction he or she was about to receive.

At the time, although it was not the focus of our research (Woolford and Ratner 2003), this seemed like a potentially stigmatizing and punitive process, especially considering the very minor nature of some of the cases presented before such panels, which included acts such as thrown snowballs, shoplifting, and graffiti. Indeed, subsequent research suggests similar panels, as used in

England and Wales, are beset by potential problems such as managerialism, in the sense that they are used as an administrative means to speed minor cases through the court system. They also contribute to net-widening by dealing with minor crimes that would otherwise be ignored by the criminal justice system. Finally, they are part of a process of reformalization, whereby lawyers are increasingly involved in these allegedly informal settings and the panels are facilitated in a legalistic manner, for example, using legal styles of questioning to obtain information from young persons (Crawford 2003; see also Crawford and Newburn 2002).

Panels such as these are here placed in a grey area because they have a potential to be restorative, but they also violate some of our key expectations of restorative justice programs. They can be restorative in the sense there is the possibility a very productive conversation will unfold between the community panel and the young offender, and this could have empowering consequences for the young person's life, helping reintegrate him or her into the community and halting what was potentially a path toward greater criminal involvement. However, there is also great risk that the panels will devolve into informal courts, where community members stand in judgment of a minor offender, enacting communal vengeance upon this young person. It also does not help matters that such panels are, in part, a repackaged form of diversion — a pre-restorative justice criminal justice reform that sought to direct youth away from the criminal justice system and toward community-based programs to spare young people the brunt of criminal stigmatization. Such diversion programs were roundly criticized by scholars like Stanley Cohen (1985), who saw them enabling an extension of the stigmatizing and social control powers of the state into everyday community life, especially with respect to providing increased state and social control over poor, minority youths.

This is but one example of a program that occupies this grey area of restorative justice. There are many criminal justice programs that pre-exist restorative justice, but which have been re-branded restorative justice, since they are believed to aspire toward similar goals. Even offender literacy and job training programs are, at times, described as part of a larger restorative justice project, since such activities are integral to offender reintegration, especially if we wish to provide restorative services for those who have been sentenced through the regular criminal justice system but seek a restorative immersion back into society upon their release from a correctional institution.

Empirical Findings: What do Restorative Justice Practices Achieve?

Today, most government-funded restorative justice programs include an evaluative component. This involves measuring the degree to which the program has met its stated goals. Therefore, a program that has the stated objectives of rehabilitating offenders, healing victims, and restoring communities may be evaluated on the basis of whether or not offenders have committed further offences after participation in the program, whether or not victims feel their needs have been met, and whether or not community members have become involved in the process.

However, these evaluative criteria are not free from political considerations. Who, for example, defines the program's goals? For government supporters of restorative justice, the desired outcomes may be described by a few key measures. Does restorative justice prevent offender recidivism? Does restorative justice reduce the costs of administering justice? Does restorative justice increase victim satisfaction? These are the matters that tend to have the best political optics for governments who are out to convince the general public they are bringing an end to the problem of crime, managing political coffers effectively, and meeting the demands of victims. However, the priority placed on questions such as these can lead to efforts at program evaluation in restorative justice that simply measure government interests rather than the actual restorative effects of restorative justice.

There is also a growing trend for government and other funding bodies to demand quantitative results demonstrating the success of a given restorative justice program, and, while it is not impossible for some restorative justice programs to provide quantified "measurables" to demonstrate their success, much of what restorative justice aims to achieve is not reducible to straightforward numeric terms. For example, a goal such as "healing" may be reflected in survey question data about victim satisfaction and the degree to which the person "feels" healed at whatever point in time after the restorative meeting that the survey is conducted, but these are most certainly imperfect measures, since healing is a process and not an either/or characteristic of the self. One's sense of healing after a traumatic event will ebb and flow; there will be "good days" and "bad days." A realistic achievement for restorative justice is to provide such persons with new frameworks for understanding the harm they experienced (or that they committed) so they may better negotiate their lives in the aftermath of the harmful event, but such frameworks are harder to gauge, especially when one is limited to quantitative analysis. It is also the case that there is no universally shared sense of healing (Braithwaite 2003). Experiences like healing and restoration are intensely individual, and it is difficult for a large survey to attend to all the various definitions of healing individuals might hold.

Beyond these more general questions about whether the tools of social scientific quantitative methodology can adequately capture the oftentimes ephemeral and deeply ontological experience of restorative justice are questions that arise in attempts to measure the success of restorative justice. Much early empirical restorative justice research was burdened by the problem that participants were not randomly assigned to either a restorative or retributive justice program, thereby allowing for measurement of the comparative success of the restorative justice program. This raised the concern that many of the participants in restorative justice may have been selected in a manner that included predominately those who are unlikely to recidivate and are more likely to feel satisfaction after participating in a restorative session. Indeed, offenders are often directed toward restorative justice programs because they are believed to be "promising" candidates, since they have admitted responsibility, and they may have a strong support network to help them with their reintegration. For this reason, it is difficult to tell whether or not these offenders would have done equally well if their cases were processed through the regular criminal justice system. In addition to this problem of selection bias, studies of restorative justice have also been criticized for lacking power in that they typically work with small sample sizes that prevent them from achieving statistical significance.

Evaluators of restorative justice have worked diligently to correct or circumvent these challenges, and, thus far, restorative justice appears to be making a favourable impact. With respect to evaluations of the role of restorative justice in helping victims of crime, several studies have shown positive results. For example, Heather Strang's (2001) research on crime victims in Canberra, Australia, compared court- and restorative-justice assigned crime victims with respect to their desires for vengeance. She found that over half of those who used the courts longed for revenge, while this was true for only 7 percent of those who used restorative justice (cited in Braithwaite 2003). Thus, those who were routed toward restorative justice were more likely to overcome some of their anger and vengefulness.

Although some programs show high levels of victim participation and satisfaction, these remain troubling concerns for many restorative justice programs. In some cases, restorative justice programs have great difficulty encouraging victims to become involved, but victim participation is usually possible if an effort is made to ensure it is convenient for victims (Braithwaite 2003). It has also been noted in various studies that victims are, at times, the least satisfied participants in restorative conferences (e.g., Maxwell and Morris 1993), although McCold and Wachtel's (1998) study in Bethlehem, Pennsylvania, showed that 94 percent of victims were satisfied with their conferences, and Strang's (2001) study in Wagga Wagga, Australia, revealed 90 percent were satisfied. Studies have also shown that victims participating in restorative justice are more satisfied than those who go through the courts (Latimer et al. 2001). This suggests that at least some restorative justice programs have managed to offer victims a more satisfying justice.

Offenders typically have high levels of satisfaction and perceive restorative processes to be fair (Braithwaite 2003). This is particularly true for offenders who participate in programs that are highly restorative in the sense that they encourage a large degree of stakeholder participation (McCold and Wachtel 2002). Reports on reductions in offender recidivism through restorative justice have been mixed, although some restorativists would argue recidivism is too blunt a measure and may not fully capture the gradual change an offender experiences after restorative intervention — a change that may include a few hurdles (or reoffences) along the way. Nonetheless, there are programs that show positive results on the recidivism front. For example, Restorative Resolutions, based out of the John Howard Society of Manitoba, is a program for adult offenders who have committed more serious crimes (crimes where the Crown is proposing a sentence of 6 months or more). In a study by Bonta et al. (1998), it was shown that participants in Restorative Resolutions had half the amount of recidivism as that exhibited by members of the control group, who were processed through the regular criminal justice system. Maxwell et al. (2006) also note that most studies show conferences have the potential to reduce recidivism, but this is not universally the case. In their view, the keys to success in preventing recidivism include active participation, consensual decision-making, lack of stigmatizing shaming, and visible offender remorse (Maxwell et al. 2006: 103).

The level to which restorative justice has benefited communities is still open to debate. Concerns that certain communities are unsuited to restorative justice, perhaps because they are perceived to be dysfunctional, appear unfounded, as even communities deeply troubled by cycles of violence and sexual abuse have been able to form positive helping networks through restorative justice programs. Here, the example of Hollow Water, Manitoba, is revealing (see Box 4.3). Although there remain concerns about the levels of community pressure upon victims to accept the restorative justice process and the presence of offenders in their midst, the program has allowed this community to begin to come to terms with its intergenerational problems of physical, sexual, and emotional violence, as well as substance abuse. In contrast, the South African Truth and Reconciliation Commission, a process we described earlier as being primarily about societal healing or reconciliation, has seen a continued rise in criminal violence in the aftermath of its efforts. While a case can still be made that the SATRC has started South Africa on a path toward healing, several commentators suggest the SATRC was too legalistic and directed toward nation-building (Wilson 2001), overlooked the structural problems created by apartheid by focusing solely on those who committed gross human rights violations and ignoring the many other "beneficiaries" of apartheid (Mamdani 2000), and left victims who did not buy into the quasi-religious philosophy of reconciliation unsatisfied and still seeking vengeance (Wilson 2001; Acorn 2004).

What remains is for more research to be conducted on the ways in which

Box 4.3 Hollow Water Healing: Straightforward, Honest

A healing movement that has roots in British Columbia has successfully taken hold in Hollow Water, Man. and is reaching to other parts of the country.

Valdie Seymour and Berma Bushie are two of the founders of what is called the community holistic circle healing in Hollow Water, a First Nation of 700 people on the eastern shore of Lake Winnipeg.

It's a process that has successfully been used to deal with dozens of cases of sexual abuse. Eighty-four sexual abuse victims and forty-eight offenders have benefited from the circle healing in Hollow Water during the past ten years. Nine out ten offenders are taking responsibility for their actions and the pain they have caused, and seldom re-offend, said Bushie. Now others want to know how it's done….

Bushie said Hollow Water's vision includes two basic values that sustained Hollow Water families in the past: children are looked upon as gifts from the Creator and women have a place of honor because the Creator has given them the gift of bringing life into the world.

The other key element was the four basic laws of the Anishinabe — honesty, kindness, sharing and respect.

In the mid-1980s, Hollow Water discovered a solution in the power of healing circles, beginning with a resource team of twenty-four, the members of which openly shared their painful personal stories with each other.

A confidential survey in a workshop of sixty community members indicated that two-thirds of the participants had been sexually victimized as children, youth or adults, and one-third had sexually victimized others.

Bushie, a victim of incest and rape by the time she was twelve, came to realize the silence regarding abuse would have to be broken if she wanted her community to live its vision.

"I lived in silence around these issues until I was thirty-eight," she said. "I came to know that the dynamics of silence in my community kept me from having a good life. I couldn't practise the laws of the Creator while I was trapped in that silence and rage."

The resource team heard its first sexual abuse disclosure from a child less than two years later, in 1996.

In search of help, twenty community members travelled to Alkali Lake, B.C. in 1988. By this time, Alkali Lake was renowned for having turned around an adult population of which 95 percent were said to be abusing alcohol to the point where 95 percent were considered "recovering" alcoholics.

When the Hollow Water group returned from Alkali Lake, it conducted a week-long stretch of workshops to share personal stories about victimization. Soon, there was a flood of seventeen disclosures from children of current abuse cases.

"They were disclosing on uncles, aunts, grandfathers. It was a scary time for the community," Bushie remembers. As a child care worker, she was faced with the scary prospect of having to bring half of Hollow Water's child population into the care of its child welfare agency. Half of the adult population could have been reported to the criminal justice system.

"We felt such actions would escalate things, not bring order," she explained. "If you're an offender, the system will protect you every step of the way. The courts will do everything in their power to rip the victim apart to support your lie."

The offender, though, is faced with the prospect of jail, where, Bushie said, healing is unlikely.

Instead, Hollow Water concentrated on setting up an alternative. Two teams were formed, one to sit in circles with the victim, another for the offender, along with their respective families. Eventually, the two groups are brought together in a larger healing circle, and later a sentencing circle that also involves community members and the usual players that would be found in a court setting.

"Victims need to get out of the trap of shame and guilt and… hear they're supported and celebrated for the things they've brought into the open," said Bushie.

Rupert Ross, an assistant Crown attorney in Kenora who travelled to Hollow Water as part of a three-year Aboriginal Justice Directorate project and wrote about it in his book *Returning to the Teachings*, knows the circles have a profound effect on the offenders.

"I heard a woman say twenty years after being abused that she still feels so dirty that she can't have her grandchild sit on her knee because she doesn't want to contaminate him or that she can't stand to look at herself in the mirror," he said. "Statements like that have immense power over an offender because the truth is part of healing. Our justice system doesn't operate at that spiritual, emotional level."

Bushie calls it a straightforward process that operates out of honesty. "There are no bargains of 'You do this and we'll do that.' Our way is not easy. To be honest is difficult."

Source: Bryan Phelan, "Hollow Water Healing: Straightforward, Honest," *Wind Speaker*, January 1, 1998.

restorative justice contributes to the formation of "social capital" as well as to strengthening community relationships. Social capital refers to helping networks that act as a resource for individuals, providing them with relationships that can be relied upon in times of need. It is certainly a reasonable hypothesis to expect that people gathering to discuss a common concern will bond in a manner that will make them resources for one another in the future, but, so far, there is too little evidence to support this claim.

In all, restorative justice programs have been subject to a great deal of evaluation, and studies tend to support the claim that restorative justice offers benefits that are not typically or widely available through the regular criminal justice system. This section has offered only a very brief sampling of some of this research, but those interested in reading more about the empirical results of restorative evaluations would find a great wealth of research at their disposal (see, for example, Elliott and Gordon 2005).

Facilitator Techniques and Restorative Practices

When we talk about VOR, VOM, FGCs, circles, and even truth commissions, it can appear as though these are spaces of spontaneous interaction. However, this ignores that the person who is in the role of the facilitator (although they may alternately referred to as a "mediator" or "commissioner" or by some other title) often makes very strategic interventions into the discussion in order to transition the parties toward a resolution. Examples of these interventions can be found in mediator training manuals, but often they are simply intuitive communicative devices that we all apply in our attempts to change the direction of a conversation. There are many facilitator techniques and models available, too many to discuss here. The model of mediation designed by Cheryl Picard (1998) illustrates the key aspects of facilitation and its limitations.

Most restorative justice sessions are comprised of several stages. These stages may not follow a discrete linear order, and one could identify other potential stages, but, generally speaking, each restorative justice session will feature an introduction, recital, transition, problem-solving, and agreement building (Picard 1998). The introduction is where the facilitator establishes a positive and productive atmosphere for the meeting by welcoming everyone and stressing the potential good that can evolve from their collective involvement in the justice process. The facilitator might also choose to remind the parties of the procedure for the session and the ground rules, such as by asking them not to interrupt one another. Once this is accomplished, the recital unfolds through the victim and offender telling their versions of the events that transpired. Other members of the restorative meeting might also be invited to speak about what happened. What is key at this stage, however, is that the facilitator help the participants move from discussing the event to discussing what to do about the event. This can happen naturally without any influence from the facilitator, but the facilitator does have at his or her disposal some techniques for helping the participants along, focusing them on problem-solving, so they can eventually draw up an agreement (Picard 1998).

The first technique is to ask *open questions*. Open questions are often "how" and "why" questions that allow respondents to explain themselves in their own terms, rather than nudging them toward a desired answer. So, rather than assuming the victim's feelings by asking, "What made you angry that day?" the facilitator would want to enquire more carefully, "How did that make you feel?" As well, the facilitator would want to avoid any line of questioning that may seem judgmental, such as "Why did you feel angry?" "Why" questions, in particular, have a tendency to sound accusatory (Picard 1998), and it would be preferable to provide room for the participant to describe his or her own feelings with a question like, "How did that make you feel?"

The second technique is to *summarize and paraphrase*. When individuals are engaged in lengthy acts of storytelling, it is not uncommon for them to get overwhelmed by the details of the discussion. A good summary helps to focus the parties on the major issues of contention and therefore helps prevent unnecessary distraction. Summary is also helpful when a party repeats him or herself incessantly because it allows this person to know he or she has been heard. Similarly, a paraphrase is a briefer summary where a statement is rephrased to ensure clarity of meaning and to let the speaker know she or he has been heard (Picard 1998).

With both the paraphrase and the summary, there is the possibility of restating what has been said in more neutral terms. Thus, if a party puts something in positional and combative terms ("he's selfish and doesn't care about anyone other than himself"), the facilitator can hone in on the interest that is at stake in the statement ("so what I am hearing is that you feel a certain level of trust and generosity is important between neighbours") (see Fisher and Ury 1991 for further discussion of "positions" and "interests"). Once the statement is repositioned in this way, a new discussion can emerge as to how the parties might achieve the general interest (trust and generosity) rather than getting bogged down in the combative claim ("he is selfish"). This neutralized summary is, in fact, a third form of intervention, *reframing*. Through reframing, the conversation is shifted toward common interests that can be resolved, stressing what is positive and focusing the parties on issues that can be resolved (Picard 1998).

A final set of techniques is used for purposes of *acknowledging, validating, and normalizing* the feelings and sentiments of participants. For example, a facilitator may acknowledge the feelings of a speaker, as well as validate and normalize those feelings. Thus, in the aftermath of break-and-enter, it may be useful for the facilitator to acknowledge the fear one may feel after one's home has been broken into, and to validate that this is a normal feeling for one to experience. Such an intervention would therefore recognize a victim's sense of discomfort, help them put a name to their feelings, and perhaps allow them to move forward in the discussion (Picard 1998).

All of the techniques are designed to help parties to transition from detailing the harm they suffered and laying blame (or providing excuses) toward finding a resolution. The goal is to subtly teach participants in the restorative justice session how to properly engage in conflict resolution. These "soft" technologies of power thus also serve as forms of modelling, with the facilitator thereby providing the participants with a model they should follow (Woolford and Ratner 2008b). These techniques are also coupled with the efforts made to prepare participants for restorative justice encounters, which often involve tips on how to communicate and listen effectively.

More broadly, these techniques are part of the "staging" or "choreography" of restorative justice (Dignan et al. 2007: 12). These interventions combine with other facilitator efforts to script and design the restorative encounter in a way that better ensures its success. In some restorative programs, actual scripts are employed for facilitators to follow, so certain questions are asked and all participants receive their opportunity to speak. As well, facilitators are careful to arrange the chairs in the room to allow for effective face-to-face communication. Thus, to reiterate, restorative justice encounters are not entirely spontaneous and unstructured. Although unscripted moments will likely arise, a great deal of planning is involved to try to produce restoration.

The Embodied Politics of Restorative Justice

Both the direct and indirect training of restorative justice participants aims to impart new dispositions in potential combatants. When we are in conflict, we often react in accordance with our conflict socialization. For example, a youngster who has observed family members being quick to anger may take on similar patterns, but, more broadly speaking, the entrenched position of adversarial law in our culture also means we almost automatically think in legal terms when confronted with conflict (Ewick and Silbey 1998). Recently, a mistake made by a roofing contractor led to rain getting into the walls of my house, destroying my paint and plaster in several rooms and presenting the risk of future mould and mildew. Although my partner and I sought to negotiate a reasonable solution with the contractor outside of the courts, we nonetheless did so in the "shadow of law" (Harrington 1985). The framework for our discussion included the legal rights we had as homeowners based upon the contract we had signed with the contractor. We did not assume this legal posture after a long period of deep strategic consideration; instead, it came to us almost naturally, as though we could sense our leverage in this disagreement could be most readily found through recourse to legal thinking.

This sort of legal reflex is becoming a more regular feature of our societies. With movies, books, and television fixated on the drama of the courtroom, and with daily news stories of happenings in the courts, a legal rationality seeps deeper into our unconscious minds. It is also the case that legal terminology has become everyday parlance, with words like liability, moot, and tort in more frequent usage. In other cases, such as with the notion of justice, the term has become synonymous with its legal sense, thereby ignoring the long history of debate about "justice" that precedes the formation of the "justice system" as we know it today. In this manner, legalism has become a largely un-thought tool that we use to negotiate and make sense of our world.

The task for restorative justice is to challenge and disrupt this legal reflex. Embedded in legalism is a confrontational and adversarial sensibility that is much different than the restorative justice ethos described in Chapter 3. Although the legal ethos and the restorative justice ethos would be in agreement that conflicts are knowable, they would differ with respect to the question of how they are knowable. For restorative justice, they are knowable through open and cooperative interaction, whereas for the legal ethos, it is through adversarialism, with defence and prosecution presenting their competing versions of the truth. Therefore, if we already inhabit a reality in which legalism is an almost automatic response to conflict, it is necessary for restorative justice to try to retrain us and discipline us according to the restorative standard. This may be less difficult for some individuals who have been socialized in accordance with spiritual or familial beliefs that stress co-operation over competition. But for others, restorative retraining will require a great deal of work. This may be especially true for some offenders who have learned to use violence as their reflex response to conflict.

Two notions drawn from the work of Michel Foucault can help us better understand the ways in which restorative justice seeks to retrain individuals and to fashion new subjects, and therefore help us to identify the ways in which the politics of restorative justice allows it to operate as a mode of governance. These notions are *techniques of discipline* and *technologies of the self*. Techniques of discipline are used to produce "normality" by creating "normal" individuals who are controlled rather than coerced in the sense that their behaviour is regulated by multiple techniques (e.g., time tables and traffic signals). For example, restorative justice practitioners educate participants in the "conduct of conduct" through the cues and interventions they use to remind participants of how they should be communicating. Through repetition of these actions, participants are drilled to become restorative rather than combative communicators. Through a great deal of preparation and frequent reminders, participants become disciplined to norms of effective listening and interest-based negotiation. Similarly, communities can play a role in disciplining their members to abide by a "harmony ideology" (Nader 1990) through which victims and offenders are coercively pressured to emulate passive, conciliatory behaviours, no matter how righteous their conflict(s) might be (see also Napoleon 2004 and Acorn 2004).

In contrast, technologies of self rely on individuals' own self-regulation as they come to internalize societal controls and to play an active role in monitoring their own conduct and being responsible for their activities (Burchell, 1993; Pavlich, 1996a). In Foucault's (1994: 225) words, technologies of the self

85

permit individuals to effect by their own means, or with the help of others, a certain number of operations on their own bodies and souls, thoughts, conduct, and way of being, so as to transform themselves in order to attain a certain state of happiness, purity, wisdom, perfection or immortality.

This may be achieved through strategies that encourage individuals to accept responsibility for their own governance and to accept rationalities of self-governance as natural and unquestionable. Certain self-help programs, Alcoholics Anonymous or anger management for example, ask participants to police their own behaviour so they halt practices of drinking and emotional displays that are perceived to be socially unacceptable. Likewise, restorative justice asks participants to become vigilant evaluators of the ways in which they approach conflicts so they might learn to "walk the talk" of restorative justice in their day-to-day lives.

This "soft coercion" employed by restorative justice practitioners may or may not seem problematic upon first glance, depending on your opinions on social control. It does, however, counter claims made by some advocates that restorative justice is "non-coercive" (Van Ness and Strong 2002). Moreover, it is necessary that we interrogate what sort of politics is at work when techniques of discipline and technologies of self are put into practice. For example, some advocates have claimed that one of the strengths of restorative justice is that it is apolitical and can appeal to liberals and conservatives alike (Van Ness and Strong 2002).

In part, the adaptability of restorative justice to conservative and neo-liberal contexts has to do with the vision restorative justice holds of the ideal citizen. In imparting its communicative techniques, restorative justice works to create individual citizens who are non-combative and peaceable resolvers of conflict. Such individuals are obviously appealing to governments that would like to have a passive citizenry more apt to engage in talk than to protest and undertake acts of civil disobedience. For this reason, it will be argued in subsequent chapters that restorative justice must not dogmatically seek to produce non-conflictive individuals. Indeed, there are times and places when restorative justice may feel it necessary to support combative relations, and it is only in ideal circumstances that cooperative communication should win out.

This conceptualization of the potential for governance to be administered through restorative justice should test any faith we had in the restorative justice encounter being a "good thing" in and of itself. The restorative encounter provides opportunities for empowerment and creative resolution, but it does not guarantee these or other desired outcomes of restorative justice (Johnstone and Van Ness 2007). Indeed, restorative justice can also be a venue for the renewal and strengthening of dominant power relations, using restorative techniques of discipline and technologies of self to fashion a population ready-made to be ruled. Or, it can be used as a soft justice option for middle- and upper-class youth, while the resources of retributive justice are preserved for more "risky" lower-class and minority young persons. Both tendencies are examples of the potential for political manipulation of the practices of restorative justice.

This chapter focused on the immediate context of restorative justice: its organizational styles, facilitative practices, and methods of evaluation. Based on this analysis, one point that should be evident is that restorative justice practices offer no certain protection against their political misuse. This fact becomes more worrisome when we look, as in the following chapter, more directly at the various participants in restorative justice, and the way in which their identities are shaped by the process — in some cases exhibiting a movement toward regulating rather than empowering these actors.

Chapter 5

Constructing Restorative Justice Identities

Who is involved in restorative justice? In Chapter 1, I described the various groups and actors that participate within the broader restorative justice social movement. In contrast, this chapter focuses on those who are present within actual restorative justice encounters or meetings: victims, offenders, facilitators, and community members. This chapter takes inspiration from the work of George Pavlich (2005), who has demonstrated that these are all problematic identities that are, in part, socially constituted through the discourses of restorative justice. Put simply, none of these actors — victim, offender, facilitator, or community member — exists in a natural sense. This is not to say people are not harmed, that people do not commit harms, that individuals do not help to mediate these conflicts, or that these harms do not take place within specific social and geographic spaces. Rather, it is a reminder that the meanings we attach to the labels of victim, offender, facilitator, and community are built through social relations. Everyday life is often incredibly complex, with each situation allowing for discernment of a plurality of harms and wrongs. In making sense of these situations, social actors draw upon condensed narratives to marshal complex facts and to make difficult situations both understandable and actionable. Thus, the sense made of a criminal event is the product of an act of interpretation that also plays a role in fashioning the identities of the actors involved in the event.

For example, it would appear on the surface that homicides would serve as relatively simple cases for interpretation of the identities of the parties involved. Say a young man kills his father after a heated argument (and since most homicides are committed by someone known to the victim, this seems an appropriate example). Here, we would have a seemingly clear-cut instance where the son is the offender (or, at this stage, the accused) and the father is the victim. The facilitator may be an individual called upon to conduct a post-sentencing mediation between the grieving wife/mother and her son, and the community is the neighbourhood in which the crime occurred. However, in assigning these identities, we have made several assumptions. First, we have treated the homicide as an isolated incident outside of a larger series of incidents — i.e., all the events that came before and led up to the murder. If, in this case, the son was subject to repeated abuse at the hands of the father, his role as offender is complicated by his past victimization, and he is both victim and offender (a combination more frequent than the simplistic black-and-white media reporting of and political grandstanding around crime would suggest).

Second, we have assumed victimization begins and ends with the person who has experienced physical or material harm. However, as restorative justice proponents often remind us, there is, in fact, a wide circle of victims of this event, as the harm of crime ripples beyond the immediate stakeholders and the geographic space in which the crime occurred. The mother is a victim, having lost her husband to homicide and her son to prison. The community is victimized by the shock they feel that such a thing could occur in their seemingly safe neighbourhood, but there is a wider circle of suffering that may include the friends, uncles, aunts, cousins, and workmates of both the son and father. Likewise, we also assume offending behaviour begins and ends with the actions of the son, but what if the mother and the neighbours long turned a blind eye to the abuse he suffered? Are there degrees of responsibility that can be assessed and unpacked? Indeed, the example above is relatively straightforward with respect to responsibility in comparison to examples that involve spousal violence or violent assaults committed upon Aboriginal reserves. In such cases, the matrix of responsibility expands to include broader structural factors, such as patriarchy, race, class, and colonialism.

This brief discussion only scratches the surface of the assumptions that are at work when we try to make sense of traumatic situations through taken-for-granted criminal justice identities, and the complexity of crime-based identity construction will become more evident as I examine separately the identities of victim, perpetrator, facilitator, and community member. Each of these populations will be understood as fractured and inchoate, so as to identify the processes by which they are given meaning. This approach allows for a critical understanding of crime-based identity construction, illustrating, for example, that the victim-offender dichotomy imported from the criminal justice system is a problematic basis on which to build restorative resolutions. In contrast, the emphasis here will be on the potential of restorative justice encounters to serve as sites for complicating and deconstructing these identities. This is a task of great political import for restorative justice, since without such critical engagement, restorative justice is at risk of complicity in the reproduction of dominant criminal justice and political conditions (see Pavlich 2005).

Victims

Restorative justice is often represented as a victim-centred approach to justice. This is because restorative justice does not marginalize the victim from the justice process while, at the same time, claiming to offer retribution on the victim's behalf. Instead, restorative justice recognizes the victim as a central stakeholder within the restorative process, and thus seeks to provide victims a prominent role in shaping the justice process and in deciding upon a just resolution to the conflict. All the while, the harm suffered by the victim and the needs of the victim in the aftermath of the criminal event are held to be of crucial importance. Therefore, a restorative approach to crime requires an identification of victim needs, which may include the following:

1. acknowledgment that the victim is blameless for the harm he or she suffered;
2. restitution of stolen items;
3. monetary compensation for damaged or unrecoverable items or for hardship suffered as a result of the crime;
4. symbolic atonement in the form of an apology or statement of regret from the offender;
5. a sense of safety and closure to assure the victim that he or she will not be similarly victimized by the offender again;
6. an opportunity for the victim to voice his or her suffering; and
7. to receive continued support from friends, community members, and/ or counselors (adapted from Johnstone 2002: 64–67).

However, it was noted in the introduction to this chapter that harm is not necessarily concentrated within a single individual or set of individuals. It can be broadly felt by all of those with some connection to the harmful event. It was also noted that harmful events are not isolated instances and often rest in a larger series of harmful events. These are important points that are widely acknowledged within restorative justice, resulting in efforts to address the broader and rippling effects of criminal harm (e.g., Van Ness and Strong 2002). In contrast, this section discusses an even more basic element of victimhood: its social and political construction.

Each of us is likely familiar with the difficulty experienced when trying to communicate a particularly painful experience. This frustration is perhaps most acute when we are very young and still learning the skills of language. A small bump or a minor disappointment can quickly cause us to unravel because of the exasperation felt when trying to express this hurt to our parents, who do not always fully understand our rudimentary language, but these experiences continue even as we mature. Anyone who has experienced a major violation or loss has also experienced the challenge of trying to articulate this hurt and may have even felt quite upset at people who said too quickly or too easily, "Yes, I understand." This upset is caused by our sense that the person does not understand and cannot understand because the experience and our feelings about it are unique and cannot be reduced to simple words. In fact, we may not even fully understand the experience ourself because it is associated with a confusing morass of sensations and memories.

This discussion has bearing on the identity of victims because the identification of a person as a victim is socially constituted through processes of verbal and symbolic communication. This means we require others to recognize our hurt so the label "victim" makes sense, otherwise we are completely alone in our victimhood, and it has no social relevance. This has further political implications, since socially unrecognized victimhood can result in one being deprived of political benefits and rights associated with this label. For instance, consider the period before various forms of family violence were fully recognized as public wrongs. Husbands and fathers were assumed to rule over their households, and therefore women and children who were subject to "moderate correction" at the hands of husbands/fathers were not considered victims of injustice, but rather the subjects of a legitimate form of political control (see Box 5.1). These sufferers therefore faced an uncertain legal context with respect to what would and what would not be considered "violence." In such situations, the power of the state to define who is and is not a victim often results in a competition among social actors to have their experiences of victimization officially recognized, as can be noted in mid- to late-twentieth-century feminist efforts to have courts take seriously the harms of domestic and family violence.

A stark example of the struggle over victim identities can be found in the case of Aubrey and Gus Lamm. When Randy Reeves killed Janet Mesner and her friend Vicki Zessin, Vicki's husband, Guy Lamm, and their daughter, two-year-old Aubrey, were left without a partner and mother. But eighteen years later, when the Nebraska Board of Pardons was considering commuting Reeves' sentence, Aubrey and Gus were denied the opportunity to speak on his behalf, as well as to voice their views against the death penalty he had been served. Why was this? Upon a District Court Appeal of their exclusion, Aubrey and Gus were informed they were agents of Randy Reeves and not victims, since they advocated for mercy rather than retribution. In contrast, Vicki's sister, who supported the death penalty, was permitted to make a presentation before the Board of Pardons and was therefore officially acknowledged as a "victim" (Kay 2006; Acker 2006). This is a clear case of the state only allowing for a certain type of victimhood — a type supportive of punitive policies — and therefore playing a role in constituting what and who may be a victim.

It is, however, not just recognition by the state that is crucial to establishing a victim identity. We also seek social recognition so our friends and neighbours understand us as innocent sufferers undeserving of the harm we experienced, for victimization often carries with it an unfair stigma, as victim-blaming is unfortunately too common in our society. In part, this is a

Box 5.1 William Blackstone on the Legal Rights of Husbands and Wives

In the nineteenth century, American and British women's rights — or lack of them — depended heavily on the commentaries of William Blackstone, which defined a married woman and man as one person under the law. Here's what William Blackstone wrote in 1765:

By marriage, the husband and wife are one person in law: that is, the very being or legal existence of the woman is suspended during the marriage, or at least is incorporated and consolidated into that of the husband; under whose wing, protection, and *cover*, she performs every thing; and is therefore called in our law-French a *feme-covert, foemina viro co-operta*; is said to be *covert-baron*, or under the protection and influence of her husband, her *baron*, or lord; and her condition during her marriage is called her *coverture*. Upon this principle, of a union of person in husband and wife, depend almost all the legal rights, duties, and disabilities, that either of them acquire by the marriage. I speak not at present of the rights of property, but of such as are merely *personal*. For this reason, a man cannot grant anything to his wife, or enter into covenant with her: for the grant would be to suppose her separate existence; and to covenant with her, would be only to covenant with himself: and therefore it is also generally true, that all compacts made between husband and wife, when single, are voided by the intermarriage....

The husband also, by the old law, *might give his wife moderate correction*. For, as he is to answer for her misbehaviour, the law thought it reasonable to intrust him with this power of restraining her, by domestic chastisement, in the same moderation that a man is allowed to correct his apprentices or children; for whom the master or parent is also liable in some cases to answer. But this power of correction was confined within reasonable bounds, and the husband was prohibited from using any violence to his wife....

These are the chief legal effects of marriage during the coverture; upon which we may observe, that even the disabilities which the wife lies under are for the most part intended for her protection and benefit: so great a favourite is the female sex of the laws of England. (William Blackstone. *Commentaries on the Laws of England*. Vol. 1, 1765, pages 442–45.)

Source: Jone Johnson Lewis, "Women and the Law." <womenshistory.about.com/cs/lives19th/a/blackstone_law_2.htm>

protective mechanism we use to assure ourselves of our own security and to preserve our sense of existential certainty. To say, "He was harmed because he was not careful," or "She was harmed because she associated with the wrong people," or "Look at the way she dressed," is also to say that such events are unlikely to befall us because we are not like the persons harmed. In this manner, victim claims to harm are made within a personal and political context. This requires victims to articulate and fashion themselves as particular types of victims (e.g., "innocent" and "undeserving") so that they might gain broader public support. Christie (1986) refers to this victim identity as the "ideal victim," which he contrasts to those who are perceived to be "deserving" of harm because of their lifestyle.

To combat these tendencies, victims will often mobilize stories to communicate their hurt and to provide other people a sense of their experience, no matter how confusing and incommunicable this experience may seem. Thus, in order to establish their innocence and to socially proclaim victimhood, harmed individuals will often *narrativize* their pain; that is, they simplify it into an understandable narrative that engages their intended audience. In so doing, they will often draw upon culturally resonant tropes that highlight the theme of innocence: "There I was minding my own business…," "Unexpectedly…," or "To my surprise…." Each such statement seeks to communicate that the victim is worthy and deserving of our empathy and support. Other statements might be used to illustrate that victims are good people who have been done wrong: "I had never imagined that anyone could be so cruel…," "His actions caught me completely off-guard…," or "I had trusted him…." These examples are offered here not to suggest that they do not contain a kernel of truth when they are used by people who have suffered harm; instead, the intention is to show there are standard communicative tools available upon which victims can strategically draw in their attempts to convince others of the legitimacy of their victimization claims.

The difficulty of communicating extreme harm is perhaps best illustrated through consideration of the Holocaust, and the intense challenges faced by memoirists and others trying to pass along to a contemporary audience their experiences of this incredibly horrific event (see, for example, Levi 1989; Delbo 1995; Wiesel 2006). Indeed, even to speak of a "Holocaust" requires an act of historical construction, since the Holocaust is comprised of a vast range of events. Although the primary image we carry of the Holocaust is of the death camps, such as Auschwitz-Birkenau, where more than one million victims were sent to the gas chambers and their corpses burned within crematoriums, this is but one space of trauma in the broader Holocaust experience. The Holocaust was also comprised of forced deportations, food shortages, slave labour, ghettoization, village massacres, sexual exploitation, rampant disease spread, and scientific and medical experimentation, to name but a few gross violations. In its totality, or even in but a fraction of its cruelty, the Holocaust is too much for one mind to process. However, people can gain some insight into its horrors through the narrativization of this complex experience. This is why generations of school children have been given *The Diary of a Young Girl* (Frank 1995) as a first text on the Holocaust. Anne Frank's story provides an account of the everyday harms contained within an individual experience of the Holocaust, and therefore offers a point of connection in what is otherwise an incomprehensible period of mass suffering. It was also the case that many Germans first connected with the mass suffering of the Holocaust through viewing an American made mini-series (titled *Holocaust*), which told the story of several families living through World War II and the Nazi-perpetrated atrocities (see Novick 1999; Cole 1999; Herf 1997). Such renderings of the Holocaust story ultimately receive criticism for being partial, but resonant narratives of the Holocaust can rarely tell more than a part of the story.

The key point here is that harm must be translated into a story to make it meaningful for others (see Alexander 2004). So, from the outset, an act of social construction is taking place in relation to the identity of the victim: the harmed individual(s) is being represented to an audience as someone worthy of their concern, and this requires that a comprehensible story be told about this harm. In addition, however, the construction of a socially recognized victim identity has further political implications, since claims to victimization are mobilized for a variety of political purposes: i.e., to build support for harsher criminal justice policies, to encourage more resources for those harmed by crime, or to reaffirm shared social norms.

Historically speaking, it is important to remember our society did not always embrace the victim identity in the way that we do today. For years, people eschewed the label "victim," associating the term with weakness and powerlessness (Garland 2001). The victim identity emerged as a key nodal point for political mobilization in the midst of World War II. During this period, as noted in Chapter 4, Jewish organizations worldwide became aware of the atrocities being committed by the Nazis in Europe. As the Allies discussed what their post-war policy might be toward the Germans, these organizations lobbied for the restitution of stolen Jewish property and compensation for Jewish individuals and organizations. These organizations convinced the Allies — the Americans in particular — that the Nazi plundering of Jewish wealth, as well as the hardship faced by Jewish organizations seeking to resettle the refugees from Nazi slaughter, deserved post-war attention. Their efforts led to a novel reparations program through which money was paid by the defeated nation not to the victors of war, but rather to its victims and "survivors" (see, Sagi 1980; Sebba 1980; Pross 1998; Goschler 1991; Kim 1999; Zweig 1987; Woolford and Wolejszo 2006). This period, however, still represented a hesitant embrace of the victim identity, and individuals were less likely to broadcast their victimhood than they are today.

"Identity politics" in the late 1960s and early 1970s opened a new stage in the valuation of the victim identity. "Identity politics" refers to a period in which social activism was guided less by one's position in the economic system ("relations of production") and more by forms of cultural identification. Marginalized groups more and more viewed their suffering and social dissatisfaction as a result not of their class position, but rather as a result of other forces, such as patriarchy, sexism, heterosexism, racism, ethnocentricism, to name but a few examples. Thus, identities based upon race, ethnicity, sexuality, and other cultural markers became increasingly prominent. Indeed, it was as an offshoot of the women's movement that the "victim's movement" began to gain its greatest ground. Feminist activists decried the lack of support offered to women who had been abused by their partners and loved ones and sought to increase services for, and advocacy on behalf of, such persons. Thus, the effort to establish shelters is one example of an emergent movement to recognize the needs of victims, not to mention to have female victims of abuse at the hands of their male partners recognized as victims. Moreover, an increased political voice for victims was found, as traumatic stories of violence and wrongdoing were drawn upon to illustrate the continuing power of patriarchy in society.

Soon thereafter victims of other crimes began to organize to press government and society to more fully recognize their suffering and attend to their needs. This was a slow process that has, in recent years, produced victories in the form of the adoption of bills of victims' rights in many jurisdictions and the increased use of victim impact statements (Achilles and Stutzman-Amstutz 2006). Policies are also being created to ensure restitution and compensation made by offenders go to crime victims rather than the state. While these advances are certainly significant, most victims' groups would agree still more needs to be done. For example, the Manitoba Victims' Bill of Rights and provincial policy on victim impact statements are both restricted to those who are harmed by only the most "serious" crimes, which in this case means crimes of violence.

The creation of victim narratives to communicate complex victim experiences and the mobilization of victims as political actors does not, however, mean victims retain full control over the symbolism of victimhood. Nearly every day in the media and in the halls of politics, the victim identity is being drawn upon to relay some pressing matter. A heart-wrenching story of victimization may be employed by a journalist to show how cold and unfeeling contemporary society has become, or politicians may use a story of a needless death to suggest more needs to be done to fight crime. In short, once a group has successfully mobilized and achieved resonance (and even repair) through its trauma narrative, it is often the case that this narrative itself becomes an object or resource for personal and political application and manipulation. That is, the stories of suffering employed by the victims to forward their cause also become resources for other claims-makers (both powerful and powerless) to use, and potentially misuse, for their own purposes.

This is a key point for understanding the reservations expressed by critical victimologists toward "conservative" or "positivist" victimology (see Miers 1989; Fattah 1992; Elias 1986; Walkate 1989), which advocates for increases in victims rights yet does not challenge the dominant assumptions about crime and punishment that govern the criminal justice system. Despite claims to value neutrality, positivist victimological research has taken for granted state-defined notions of crime and victimhood, and state-sponsored means of criminal punishment, and this allows for the co-optation of victim narratives by conservative political actors to promote retributivist ends, since the trauma narrative becomes neatly embedded within the common sense of criminal justice and control (Garland 2001). Simply put, the only victims considered worthy of study by positivist victimologists were those who were harmed by street crime rather than state or corporate crime, and their post-victimization needs were viewed as synonymous with state punishment. This is not to deny that some victims may demand punitive and vengeful responses to their trauma, and their trauma narrative may be designed to elicit these sorts of responses, but victim movements are not unified and do not speak with one voice. For each victim, in fact, there may be multiple and competing trauma narratives that articulate their suffering; however, certain narratives achieve broader resonance because they are consistent with or complementary to existing social and discursive conditions and therefore receive broader support. Thus a neo-conservative discursive context may provide greater resonance for those trauma narratives that fit the overarching themes of neoconservative morality — e.g., vengeance and individual responsibility.

Along these lines, Alcoff and Gray (1993) note how survivor narratives can be subsumed by dominant discourses and redeployed in a manner non-threatening to the status quo, thus demonstrating that suffering is negotiated between actors and in relation to dominant social conditions. They cite examples in which rape victims who make their stories public often face questions or statements (whether in a family, legal, or therapeutic context) that direct these narratives away from male responsibility for the acts towards gendered assumptions reflective of the patriarchal social order. Thus, in courtroom questioning, emphasis was placed on the "emotional" or "hysteric" nature of the survivor in that she was held to be in a fragile state of mind that left her susceptible to assault. The gendered order was also preserved by highlighting her passivity — she was vulnerable because she was without a male companion. In other cases, victim narratives might be useful tools for governments that want to encourage public fear as a way to drum up support for increased government controls (Walkate 2006). Certainly, in the aftermath of 9/11, we witnessed a Republican U.S. administration that drew on the horrors of this event whenever its foreign policy decisions were called into question. In sum, the problem is one whereby trauma narratives can be used to empower the state or other already powerful actors and to reinforce structures of inequality rather than to empower victims.

The process by which a harmful experience is narrativized, and that narrative is appropriated for political purposes, can be illustrated as a process that feeds back into subsequent narrativizations of harmful events (see Figure 5.1). In other words, the political use of victim narratives will often affect the way in which victim narratives of harm are subsequently created, such as when victims draw upon a "law and order" rhetoric to express their frustration with the criminal justice they have experienced and the lack of an adequate societal response.

So what does this all mean for restorative justice? In its efforts to be "victim-centred," restorative justice immediately enters into a field of competition over victim identity, and restorative justice practitioners must be aware of this and tread carefully. For example, restorative justice attempts to define more subtle notions of victimhood that allow for recognition of multiple levels of victimization (including the offender's suffering) are likely to have little traction in a political realm where victim and offender are assumed to be discreet identities, easily identified. Under these conditions, any mention of the past sufferings of the offender can be perceived as offender-centric and insensitive to the "true" victim. Indeed, it may be the case that the language of victim and offender is too corrupted by its frequent application in formal criminal justice systems that restorative justice must strike out and find a new language.

In fact, some restorative justice theorists and practitioners have done just that, referring to participants as "clients" or "agents." However, such refinements come with their own ideological baggage. The term "client," for example, suggests a consumer of justice services, who shops for an appropriate justice response. This fits all too snugly with a neoliberal project of redefining citizenship around notions of consumerism and entrepreneurism. In the neoliberal ideal, the balance between citizen rights and responsibilities is shifted preponderantly toward a notion of citizen responsibility, where the citizen is empowered to make choices, but these choices are circumscribed by an economic rationality and therefore not wholly "free" (Rose 1996 and 1999). Thus, whatever gains are achieved by using the term "client," such as an emphasis on individual choice and agency, are undone by the association of this term with an overly economistic model of choice.

It may well be that any alternative terminology is likely to be saddled with some ideological residue. Criminal harm is highly politicized, and there is no fully neutral wording that can take us beyond its reach. What may be more important, as we continue to grasp at terms and categorizations that allow us to narrativize harm, is that we do as Derrida recommends (see Chapter

Figure 5.1 Victim Narrative Feedback Effects

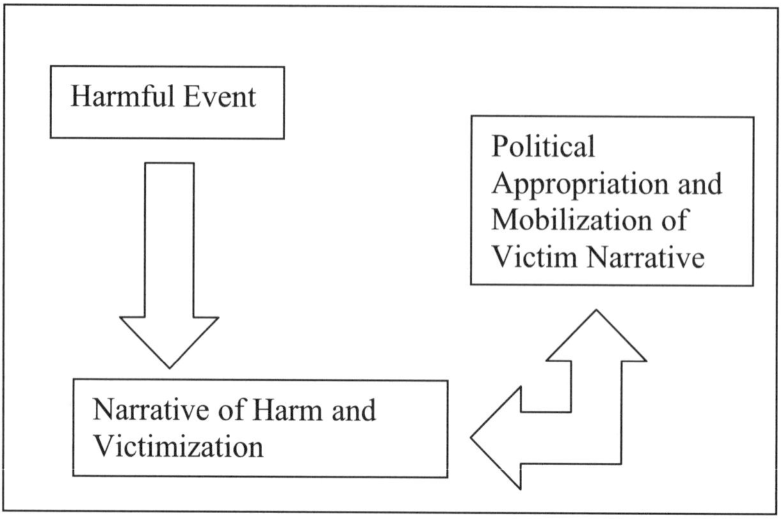

3) and keep these calculations of justice open to deconstructive criticism and revision. This means reflecting upon the ways in which we imagine the victim: do we construct this person as an "ideal" victim? Do we exclude some members of our community from assuming the victim status? What are the political expectations and assumptions in our use of the term "victim?" In part, an adequate response to victim claims, as well as claims of a public or state failure to recognize victimhood, requires that we understand the victim identity as the result of social, legal, and political processes, and not as simply a by-product of the criminal or harmful act. Only through such a detailed approach can we understand the oftentimes arbitrary decisions that result in the elevation of certain victims, and certain types of victimhood, over others.

Offenders

As can be seen above, the victim is a heavily politicized figure, who of necessity must be socially constructed so that the victim experience becomes communicable and a source for social and political support, but what about offenders? Certainly, there is no figure more heavily politicized in our culture. A glance at most newspapers and news telecasts quickly confirms that few subjects cause more anxiety and consternation than offenders. For example, the issue of automobile theft in Winnipeg has long been a matter of great public concern. With Winnipeg ranked year after year as among the cities with the highest rates of automobile theft, people are legitimately fearful of having their cars stolen or damaged in the attempt. However, public panic reached a higher pitch when stories appeared about deadly police car chases, stolen cars being set in neutral and sent unoccupied to crash into buildings, and of car thieves terrorizing (and even hitting) joggers during their joyriding escapades. This perception of heightened danger combined with increased frustration as information came forward to suggest that a small group of young people were the perpetrators of a large percentage of Winnipeg automobile thefts, and that even when apprehended, these youth rarely spent more than a short time within correctional institutions. This resulted in opposition criticism of the governing Manitoba NDP for their "catch and release" policies. The inability of the government to properly punish these young offenders was viewed by critics as evidence of their "soft on crime" policies.

In this example, young offenders guilty of automobile theft become a political football to be kicked around. In response to critics during legislative debate, the NDP Minister of Justice would often cite the successes of NDP programs for dealing with automobile theft, and counter that the problem grew under the previous Tory government, leaving a huge problem with which the NDP had to contend. During such debates, however, the young automobile thief quickly disappears and, after some initial discussion of their home situations, or whether or not they suffer from Fetal Alcohol Spectrum Disorder, we hear little more about the broader motivations of these individuals. Why is it that they are attracted to automobile theft? Why has a culture of automobile theft become prominent in Winnipeg? What are the social and economic conditions of these young people? The offender is reduced to a simple mask of dangerousness and presented as someone who has little substance to their character, other than the fact that they are out to cause public harm and mischief. The young offender thus becomes a "risky" subject, someone to be managed and administered to rather than reformed and rehabilitated. Indeed, some young people need not even commit crimes to be considered "at risk," as they may possess specific qualities or characteristics that lead them to be considered "high risk" and therefore more likely than others to commit crimes (Hudson 2003; Hannah-Moffet and Shaw 2001). In this sense, they are criminalized because of who they are rather than based on actual criminal activities.

Thus, while victims' groups have at times succeeded in constructing resonant narratives to communicate their experiences, offenders and their advocates have had a tougher time reworking their image. In the reigning philosophy of liberal individualism that conditions much of our political thinking, offenders are viewed solely as individuals who have made poor choices and are lacking in moral character. Therefore, they must be held individually accountable for their actions. While our justice system admits more detailed information about the offender's background for consideration during sentencing, the court of public opinion does not necessarily go so far, as the public is often more content to view the offender as a dangerous Other with no real connection to the regular world. Such a rationale makes it much easier to support policies of exclusion and imprisonment, since these actions provide a sense of comfort that the source of harm — the offender — has been removed from community life.

Offender advocate groups have long wrestled with such views of offenders. For them, the societal response to offenders is often nothing short of paradoxical. The public fears (and is encouraged to fear) offenders, and therefore, we come across a significant number of people who want nothing more than to see offenders placed in correctional institutions for as long as the law will allow. Yet, inadequate emphasis is placed on "correction" within such institutions, and offenders are released back into the community, more embittered, with more criminal contacts, and with fewer prospects for gainful employment and pro-social relationships. Thus, the system of punishment we desire, which is alleged to make us safer, in fact often makes us less safe. Indeed, the situation of offenders goes beyond the warnings of "labelling theory" (see Chapter 3). To review, according to labelling theory, an individual who commits a primary act of deviance has not yet invested in a criminal identity. However, the criminal justice process can encourage them to make the transition from primary to secondary deviance — a stage at which "criminal" becomes their "master status" or primary form of identification. It is also noted that the correctional institutions can contribute to a process of "prisonization" or "institutionalization," whereby the offender's behaviour becomes shaped by the institution, making it very difficult for him or her to re-adapt to society upon release. They become accustomed to the schedules, sociability, and patterns of prison life, and find it very hard to resume a law-abiding life in the community. These problems are exacerbated by the difficulties offenders face on account of public stigmatization, whereby their status as "offenders" makes it very challenging to establish or re-establish non-criminal contacts, to secure gainful employment, or to find a positive living situation, away from the influences that might have contributed to their previous criminal behaviour (e.g., drugs and alcohol). But, as suggested above, this process has, in some cases, become more severe in contemporary prisons, where a programming vacuum has left inmates more susceptible to forces such as gang recruitment and drug addiction within prison walls. For those already stigmatized by the criminal justice process, gangs provide, in addition to immediate protection from other gang-affiliated prisoners, a seductive source of identification, providing a prisoner with a similarly situated cohort who will positively value the forms of capital (or wealth) the prisoner possesses in great abundance. That is to say, they can achieve status for their daring, for their toughness, and for the audacity of their criminal acts.

This pattern of revaluation of the criminal identity among gang-members and other outcasts has been the topic of great discussion among criminologists (e.g., Cohen 1965) and is a persistent criminological phenomenon. However, it is important to recognize that at the root of this process of revaluation is a contest over the power to name and categorize in our society. Critical criminologists have long noted the "power to criminalize" (Comack and Balfour 2004) is unevenly distributed. In this view, law is not the natural and unproblematic reflection of our shared beliefs but, rather, the political creation of powerful actors. This is not to suggest we do not all, on some level, agree with many laws. We have been deeply socialized to hold dear the norms that are codified within our legal systems. Rather, laws, and our socialization into the normative system upon which they are based, are influenced by the hegemonic values of dominant groups within our society. The nature of "hegemony" is that it becomes so widespread, so second nature, that certain ways of seeing and knowing the world appear common-sensical and almost unquestionable (Gramsci 1971). Thus, the fact that law reflects the interests of dominant groups is not so much a matter of individuals from these groups conspiring to create laws in their interests (although there are certainly historical instances of this), but more often a matter of law being made on the basis of certain assumptions about the world, or an orientation to the world, that is already tinged by power.

We see such biases at work in attempts at "criminalization." Criminalization refers to the processes through which certain individuals are categorized as criminals while others are not. Consider for a moment who in your life you would brand as a "criminal" and who you would not. Do you know anyone who illegally downloads music or movies from the Internet? Do you know any casual drug users? Are these individuals who break the law criminals? If not, why? Is it because they have not been caught or sent to a correctional institution? Such questions begin to reveal the fact that the label of criminal or offender is not as clear-cut as we may like to believe. Indeed, we are surrounded in our day-to-day lives by a whole cast of tax evaders, petty thieves, perpetrators of violence and other harms, who we do not brand "criminal." In part, what appears to be at work here is that certain people are more able to resist the label than others. For the most powerful, the law often defines the harms they cause in other terms, such as regulatory offences. So, despite the fact we have seen some high profile white-collar offenders taken to task in recent years (e.g., Conrad Black and Martha Stewart), these likely only represent the tip of the iceberg of such offences, some of which are still unrecognized as "crimes" (e.g., misleading advertising), or skilfully hid through offshore holdings, jurisdiction shopping, or through their diffusion within the practices of a large corporation. Others are able to use the resources at their disposal to spread the idea that their actions were accidental. Take, for instance, the way in which Michael McCain, CEO of Maple Leaf Foods, was

Box 5.2 Selections from "The Testing of Michael McCain"

On Saturday, Aug. 23, the head-office lobby of Maple Leaf Foods in midtown Toronto should have been quiet — it was, after all, the middle of a sleepy summer weekend. Instead, the air was electric, the scene tumultuous. Maple Leaf, Canada's largest meat company, was facing the most serious crisis of its 100-year-plus history. It had been confirmed: Packaged meat from its Toronto plant was killing people.

It was the nightmare scenario for any consumer-products company. Maple Leaf's crisis plan was duly put into play. A camera crew was dispatched to the office lobby, where president and CEO Michael McCain, tall, lean and attired in an open-neck blue shirt with a white undershirt, taped a televised statement.

After announcing that he had closed down the plant and ordered a recall of its products, a grim-looking McCain apologized and expressed his sympathy for the victims of the nationwide listeriosis outbreak. He followed up with a press conference the next day. "Going through the crisis, there are two advisers I've paid no attention to," he told reporters. "The first are the lawyers, and the second are the accountants. It's not about money or legal liability — this is about our being accountable for providing consumers with safe food."

McCain's appearances and statements seemed perfectly natural to the public. To crisis management experts, they appeared to be expertly crafted. The contrite message resonated so strongly in public opinion that even as the number of deaths caused by listeriosis mounted and the entire Canadian food safety system came under attack, McCain seemed insulated by his statement that "the buck stops here." His sad, sober visage became standard fare on the evening news, on YouTube and in newspaper photos. He emerged as the human face of a company that cared about its customers….

Ken Wong, a marketing professor at Queen's University's school of business, admired McCain's public-service ad because it had the look of amateurishness. "The text was dull and dry," Wong wrote in a commentary. "McCain was clearly reading off a teleprompter, and his unpolished appearance gave every indication of being tired and weary. I don't know if it was intended, but the ultimate message was, 'We're concerned and this is not about advertising.' Interestingly, a non-ad was exactly what was needed to be the best ad."

The TV spot felt artless and genuine, right from the declaration of culpability to the un-slick presence of Michael McCain in his open-collar shirt. Yet Maple Leaf officials insist there was no premeditated attempt to make it look "real." "We never had the time to overthink anything," says Linda Smith, a communications consultant who has worked with the company for a dozen years. "We weren't that smart, believe me."…

Bob Kingston, the union leader, sees nothing heroic in Maple Leaf's performance — if McCain had not ordered a voluntary recall, he would have faced a mandatory recall by the food agency, Kingston points out. In that case, McCain could not have taken the high road and portrayed himself as a good corporate citizen. In Kingston's eyes, what was done was motivated by necessity, not altruism.

So McCain can't really win. The crisis management experts describe his action as "a textbook case" and "boiler-plate crisis management." It is faint praise, for it sounds like he is following a proven formula instead of acting from the heart. Yet surely he cannot be faulted for doing what was right to protect his company. In effect, the Maple Leaf case confirms what corporate reputation consultants say: Doing good is good business. Taking responsibility for a corporate failure is particularly laudable in an age when corporate executives shun accountability.

Source: Gordon Pitts, "The Testing of Michael McCain," *Globe and Mail Update*, November 28, 2008. <www.business.theglobeandmail.com/servlet/story/RTGAM.20081124.rmmccain1124/BNStory/specialROBmagazine/home>

able to present himself and his company after meat from his plants caused a listeriosis outbreak and the deaths of multiple Canadians in 2008. In Box 5.2, McCain is drawn as either a skilful crisis manager or a sensitive human being (depending on one's perspective) rather than as someone potentially criminally liable for harming consumers — or as someone whose company helped lobby the federal government for greater privatization and deregulation of food inspection. McCain possesses the wealth, the language skills, and the socialization required to represent himself as a responsible person of integrity, and factors such as these make all the difference when it comes to resisting criminalization.

Even our friends and family often possess the resources needed to resist criminalization. We have access to exculpatory discourses that allow us to explain away or rationalize our actions. Thus, the ability to effectively employ the "techniques of neutralization," identified by Gresham Sykes and David Matza (1957), is differently possessed by different actors. Techniques of neutralization are meaning frameworks designed to alleviate guilt and blame within a potentially stigmatizing context. For example, a person accused of a crime might offer a "denial of responsibility" ("it was an accident"), a "denial of injury" ("their insurance will cover it"), a "denial of victim" ("they got what they deserved"), a "condemnation of their condemners" ("who are you to judge me?"), or an "appeal to higher loyalties" ("I didn't do it for myself"). Statements such as these are used by individuals from all segments of society when they are accused of wrongdoing, but some have more power than others to make them stick. A lawyer or corporate executive for example might cite the stresses of their high-pressured jobs as the source of his cocaine addiction (an "appeal to higher loyalties" since their drug use becomes less about their own desires and more about their commitment to their work), whereas as a crack or heroin addict living on the street has no such recourse. Moreover, this power imbalance is further reflected in American drug laws, whereas punishments for cocaine use are much lower than those for crack, despite the similarities between the two substances (Stern 2006).

"Criminals," therefore, often possess less power in terms of being able to resist categorization, and for this reason, they are an easy population upon which we can heap many of our anxieties and fears. They are transformed into dangerous Others, people who, because of their careless disregard for others, should themselves be removed from the community. However, as mentioned earlier, branding individuals with the indelible mark of "criminal" has the effect of excluding them from society, leading them to commit more strongly to the criminal lifestyle. Thus, through criminalization, we contribute to the creation of the very thing we fear.

Restorativists have largely accepted the version of criminological analysis presented thus far in this section, and respond to it by recommending we forge relationships with offenders to help them reintegrate into our societies and form pro-social ties with others. A first step in such a process is changing the way we apportion blame in reaction to harmful acts. Morally speaking, it makes little sense to pretend the harms did not occur or they were not harmful. Such a denial of harm would only serve to weaken our sense of self-respect as actors undeserving of harm (Hampton 1998; Murphy and Hampton 1988). However, the need to lay blame and to be tough on wrongdoing does not handcuff us to stigmatization. As John Braithwaite (1989) has long suggested, we can aspire toward a justice that is hard on the act, and not the actor. This is the foundational premise of his theory of reintegrative shaming, which was discussed in Chapter 3. When we condemn the act and not the actor, we recognize the act does not define the person in his or her entirety. This allows him or her the opportunity to distance him or herself from the act and to reintegrate into the harmed community. This view has become a central tenet of much restorative justice practice, opening a space for people who commit wrongs to prove themselves something other than "criminals."

Pavlich (2005), however, notes restorativists are still engaged in the process of constructing the "offender" as a subject, and they do so in manner that reproduces the governing rationality of the criminal justice system. At the root of restorative notions of the offender is a harm-causing individual who needs to be reintegrated into the normative order, but for Pavlich this assumption must be unpacked. To begin, one could critically interrogate the notion that harm causation can be isolated within a single individual. Such a manoeuvre ignores that harm often has many sources, including structured patterns of social inequality that contribute to an individual's motivation to commit harm or that are themselves the source of grave harm, such as the structural violence committed against poor and working people in the name of preserving the capitalist system. For example, our capitalist economy depends upon unemployment so there will be competition for jobs and wages will be kept low. Therefore, this system and its supporters militate against ideas such as cost of living allowances and other substantive guarantees of general social welfare, thereby accepting the inevitability of child poverty, homelessness, and other social ills.

In addition, the construction of the offender helps create a subject who can then be the target of disciplinary governance. Through the techniques of restorative justice, offenders' behaviour is to be reshaped, re-making these wrongdoers as "responsibilized" (that is, as actors made responsible for their self-governance) and non-conflictive individuals. What this amounts to is a process that works in a very similar fashion to the regular criminal justice system in that its ultimate aim is to pacify and discipline those branded as "offenders." For Pavlich, this is problematic since it contradicts restorative justice claims to be offering a justice that is distinct from, and even oppositional to, the criminal justice system. Restorative justice, therefore, reproduces and is very much a part of the system it claims to challenge, and Pavlich hopes to push our thinking beyond the limits of our current justice horizons.

Following Pavlich, restorativists should be wary of the offender label and seek instead to understand the perpetrator of harm as an accountable individual situated in a broader context defined by forces and influences that play a role in shaping this individual's behaviour. This requires a degree of sociological sophistication, since the objective is to treat this harming actor both as an individual agent and as a person susceptible to/embedded in structural processes. The wrongdoer is directly responsible to his or her fellow citizen for causing them harm, but this harmful behaviour can only be fully corrected through a thorough analysis of the conditions that brought about the wrongful acts. For example, how did the individual come to accept abusive behaviour toward women as normal? Why did the drive for corporate profit lead to the marketing of unsafe products? How did economic downturn and job loss contribute to the gambling addiction that was the motivator behind credit card fraud?

Communities

When restorative justice practitioners claim community is an essential pillar of their practice, the obvious critical response to this claim is to ask: what community? Where do such communities exist? Certainly not in contemporary urban settings, some would argue, where a complex division of labour has deprived us of the most intensive bonding mechanisms of traditional community life (see Durkheim 1984). We no longer possess shared belief systems, we no longer depend as immediately upon one another for our daily survival, and we no longer remain settled in the same communities for extended periods of time, to list but a few of the changes that characterize contemporary urban life (Bottoms 2003; Kueneman 2008). This criticism is particularly applicable in those urban settings most prone to crime: inner cities. Here, urban deindustrialization has moved decent-paying, working-class employment opportunities from city centres to the outskirts of town, creating a vacuum of poverty within the inner city. Bereft of opportunity, inner city communities have become more fractured (see Anderson 1999). Drugs, violence, vandalism, prostitution, and the other social ills are conditions better suited for the formation of illicit subcultural communities than the sort promoted by restorative justice practitioners.

Other critics wonder if the concept of "community" is itself problematic. When we place ourselves "within" a community, we are presuming that there are others who do not belong to this community. Indeed, the identity of a given community, or an "us," is often dependent upon a notion of those who do not belong to this community, or a "them" (see Pavlich 2001). This "them" is therefore essentially excluded from our communal world and, more severely, potentially from our "universe of moral obligation" (Fein 1993) in the sense that we only feel responsibility toward those with whom we share communal ties. Nazi fascism is often used as an example of a project of exclusionary community formation. The Nazi vision of Germany (and later Europe) was built upon the exclusion of Jews, Roma, Slavs, homosexuals, and "Others" not perceived to meet the criteria of their Aryan community ideal. Based on this example, one can see the potential danger that lies within the idea of community: it promotes an ethics whereby within the community, like looks after like (e.g., I watch out for my neighbour and vice versa) (see Koontz 2003), while at the same time placing limits upon this ethics, drawing a line beyond which all obligations of caring stop (e.g., I no longer need/feel responsible for those outside of my community).

The restorative justice response to these criticisms has been to redefine community or, at least, to redefine the purpose of community within restorative justice. Some restorativists, for instance, prefer to speak of micro-communities, or "communities of care," by which they mean our close relationships to family, friends, and other significant persons who possess the moral force needed to influence our behaviour (McCold and Wachtel 1998). It is often presumed we all possess such connections to positive support persons who can come to our assistance and stand beside us at a restorative justice meeting, but this is, perhaps, overly optimistic. As Johnstone (2002) notes, we cannot discount the possibility that there are people who are largely deprived of positive social relations. Rather than presume the existence of such networks, others have used Robert Putnam's (2000) notion of "social capital" to argue restorative justice is more about building communities and creating networks. A person who possesses a high degree of social capital, for example, will find her job search much easier, since she will be able to use her network of friends and family to learn about openings and to gather glowing references. In contrast, a person with low social capital may be able to enter the workforce at only the most menial levels, since he will not be able to rely on his social network as a resource. Social capital is, therefore, a form of social power that can be cultivated in community settings. Applying this notion to restorative justice, it is not necessary that the community exist fully formed at the initiation of a restorative justice process. In fact, it may be possible to build such a community through restorative justice, as people form relationships with one another through addressing local injustices. By offering opportunities for the creation of social relationships, restorative justice enables social networking that will ideally continue to function long after specific restorative meetings have reached a conclusion.

The problem here is that all of these notions of community lack anthropological specificity. That is, they have not fully grappled with the notion of community as an "essentially contested" subject possessed of a variety of meanings (Johnstone 2004). Put in the most basic of terms, community is something defined by communities. We are part of a community because we share some common qualities with our fellow members (such as a location and/or culture), but also because we identify ourselves as part of that community. Community, therefore, is an active process of identification with others. This process can take an exclusionary form, as suggested by critics of restorative justice. However, this is not necessarily the case. While there has been a tendency for communities to form through an us/them binary, not all communities follow this strategy. There are indeed some communities that fit what some would refer to as "becoming communities" (Nancy 1991; Agamban 1993). This form of community life entails a sense of common identity that is not bound by rigid borders. Here, community represents something much more fluid, definable only in the experience of it.

Indeed, there are examples of community life that are defined by guidelines of hospitality and mobility rather than in stark contrast with an external Other. For example, some Coast Salish communities in British Columbia remain open to membership of individuals from other cultures and, in fact, encourage intermarriages between their members and members from other communities as a means for creating inter-group ties. Moreover, the borderlands between these communities were traditionally not defined by fixed boundary lines, but rather by spaces that were "shared territories," as much under the stewardship of one community as another. As Thom (2006: 21–22) states, Coast Salish members

> see boundaries and borders as arbitrary and artificial at best, and
> at worst a part of a recurring colonial mechanism of government

to create division between communities and kin and weaken the potential strength of the Coast Salish people as a Nation. These people are concerned that the power of such maps and terms will have the effect of severing their connections to place, framing the future of engagements with the land exercised as rights negotiated under land claims settlements firmly in western ontological terms.

In these cases, the identification with the community does not necessitate an exclusion of others, since there exists recognition that the boundaries of the group are fuzzy and permeable.

This form of open community does not simply reflect a romanticized view of indigenous peoples. Rather, it recognizes that notions of collective and community identity have often allowed for a certain degree of play. In some communities, one can shift ethnic identity. Prior to colonization, this was possible in Rwanda. A person could go from Hutu to Tutsi identity by acquiring certain goods (in particular, cattle), and these identities only became rigidified and exclusionary through the imposition of colonial racial science and the subsequent politicization of identity (Mamdani 2001). In such cases, identity is not an essential quality of the person, but rather a marker of certain material attachments (either to economic wealth or the land).

What this suggests is that community is not necessarily exclusionary. We can conceive of community rather as a process of becoming. That is, community is a dynamic process that takes place within particular social, cultural, economic, political, and historical circumstances. Within these contexts, the process of community negotiation can indeed turn exclusionary, particularly when particular forms of community identity are politicized and prioritized. Take, for example, the politicization of identity in Bosnia-Herzegovina. Sarajevo, the largest city in this region, was a multi-cultural and cosmopolitan metropolis before the dissolution of Yugoslavia. After the death of Tito and the fall of communism, the many ethnicities of Yugoslavia lost these two key sources of political solidarity. This resulted in some provinces within Yugoslavia, namely Croatia and Slovenia, seeking independence. The breaking away of these two republics left Bosnia-Herzegovina on a precipice. Would it, too, secede? During this period, Yugoslav president, Slobodan Milosevic had been fomenting the ideology of Serbian nationalism in order to secure his rule. This left non-Serb populations, such as Muslim and Croat Bosnians, feeling insecure. Ethnic communities then became more rigidly bound, and long-standing grievances that had been forgotten or placed aside in the day-to-day life of cosmopolitan Sarajevo re-emerged with a vengeance. Terrible stories of the war abound: neighbour turning violently upon neighbour, when only weeks before they sat in the same cafes and shared a conversation (Power 2002).

As we can see from this example, community closure and exclusionary politics are not necessary facts of community life. Community identity does not have to define itself in opposition to an always excluded Other; instead, it can be defined through relations, and the strength of these relations allows one to identify oneself as part of several communities, each of varying intensity. These identifications become dangerous and exclusionary when they are politicized and made exclusionary; that is, when they are treated as an essential difference between one group and another.

Based on the above analysis, it is clear restorative justice must aspire to a different ideal of community life. The goal is not to draw upon or to fashion fixed, static communities of support; rather, community is the process of relations through which we negotiate our identities. Therefore, restorativists must be extremely careful in the image of community life they construct when advancing their programs. As Zygmunt Bauman (2001) notes, community "feels good," it reminds us of a time (possibly one that never existed, or that we never experienced) when people got along and could trust one another. For this reason, there is an inherent appeal to selling restorative justice on the basis of it being community centred, but whatever is gained by such an appeal is quickly lost if restorative notions of community lead to the drawing of strict social or spatial boundaries. If the community of restorative justice is thought to be a specific town or neighbourhood, exclusionary principles are likely to obtain, and a restorative justice program could become tempted to restrictively define their clientele. As well, it is important to recognize that service providing and not-for-profit organizations currently operate in "quasi-market" conditions (Bartlett and LeGrand 1993), in which they are required to compete with other organizations for funding and resources (see Chapter 6). Under these political conditions, one could imagine a situation in which restorative justice programs, and their corresponding communities, compete with one another, each vying for a larger share of a perceived limited pool of public resources. The well-being of one restorative justice program/community could therefore be perceived to be at the expense of another program/community. Again, restorative justice must work with a notion of community that is open, multiple, and flexible.

Facilitators

The traditional image of the restorative justice facilitator is that of the community notable — a person of some standing within a group who has the moral authority to help guide others in their decision-making. In contemporary restorative justice practice, there are some such figures who still reside within communities: e.g., trusted elders or religious leaders. Indeed, the initial renewal of informal justice practices was designed to empower such figures to serve as facilitators in neighbourhood justice programs (see Chapter 4), but modernization has taken a toll on the forms of legitimation required for the exercise of power in our societies (and facilitation is a modality of power). As Max Weber (1946: 78–79) outlines, the ideal typical legitimations for power are "traditional," "charismatic," and "rational-legal." Traditional legitimacy belongs to those whose power stems from the traditions and customs of a specific society. Thus, an elder may be granted special status because of her connection to and knowledge of the group's traditions. Charismatic authority is based upon the personal qualities of the individual, such that he or she is able to appear a legitimate authority because he or she exudes a magnetism that attracts the engagement and obedience of others. Many such figures have come to fill roles within restorative justice programs, relying on their charisma to ensure the participation of the disputing parties. Finally, rational-legal authority is the product of official process or qualification, and it is this form of legitimacy that is becoming more commonly sought in restorative justice programs.

As Weber (1946) notes, charismatic authority is often short-lived. Once the charismatic figure dies or retires, their followers must seek other means to ensure the regular operation of their projects. This often results in recourse to rational-legal authority, since such authority can be formalized to ensure certain standards of practice are maintained. In the case of restorative justice, we increasingly see more emphasis placed upon facilitator training and qualifications. It is no longer assumed any community member is competent enough to help his or her fellow members negotiate their conflicts. Instead, such a person requires a specific education to prepare him or her to facilitate in potentially difficult situations. For example, when facilitating a conflict between husband and wife, where family violence may be evident or suspected, a lay facilitator may not be sufficiently attuned to the subtle intimidations an abuser might use to ensure he gets his way and therefore may not do enough to advocate for the wronged party in the meeting. It is also the case that community facilitators may not be fully aware of the programs and services available within their community. If this is so, the restorative meeting may result in a recommendation for addiction counselling or anger management training, only to discover these services do not exist or are overbooked. Therefore, many restorativists now claim that it is to the advantage of all parties if the facilitator is a trained professional.

It is also true that facilitators are no longer necessarily assumed to be trustworthy based upon their status within the community. Given the fractured nature of modern urban communities, interpersonal trust has come to be replaced by contractual trust, meaning that what makes a facilitator seem trustworthy is not the product of a long-standing relationship but, rather, built upon her contractual guarantee that she will facilitate the conflict in a fair and equitable manner (see Durkheim 1984). For this reason, more and more restorative justice agencies are investing time and energy in developing facilitator codes of ethics that provide a set of behavioural expectations to which facilitators must abide. Of course, since there are seldom national or regional licensing bodies for facilitators, there is still some question of whether or not such codes carry any weight. A centralized licensing body would be able to withdraw the professional credential of a facilitator after an instance of ethical violation but, at the moment, no such body exists in Canada, or in most other jurisdictions.

These, and other factors, speak to the professionalization of restorative justice. Indeed, restorative justice can no longer be seen solely as a lay practice, since it is now the subject of countless training programs and practitioner guides. For state-supported restorative justice programs, restorative practitioners are often expected to have training in victim-offender mediation, risk assessment, motivational interviewing, trauma counselling, and other such skills, but what are the consequences of the professionalization of restorative justice?

The image of the facilitator as a lay practitioner has much different connotations than the facilitator as a conflict resolution professional. The lay practitioner is someone who is reasonably familiar with you and your family. Their lack of professional status means the process is more "informal" in the sense that the problem of the injustice(s) is worked through by people who know one another. However, this changes when the facilitator becomes a conflict resolution professional. The involvement of this person, unfamiliar and yet to be trusted because of his or her experience and training, results in the conflict appearing more closely connected to the field of formal law. The conflict resolution professional then becomes perceived as a potential competitor with those professionals who have traditionally possessed monopoly control over the field of law: lawyers and judges (Bourdieu 1987). Also, as restorative justice competes for clients and resources within this broader field of law, it tends to model itself on other "professional" groups, most notably lawyers and doctors, to make itself seem "serious."

Thus, the construction of the restorative facilitator as a "professional" presents the danger that restorative justice will lose its local and informal roots and become more fully part of the formal criminal justice system. Such has been the case with the practice of mediation in civil law. Mediation was first touted as a community-based process for resolving conflicts between neighbours, whereby lay mediators would help people negotiate the conflicts that interfere with civility and sociability in community life (see Chapter 4). For example, neighbours in a dispute over a contested property line could talk things out with the help of a respected community member rather than pursuing their case in the courts. However, the state came to view mediation as a cost effective means for reducing backlog in the courts (Burger 1979).

Moreover, once the state lent its support to mediation, its practice became potentially more profitable. A mediation market thus emerged, with lawyers and other justice professionals adding mediation to their skill-sets and thus advertising their service. In a relatively short period of time, community-based mediation became less prominent, largely eclipsed by a growing cadre of professional mediators, who could charge upwards of $200 per hour for their services (Woolford and Ratner 2005).

There is also the risk that formalized restorative justice training will reduce restorative justice to a technical practice, offering practitioners very pragmatic tools for preparing for and intervening during facilitated meetings, but not preparing them for understanding the broader context of the conflict. Thus, a facilitator could be trained to possess a large toolbox of tactics she or he would apply to a crime involving an Aboriginal offender who has found himself drawn toward gang involvement. However, the facilitator may have little understanding of the forces of colonialism, the difficult transition from reserve to city life, and the racism experienced by Aboriginal persons in the inner city.

Given the complexity of the injustices with which restorative justice practitioners must deal, it would be naïve to expect them to work within this field without training. However, restorative justice must resist the course taken by other "professions," and not make training and credentials the primary source of legitimacy for facilitators. Instead, even trained facilitators should derive their sense of legitimacy from the satisfaction and empowerment they provide to participants in restorative justice, as well as from their ability to plot the linkages between private troubles and public issues (Mills 1959).

Opening Restorative Identities

Restorative justice has typically been defined as a process that involves victim(s), offender(s), and community members in resolving the harm caused by a criminal event. However, buried in such definitions are assumptions about these so-called "stakeholders." Victim, offender, community member, and facilitator are not unproblematic identities, and the assumptions we make about each has distinct political consequences for the practice of restorative justice. The argument presented in this chapter is that each of these identities must be held open for reconsideration. It is less a matter of doing away with the language of victim, offender, community, and facilitator than it is of broadening our sense of what we mean when we use these terms. These are not fully formed identities, since each is the result of a socio-political process through which the label is given meaning. As well, these are not distinct identities since it is possible for actors to fill more than one role.

Keeping these identities open and even allowing them to be potential topics of discussion within restorative justice meetings would enable restorative justice participants to address and challenge their own preconceptions of these terms. If the person who has committed an injustice is not reduced and individualized by the label "offender," there is then the possibility of speaking more broadly about the structural factors that are the wider context of injustice. Only in this way can a community contemplate transformative action, taking the private trouble of the crime and transforming it into a public issue to address (Mills 1959).

In addition, the restorative justice meeting could then serve as a venue in which each of these identities is broadened and complicated. A community member could also be understood as a victim of injustice, since she now lives in an environment that seems more dangerous. The offender, although responsible and accountable, could also be understood as a victim of personal and structural injustices that have left him with little opportunity, or with an overwhelming sense of anger. Thus, by keeping these identities more fluid and open, restorative justice can help participants negotiate what these terms might mean at the local level, rather than to have these statuses imposed through a quasi-criminal justice process.

Chapter 6

Restorative Justice Contexts

As should be amply clear from discussions in preceding chapters, restorative practices are directed toward a variety of injustices, ranging from petty theft and zoning disputes to murder and mass violence. How does restorative justice differ when it is practised with individuals in conflict from when it is used for groups in conflict? Does restorative justice operate the same way in rich and poor communities? Does it operate the same way in highly integrated and disordered communities? Why are youth the primary targets for restorative justice? Finally, I will address the question of the place of restorative justice within neoliberal capitalist democracies. What goals of state and governance are served by restorative justice in this context? What pressures does neoliberalism place on the values and practices of restorative justice? Answering these questions will allow us to begin to consider some of the social and political limitations of restorative justice, which is essential for purposes of developing a transformative political strategy.

Restorative Justice Between Individuals

The paradigmatic case of restorative justice is a meeting between individuals who, although perhaps members of a community, are there to represent themselves as distinct social actors. In such cases, the restorative justice meeting takes on particular characteristics of interaction that distinguish it from group- and nation-based forms.

In making this distinction, I follow in the footsteps of Nicholas Tavuchis (1991), who has identified the analytical differences between individual-to-individual, individual-to-group, group-to-individual, and group-to-group apologies. In fact, much of Tavuchis' analysis could be brought to bear on the subject of restorative justice, since apologies and statements of regret are a desired feature of restorative justice.

When meeting with another individual to discuss a harmful incident, there are several hard-to-define, yet socially meaningful qualities we might look for in our fellow participant. Does she show "integrity?" Is he "trustworthy?" Is she "sincere" in what she says? These and other human characteristics are difficult to operationalize in a social scientific manner, but we nonetheless tend to believe they are discernable within interactive contexts. In evaluating them, we often seek out clues. We examine body posture (e.g., are they sitting upright and being attentive?), tone of voice (e.g., does their voice communicate deeply felt sentiments?), a willingness to take ownership for their deeds (e.g., does the person make excuses or take responsibility?), and, perhaps afterwards, their actions (e.g., are their subsequent actions consistent with their representation of self within the restorative meeting?). Through this examination, we gain either a sense of trust or distrust for the speaker, as well as an opinion on their level of sincerity. Thus, in a restorative justice meeting between individuals, part of the facilitator's work will be to encourage honesty and openness, to invite people to express their feelings, and to make sure they remain actively engaged in the discussion. In this manner, the facilitator hopes to build trust between potential combatants. This need for trust also speaks to the strategic reason for using tools such as "ice breakers" or humour at certain points in the meeting, or, perhaps, a prayer or opening song. Whereas ice breakers and humour might help relax the parties and make them feel more at ease (and therefore more willing to expose their "true" selves within the meeting), a prayer or opening song can help remind participants they are all members of a common community with shared norms and values.

Thus, in the individual-to-individual restorative meeting, the facilitator wants to instruct participants on how to assume, as well as to model him or herself, a conciliatory performance of self. The goal is to encourage each participant to present his or herself as an open and communicative actor — as someone who says what she means and means what she says. Otherwise, the parties will have greater difficulty reaching an agreement and are more likely to leave the meeting unsatisfied.

If one's goal is to encourage societal transformation through restorative justice, however, a potential negative consequence of individual-to-individual meetings is their tendency to focus on personal differences without connecting these differences to wider structural inequities. For example, much transformative potential would be lost if a conflict between two youths from different ethnic backgrounds that has resulted in a violent assault was addressed solely as an interpersonal issue rather than an intergroup conflict emanating from broader ethnic tensions in the community. Therefore, if transformation is indeed the goal, it is necessary that facilitators and community participants make attempts to connect such conflicts to their structural conditions so the restorative justice meeting does not merely ameliorate the immediate problem while leaving the broader conflict unaddressed.

Restorative Justice Between Individuals and Groups

The "individual-to-group" and "group-to-individual" forms of restorative justice can slightly alter the interactive patterns discussed above. In an "individual-to-group" setting a lone wrongdoer faces a group or community he has harmed. For example, imagine a young person who has defaced a local ethnic community centre with racist graffiti. If a restorative justice session were initiated for this individual, this young person would likely meet either with one or more representatives of the group that was harmed, who would be charged with the task of speaking on behalf of the group. In such circumstances, the facilitator would still want to establish the conditions of trust and sincerity that are the goal of individual-to-individual meetings, but it is not possible to speak of a group being "sincere" or "trustworthy" in the same way we use these characteristics to describe individuals (Tavuchis 1991). As well, coming up against the perceived anger and resentment of the group could potentially be a frightening experience for the youth, even if the group representatives at the meeting seem quite approachable. Moreover, since the youth's crime was one of expressing hatred for the group, one can expect he will enter the restorative justice meeting with preconceived notions about and lack of trust in members of this group. The consequence of these factors is that the restorative justice meeting may need to be more gradual in developing trust among the individual participants, perhaps by slowly educating the youth about the group and exposing him to members of the group so he understands that they are not innately harmful. As well, efforts must be made to ensure the group, whether by its actions or by the sheer force of its numbers, does not intimidate the youth. Thus, the individual-to-group restorative justice session cannot rely on the prompt formation of an interactive trust between participants, and may need to take a more gradual approach to establishing reconciliation.

Similarly, we can imagine a group-to-individual restorative justice meeting in which a group of kids has bullied an individual outcast. Here, the outcast's separateness from the group, and the pain he has suffered through their taunts and violence, will make it very difficult for him to trust the individual members. Even if, one-by-one, the group members acknowledge they have done wrong, it will still be hard to tell whether or not they will return to their malevolent behaviour when they are once again assembled as a group. As with our example above, such trust is less likely to arise in the context of the restorative justice meeting, and is more likely to need reinforcement through the changed actions of the members of the group to show they are indeed sorry for their actions and have become trustworthy in the eyes of the victim.

The major point here is that group involvement in a restorative justice meeting changes the context of restorative justice and will likely require the facilitator to use different, and perhaps more patient, strategies to encourage cooperation among participants. However, returning to the goal of transformation, group involvement does present more direct opportunities for addressing structural inequities than would be the case in a meeting between individuals, since injustices committed by or against groups are typically the result of patterned behaviours — as is evident in the examples of hate crimes and bullying offered above. In such cases, the restorative justice meeting is

clearly required to address matters that extend beyond interpersonal relations by discussing how it is that bullying or hate crimes came to be problems
in these communities. Thus, even though such conflicts may be trickier in
the early going and require greater time commitments, the payoff is that
such meetings have better potential to link with injustices of broader public
concern.

Restorative Justice Between Groups

Some of the challenges presented in individual-to-group and group-to-individual restorative justice are also evident in restorative encounters between
groups. A facilitated meeting between two groups of people, especially if
they are large groups, will typically take place through their representatives. Here, the focus is not upon restorative justice meetings that take place
within groups, as with family group conferences and circles, since in such
instances the group is usually assembled to attend to a conflict between two
individuals (even if the FGC or circle broadens discussion to include matters
of community interest). Instead, it is upon what is more appropriately called
"intergroup" conflict. Such conflicts are not uncommon in our society and
can take a variety of forms: Aboriginal peoples and city police officers may
be in dispute over perceptions that racial profiling practices are resulting in
Aboriginal overrepresentation in the criminal justice system; tenants of an
apartment complex may be in conflict with the owners of the complex, as
well as the architects who designed it, the contractors who built it, and the
municipal inspectors who failed to notice the many code violations appar-
ent in the building's construction; or two ethnic communities who share a
common neighbourhood may discover their children are engaging in an
ongoing "turf" war that results in multiple acts of violence and aggression.
Any of these cases could serve as an opportunity for restorative justice, but
they may potentially involve numbers of people that would make it difficult
to establish a fully inclusive restorative justice encounter. For example, circles
have been used to engage police representatives and Aboriginal leaders in
discussions over policing practices; however, the circles are not inclusive, nor
could they be, of all police officers and all Aboriginal people within a region.
In these cases, representatives speak on behalf of a community of people,
and when this occurs, there is a degree of loss in terms of the interpersonal
and emotional intensity of the meeting. This is not to suggest emotions cannot and do not arise in such settings. Aboriginal leaders are likely to have
their own stories of being pulled over for "DWI" (Driving While Indian) and
hold resentments for the suspicion they might arouse in police officers for
being successful Aboriginal persons within a colonial society. However, they
cannot relate the stories of every Aboriginal person and are instead required
to summarize this information to facilitate understanding among the police

representatives. They may do so by recounting emblematic and anecdotal stories of police abuses, or by presenting data gathered to show the number of Aboriginal persons who have been pulled over and searched based upon unfounded suspicions. Likewise, the police representatives cannot speak in the voice of every officer. What they can do is give the Aboriginal leaders a sense of how their officers are trained to be culturally sensitive, as well as remind them that officers must respond to any behaviour they deem to be suspicious. Through this discussion, the two groups ideally move toward creating an agreement (or policies) to guide future police/Aboriginal interactions to help ensure fewer Aboriginal people are wrongfully suspected of or arrested for crimes.

The group-to-group restorative justice meeting hinges on the ability of representatives to speak on behalf of their communities. This means the relationships between the parties to the restorative encounter are less direct and immediate, and instead general; that is, the meeting seeks to establish general guidelines or policies for future interaction rather than building an interpersonal relationship between two or more individuals. In this situation, establishing trust is a greater challenge because, once again, it depends on the future interactions of the two parties and is more difficult to build based upon interactive clues (such as the seeming sincerity of the police or Aboriginal representatives). However, it is also the case that this loss of interpersonal intensity brings matters of a more general or structural nature to the forefront. Since participants do not have the time to explore each and every instance where a police officer is suspected of racial profiling an Aboriginal person, the meeting will need to explore questions of racism more broadly: what does it mean to use racial profiling? What are the explicit and implicit ways racialized thinking affects one's judgment? What assumptions about Aboriginal persons guide police officers' thoughts and actions?

Restoring Transitional Societies

Group-to-group restorative justice processes take their most macro-societal form in post-war and post-oppression contexts. In this vein, so-called "transitional societies" present a series of distinct challenges for restorative justice practice. Most certainly, the move from authoritarian regime to democratic government is rarely a smooth one. In such cases, the justice infrastructure is often either too poorly developed or too corrupt to be expected to pursue all of the perpetrators of violence and suffering. As well, significant power often continues to rest in the hands of members of the previous regime, especially if they maintain control over the military, police, or economy (Villa-Vicencio 2006). For these reasons, transitional societies often seek a path to justice that allows them to use the resources they have and to advance the cause of societal reconciliation.

Such a project is nonetheless marked by many further complications. McEvoy and Eriksson (2006: 322) note that:

> Restorative justice in transitional societies faces a number of additional difficulties to those traditionally associated with more stable jurisdictions. For example, state-based initiatives may be regarded with some cynicism by affected communities where the state justice system has been contorted during the conflict (e.g., through emergency legislation) or where the police or state security forces have been guilty of human rights abuses in their war against non-state forces.

In such cases, citizens may have trouble regaining trust in their government, and yet, on the other hand, a transitional restorative justice process, such as a truth and reconciliation commission, is unlikely to move forward without a degree of state support, especially in terms of state resources (Cunneen 2006; Woolford and Ratner 2008a). Therefore, to ensure the legitimacy of the restorative process, it is often essential that it be perceived to be independent of excessive state influence. This may be partially accomplished by placing the process in the hands of an independent commission, as was done in South Africa, but questions are still likely to rise about connections between the commission and the past or current government. As well, an emphasis on "truth" can serve as a means for establishing legitimacy and building trust in such a process. Due to the fact the commission cannot develop interpersonal relationships with all stakeholders, nor is it possible to form such relationships between those victimized and those who committed wrongs, a more modest project for a restorative process is to work on establishing an accurate official historical record of the events (Tavuchis 1991; Minow 1999). This emphasis on truth provides a degree of recognition of victim suffering without necessarily igniting conflicts or appearing overly partisan; instead, the commission simply records the events reported to and investigated by it, thereby proving itself an impartial compiler of facts. Finally, McEvoy and Eriksson (2006) also suggest restorative transitional processes need to be accompanied by local initiatives reflective of community-based cultural values so there is a sense of local ownership of the process and so that it does not appear to be state imposed.

Given the scale of the conflict dealt with in transitional restorative justice settings, it cannot be expected that the restorative process will be able to simply follow the same methods used when mediating between victim and offender. Although the goal is still to facilitate a discussion about past injustice and to provide opportunities for creative problem-solving, transitional restorative justice approaches this task with much broader scope and over a lengthy time period. Simply put, societal healing may require a more long-running conversation than what is needed for individual healing.

Moreover, transitional restorative justice practices should, by their very definition, be transformative. This is true to the extent that these processes are meant to be part of a larger transition away from an unsavoury past. Their goal is, therefore, to engage the public in the project of societal change. However, such projects are very susceptible to political co-optation. The fact the nation is "transitioning" invites several actors interested in placing their own political or ideological stamp upon the transition, which may include more conservative goals, such as renewing nationalist sentiments or ensuring that status quo economic and trade relations will continue throughout the period of transition. In the case of South Africa, both conditions were noticeable as the SATRC became directed toward constructing a unified South African identity and reparations demands were curtailed to prevent harming the South African investment environment and the corporations that populate it (Wilson 2001).

Restoring Integrative and Disintegrative Communities

Moving away from the quantitative context — i.e., whether restorative justice is dealing with individuals or groups — we can now examine some aspects of the qualitative context — i.e., specific features of the social world that present challenges for restorative justice.

The criticism is often made that the term "restorative" assumes there is something to restore, but what can be restored in a situation where one's entire social network is not strongly opposed to criminal or harmful behaviour? Or what if the status quo of community life is defined by dysfunction rather than harmony?

The notion of "reintegration" also assumes one has a morally upstanding and law-abiding community into which one can be reintegrated. In strong communities, where a dense network of relations connects neighbours and families, an offender can rely not only upon his family to help him walk a more positive path, but also on his neighbours to assist him in reforming his behaviour, but what about a community rife with drug use and violence? Of course, such communities are rarely entirely bereft of law-abiding and morally upstanding people, and some of these communities still exhibit strong networks (e.g., as is the case for some Aboriginal reserves), but there are pockets of city life across the globe where primary networks are rife with illicit activities and interpersonal violence (see Anderson 1999; Wacquant 2001). In such situations, an offender may not possess an abundance of moral supporters to help guide her in reintegration. There is no positive normative situation to be restored and few conventionally "upstanding" community members with whom she can be reintegrated.

Similarly, a family group decision-making meeting to deal with family violence is unlikely to be very effective if all the people in attendance are not strongly opposed to family violence. If one seeks to establish such a meeting in a community where family violence is the norm, or where it is a "well-known secret" that community members would prefer not to discuss, then the participants in the meeting are unlikely to be able to fully "shame" the act of family violence (without appearing to be hypocrites), nor will they present a law-abiding community into which the perpetrator of this violence can be reintegrated.

As noted in Chapter 5, restorative justice practitioners might respond to this situation in one of two ways. First, they may emphasize "communities of care" and seek out positive connections for restorative justice participants that exist beyond the dysfunctional boundaries of the community in question. Along these lines, a trusted uncle or a former basketball coach may be called upon to act as a support for a young offender whose family and community life provide him with few positive role models (Braithwaite 2003). If such connections cannot be found, then the restorative justice practitioner must engage in the second, and more difficult, process of establishing "social capital" and rebuilding strong communal ties. Thus, an offender may lack a positive social network upon which he can depend, but, perhaps, he will make connections with the victim or the community members in attendance at the restorative meeting that will help him advance his life. In this sense, the restorative justice meeting is looked upon as a form of community-building rather than as a discussion taking place within an already established community.

Either approach requires that the restorative justice agency possess the time and resources to undertake either community-finding or community-building efforts. Especially with respect to the community-building option, agencies are often not in a position to help build the social capital to make restorative justice viable. For example, not-for-profit and citizen-led justice agencies, such as the John Howard Society of Canada, which in some jurisdictions adopts restorative justice practices for offenders and ex-offenders, receive most of their funding from sources that expect them to work with offenders. Their mandate does not typically include victim services or community building. Likewise, victim support agencies that support restorative practices tend to work in isolation from offender- and community-focused agencies. Such agencies would do well to link up and cooperate with other agencies involved in the work of community social and economic development. Indeed, the project of restorative justice cannot be isolated from the social and economic health of community, and support for broader ongoing projects to increase community capacity, to empower local residents, to create economic opportunities, and to forge ties between community members will only serve to help restorative justice programs better respond to specific crimes and injustices. In this sense, the challenge is beyond simply establishing social capital — it also must centre upon increasing other forms of power within the community, including the economic strength of the community.

This brings us to consider the broader class context that has the potential to shape the delivery of restorative justice. Given the challenges presented to restorative justice programs in so-called "disorderly" communities, there is the risk that restorative justice gatekeepers will instead direct their services toward middle- and upper-class offenders. Indeed, the criteria of what makes a person "suitable" for restorative justice is weighted upon factors that advantage people of higher economic standing, in that, for example, these people are more likely to have the social networks and resources that make them seem good candidates for restoration. Therefore, middle-class and upper-class youth may appear more redeemable in the eyes of those who refer people to restorative justice programs (e.g., judges, lawyers, and police officers), since they not only possess the economic resources to pay for any damage they may have caused, but also class dispositions that make them appear ready for redemption. For instance, they may have internalized mannerisms of politeness and practices of speech that make them seem more outwardly remorseful for their actions.

A class dimension can also be identified in the move to use restorative justice for white-collar crimes like "breach of trust" or embezzlement offences. Such cases seem quite attractive on several levels. First, restorative justice can be presented to businesses as a practical way for them to recoup some of the money or goods stolen. Second, employees who have stolen from their employers typically possess skill sets that allow them to earn money and to pay off their debts. Finally, these offenders are viewed as being less of a risk to the public, since their white-collar status gives them the appearance of being less "dangerous" because their crimes took place outside of the public limelight. However, when such cases become prominent parts of a restorative justice program, one must be wary of contributing to a two-tiered justice system where the poor offenders get prison while the white-collar offenders receive restorative justice.

Youth and Restorative Justice

Age, like class, is an overarching context of restorative justice, and, once again, the most disadvantaged in this hierarchy, namely, young people, receive differential treatment through existing restorative justice programs.

The category of youth is itself a social invention (Cote and Allahar 1995). There is no biological category that necessitates a clear distinction between those with ages ranging from twelve to eighteen (and this range may vary according to region) and those who are younger or older. Youth is a purgatory in between the supposed innocence of our younger years and the workaday world we will be immersed into thereafter. It is "liminal" in the sense that it is a space of transition, when we are said to seek out our identities, to experiment, to drift, but hopefully come out on the other side properly socialized into the normative world.

Youth is the primary terrain upon which restorative justice operates. When restorative justice is considered in most political jurisdictions, youth are typically its first intended targets. Why is that? Some would suggest the transitional nature of youth makes young people ideally suited for restorative interventions. Since young people are still in a process of formation, they are considered malleable and open to change. It is at this point we can seek to halt their initial "drift" (Matza 1990) into deviance and return them to a "proper" lifecourse, preventing their movement from acts of "primary deviance" toward accepting a criminal "master status" and entering the realm of "secondary deviance" (see Chapters 3 and 5).

At work in this seemingly logical rationale for youth-based restorative justice are several assumptions about youth. To begin, the category of youth is "essentialized" — that is, it is treated as a foundational essence or truth about individuals rather than something that is socially constructed. Thus, the implementation of youth restorative justice plays a role in reproducing the category of "youth," and thus of reproducing a category of people who can be targeted with specific forms of governance. We must always be wary of attempts to construct a population for governance, since these efforts of categorization are means by which social control can be established to target certain individuals more than others. Indeed, youth have been increasingly criminalized in recent years, as moral panics about youth crime have painted a broad stretch of the youth population as "at risk" (see Hogeveen and Minaker 2008). The language of describing young people as "at risk" serves to extend the reach of the criminal justice system beyond the world of actual offences and into the realm of potential offences, making heretofore law-abiding members of society into subjects of criminal justice concern. Along these lines, even programs intended for children, such as "head start" or "healthy child" programs directed toward helping parents bond with and socialize their children, are often justified through a criminal justice rationale that views young people as potential future criminals before they have even entered elementary school.

Second, too many restorative justice programs still treat youth as passive objects within their justice processes. Young people typically enter the restorative justice programs surrounded by adults. Adults refer them to the programs, adults facilitate the meetings, and adults attend as the support persons for young offenders. In the worst case of community accountability panels (see Chapter 5), the young offender comes face-to-face with a panel of community notables who "advise" the youth on her wrongdoing and how she might make amends. Whatever the rules of inclusion and participation are in these processes, one can expect that the young person is likely to feel intimidated and pressured by the "moral scolding" they receive at the hands of the panel (Crawford 2003). The young person is also likely to look to the adults for clues as to how he should and should not act. In this sense, the intergenerational character of most "youth" restorative justice leads to imbalances of power that cannot be easily masked through rhetoric of "open and noncoercive" participation.

A more youth-centred approach to restorative justice is offered by programs like the Youth Restorative Action Project (YRAP) in Edmonton, Alberta. Run by youth, for youth, YRAP seeks to empower young people rather than adults. Although YRAP is reliant on the criminal justice system for referrals and needs judge approval for the agreements it achieves, it still provides young people with a great deal of autonomy with respect to how they deal with the conflicts in their midst. The young people at YRAP have also committed to selecting cases that reflect broader challenges within their communities, such as racism and sexism. For example,

> Riff, a relatively recent addition to the YRAP team, suggests that: "I vote to include a case when it is something that I feel is a racially motivated crime, something with abuse. Usually, I will try to vote yes for that because I think it is important to get that issue in the forefront." By mobilizing their resources around such forms of social injustice, members see themselves providing a forum for the education and reconciliation of troubled youth. (Hogeveen 2006: 59)

Thus, YRAP empowers young people to not only be agents with respect to specific conflicts, but also in relation to prominent issues that trouble the places in which they live. This also allows YRAP to serve as a space in which young people can challenge and contest a wide variety of issues, including the social construction of the category of "youth," as well as racialized and class-based assumptions about crime and victimization (Hogeveen 2006).

Although youth crime appears, on the surface, a natural target for the practice of restorative justice, it is necessary that this be denaturalized and criticized so restorative justice can achieve a broader empowerment, which includes the empowerment of young people, as illustrated by YRAP, rather than simply offering new tools for targeting and criminalizing youth.

Restoration and Neoliberal Politics

With respect to the economic and political context of restorative justice, the most salient tendency governing contemporary economic and political life is neoliberalism. Neoliberalism is a wide-reaching phenomenon. To fully understand the consequences of this political-economic context for restorative justice, it is necessary that some care be taken to describe exactly what neoliberalism is, since it remains a contested notion.

Over the past thirty years, corporate power has become more mobile or "globalized," pressuring regions to create regulatory conditions inviting investment. As well, a "neoliberal international" (Wacquant 2004: 100), with its institutions (e.g., World Trade Organization, General Agreement on Tariffs and Trade, the International Monetary Fund, all of which work toward advancing neoliberal monetary policies) and think tanks (e.g., internationally, the Organization for Economic Cooperation and Development, the Heritage Foundation, American Enterprise Institute; in Canada, the Conference Board, the CD Howe Institute, Canadian Council of Chief Executives), has spread the economic and political principles of neoliberalism to the furthest reaches of the planet. This movement is argued to represent something distinct from liberalism, the political philosophy that has dominated Western governments for some time. Under liberalism, emphasis was placed upon *laissez faire* governance, a call that inspired earlier attempts to roll back state involvement in economic and social relations. However, in the late twentieth century, this philosophy shifted to challenge welfare-state provisions of health care, education, unemployment, retirement, housing, and other benefits that had been won by the working classes through their demands that the state address the hardships brought by unregulated capitalism. These welfare state provisions were dominant in Western nations following World War II, and they demonstrated the state could play a vital role in directing capitalist production by offering workers the security and spending power required for them to contribute to a stable national economy (see Tickell and Peck 1995). However, in the 1970s, these policies were perceived to be in crisis, as the social programs of the welfare state appeared cumbersome, and attempts by nation-states to regulate matters such as labour or environmental policy came to be viewed as a burden by increasingly mobile and globalizing corporations and investors. Moreover, with the fall of the Berlin Wall and the rise of Glasnost in the U.S.S.R., the demise of the communist alternative led a triumphant capitalism to take an even more aggressive stance against state involvement in the economy. Thus, *neoliberalism*, a political rationality often seen as originating in the economic policies of Thatcher and Reagan, became the new reigning philosophy. Other economic systems, it was argued, had fallen onto the scrap heap of history, leading to the neoliberal mantra that "there is no alternative" (TINA).

One should avoid forming an overly simplistic concept of neoliberalism, as it is a flexible approach to economic and political policy that adapts to specific regional contexts. For this reason, some scholars prefer to speak of there being multiple "neoliberalisms." However, across all of these varied applications of neoliberalism, one can discern a "neoliberal ethos," just as we spoke in Chapter 3 of a "restorative ethos." Within the neoliberal ethos, neoliberalism refers to a collectivity of discourses and practices that serve to monitor and regulate the capitalist system in a manner that encourages free mobility and maximal profit for capitalists (Hardt and Negri 2004). In this sense, neoliberalism, as a political project, is intertwined with globalization as an economic project (Jessop 2002). Neoliberalism provides globalization with a political strategy directed toward toppling labour, environmental, and other regulations that are viewed as prohibitive to investment. It also suggests a strategy of governance (or "governmentality") that operates by shifting responsibility from the state onto individual and community actors. As Rose (1996: 41) writes:

> Advanced liberal rule... seeks to degovernmentalize the State and to de-statize practices of government, to detach the substantive authority of expertise from the apparatuses of political rule, relocating experts within a market governed by the rationalities of competition, accountability and consumer demand.... "Community" emerges as a new way of conceptualizing and administering moral relations amongst persons.

In addition to calling upon states to reduce their levels of regulation (particularly with respect to regulations that hamper the profit of capital), the neoliberal ethos inspires broader self-regulation and so-called "responsibilization" amongst citizens and communities, enlisting these actors into the neoliberal economic project, while allowing the state to retreat into a role of merely managing and more subtly directing the national economy. For example, communities and individuals are asked to help manage and police the consequences of neoliberal rollbacks — that is, as social security is removed and more people find themselves without adequate financial or health support, individual community members are encouraged to care for their neighbours, to "look out for one another," to form neighbourhood watch groups, and to participate in "community policing" and "community justice."

Despite the rhetoric of neoliberalism, which suggests an opening of and a freeing of economic markets, the neoliberal ethos is often coercive in its application. In this regard, states and actors do not, in all cases, simply volunteer to privatize state-run industries or to expand the realm of "property" to include more and more public goods. Indeed, governments that stubbornly cling to socialized businesses or services, or that resist the patenting of traditional knowledges or genetic material, will find themselves facing the full brunt of neoliberal power, whether administered through austerity programs imposed by the International Monetary Fund that require privatization in exchange for aid, or through a growing body of trade agreements designed to push open the door to global commodification. In terms of the latter, we see the emergence of the Agreement on Trade Related Aspects of Intellectual Property Rights (TRIPS), the Agreement on Trade Related Investment Measures (TRIMS), and General Agreement on Trade in Services (GATS), which all play a part in restricting the ability of governments to control the patenting of products (including biological life forms) to insure foreign investment brings with it some benefit to the nation (through employment or technology transfer strategies) and to protect national services from foreign competition (such as socialized medicine) (Hart-Landsberg 2006).

In addition, the neoliberal ethos is sufficiently malleable that it can even assimilate seemingly contradictory political philosophies into its operations. In this regard, the neoliberal ethos represents, to some degree, only a partial assault on the welfare state that does not necessarily amount to its absolute disappearance. Instead, some welfare state protections are maintained under the direction of the "left hand" of the state (Bourdieu 1998), although they are reconfigured so emphasis is placed on the responsibilized obligations rather than entitlement of citizens (Hartman 2005). In this manner, for example, forms of unemployment benefits are likely to continue under neoliberal systems because they play an important role in allowing for greater worker flexibility, especially for those workers whose employment is irregular, temporary, or casual. However, these benefits are then coupled with workfare or similar programs that reinforce the message that the citizen has an obligation to work, no matter how insecure or low-paying his or her job (Hartman 2005), or unemployment benefits might be reduced to insufficient levels so they no longer provide an adequate safety net and compel people toward poverty-level wage jobs. In part, the dregs of the welfare state are preserved to mitigate the contradictions, crisis tendencies, and consequences of neoliberalism for everyday life. These include:

- Growing rates of un- and underemployment, as well as numbers of those who have dropped out of the workforce altogether;
- A worsening of unregulated environmental devastation, resulting in loss of habitat and a decline in global liveability, including the spread of new diseases and the intensification of others that accompany ecological destruction;
- Zero-sum competition between regions seeking investment, resulting in greater inter- and intra-national geographical disparities;
- Growing volatility and instability within the global financial system, as well as the fact that downward economic cycles and crises spread rapidly across the globe;
- The power of the nation-state to regulate its territory is further under-

mined at the hands of supranational institutions and agreements;

- Individualizing tendencies of neoliberal governmentality result in a further erosion of social cohesion;
- A magnification of the divide between the rich and the poor;
- A commodification of heretofore untouched areas of our lives and worlds, including life forms, plants, and seeds;
- A stepping-up of global policing operations and an intensification of war, as the terrain of war shifts toward a greater frequency of attacks on non-combatants (and the line between combatants and non-combatants becomes more blurred);
- Greater corporate/capitalist influence in electoral politics, causing wider cynicism with regard to democratic representation and lower political participation amongst the citizenry;
- The mobility of corporations is not coupled with a mobility of people, which, along with the growing ferocity of war, leads to larger numbers of refugees (economic and political), *sans papiers*, boat people, and others seeking the right of movement;
- Previously secure groups will find themselves suddenly prone to economic or social exclusionary policies that detract from their former, more stable, social status (e.g., beneficiaries of welfare state policies in the western world).

This list could go on, but the aforementioned points are sufficient to illustrate the "ontological insecurity" (Giddens 1991) that is provoked by neoliberal-inspired harms. Such insecurity is likely to produce greater social instability unless neoliberalism can attach itself to a mode of social regulation that allows for the effective management of potentially unruly populations caught within and reacting to these dangerous and very uncertain circumstances. For instance, as people become more desperate for sustenance, but also for all the goods and services sold to them through the capitalist marketplace, they may be increasingly drawn to crime when other legitimate avenues are closed off. To address such risks at both the global and local level, new forms of social control are emerging (Fraser 2003: 167). On the one hand, the International Criminal Court, the United Nations, NATO, and other such bodies are increasingly involved in the project of global policing. On the other hand, local community justice programs, "alternative dispute resolution," and similar projects are being designed to enlist community members in the mediation and resolution of justice issues (Fraser 2003; Hardt and Negri 2000).

Critical criminologists and socio-legal scholars have often noted the coincidence between the ascendancy of neoliberalism and the rise of restorative justice. Moreover, they have pointed to overlaps between the two (see Pavlich

1996b; Woolford and Ratner 2003). For example, restorative justice promotes the devolution and decentring of state criminal justice powers in a way that fits the neoliberal rhetoric of reducing state infrastructure and involvement. It is further argued that by responsibilizing citizens to attend to their own criminal justice problems through "technologies of self" that are designed to fashion docile citizens, social projects, such as restorative justice, serve as much to reinforce the logic of criminal justice and adapt individuals to the neoliberal era as they do to challenge the dominance of so-called retributive justice (Pavlich 2005).

Once again, however, like most aspects of neoliberalism, its position on criminal justice is flexible and multifaceted. For, although neoliberalism makes room for restorative-type practices, especially when they appear to have some practical value in terms of managing minor offenders, it does not forsake punishment. Indeed, punishment is intensified under neoliberalism, since retribution continues to have positive value. This is not a value in terms of reforming offenders, as imprisonment and harsh sentences have rarely achieved this goal. Rather, the value stems from warehousing those who are viewed to be incorrigible, removing them as potential "risks" to law-abiding society. As well, the value is a symbolic one, since it allows neoliberal politicians to demonstrate their tough-on-crime mettle, and with this, politicians can make the populist claim to represent the everyday interests of citizens, who are represented in political discourses as being ever fearful of crime. Moreover, the sensationalism of crime comes as a welcome distraction from the deeper and more widespread harms produced by neoliberal economic and social neglect. Finally, retribution is itself a neoliberal growth industry, evidenced by the rise of for-profit prisons in the United States (Stern 2006). The trend toward having states outsource punishment to private industries is consistent with a neoliberal philosophy that seeks to reduce the size of government.

These criticisms of restorative justice and its relationship to neoliberalism will receive greater attention in the next chapter. What is important here is that we recognize that restorative justice operates in a distinct political and economic environment, and that this has implications for how restorative justice goes about its business. To illustrate this point, one must have some conception of how restorative justice agencies work. As noted earlier, such agencies may be run by not-for-profit or non-governmental organizations, or they may be state-run. Whatever the case, the agency is dependent on government resources, primarily in the form of funding and case referrals. To ensure a steady and reliable flow of funding and referrals, it is important for restorative justice agencies to speak in a language that makes sense to, and appeals to, those in power. Therefore, restorative justice advocates looking to promote their work may decide to focus less on the idealistic aspects of their philosophy and more on how to market themselves in terms that will appeal to the neoliberal palate. For example, the word "accountability" has great currency in contemporary neoliberal times. Everyone and everything must be accountable, from governments and their sub-agencies to citizens. Thus, we find restorative justice agencies emphasizing to government that their programs offer accountability in the sense that having the offender face his or her victim is a way of holding that person accountable for the harm they have caused. Furthermore, having the offender make reparation to the victim is a more far-reaching form of accountability than that achieved through the regular criminal justice system, and it also fits the compensatory logic of neoliberalism by translating an injustice into monetary terms, thereby, in part, transforming justice into an economic transaction. As well, a restorative justice program might highlight the fact that it can save the government time and money through its use of volunteer workers and community resources to address the problem of crime. Sales pitches like these have become increasingly necessary in the field of not-for-profit agencies because there are a great number of such agencies competing for a limited pool of government funding. In this context, a "quasi-market" (Bartlett and Le Grand 1993) structure unfolds, meaning agencies must seek to outbid their competitors to ensure they receive and maintain their piece of the pie. This makes it increasingly difficult for agencies to hold a principled stance in relation to the services they provide and leads many to adapt so as to better serve the desires of government.

What this all means for restorative justice is that practitioners must be very savvy in terms of what sort of compromises they are willing to make in order to ensure the well-being of their agency. For some, the principles and practice of restorative justice may appear so crucial to the needs of victims, offenders, and communities that compromising some restorative justice principles may be a necessary trade-off for exposing a greater number of people to a form of justice that is still widely unknown. However, for others, these compromises will appear little more than a "selling out" or appropriation of restorative justice, which redirects the transformative potential of restorative justice toward the task of increasing social control and further solidifying neoliberal domination. In other words, restorative justice cannot just accept the downloaded task of making communities responsible for their own crime control — it must also initiate discussions and actions that have the potential to foment wider social change. Along these lines, it should not be beyond the reach of a restorative justice movement to counter neoliberal policies — e.g., to advocate for liveable wages and adequate levels of welfare payment since the lack of these elementary protections is often a primary source of community insecurity.

Culture, Meaning, and the Politics of Restorative Justice

Frederic Jameson (1991), the literary critic and social theorist, famously spoke of the "cultural logic" of late capitalism — a term he used to articulate how the cultural conditions of postmodernism provided a meaning framework for a globalizing capitalist system. Indeed, critical scholars have long studied how culture plays a role in the preservation and reproduction of social domination. Culture provides us with a source of meaning-making, with ways of seeing and interpreting the world, and therefore, we must not ignore the cultural context of restorative justice.

Culture, however, should not be understood here in an essentialized and bounded sense. Following Clifford (1988), culture is a "deeply compromised" notion that has been used to place limits on what is, in truth, a complex set of relationships. Culture is not as a thing, but, rather, a loose assemblage of values, practices, and behaviours that are never wholly fixed, but, rather, always in interaction with historical processes of "appropriation, compromise, subversion, masking, invention, and revival" (Clifford 1988: 338). However, despite its dynamism, culture also provides us with a persistent means for making sense of the world — it offers us a store of meanings upon which we can draw to understand and interpret the unfamiliar present.

It is culture as a system of meaning-making that is most important for proponents of restorative justice. Contemporary western societies are often characterized by anger, suspicion, and heightened intolerance. In this atmosphere, Bottoms (1995) has noted the "popular punitiveness" of contemporary Western cultures. In the wake of sensationalized crimes, it is not uncommon to hear media pundits and radio callers demanding only the harshest of punishments. These sentiments appear to have increased in the aftermath of 9/11, as the atmosphere of distrust and fear has become more pronounced. In these cultural conditions, crime and the criminal have come to occupy a special place in our growing list of anxieties. Politicians and the media understand this. They capitalize on these anxieties by feeding us stories to confirm and exacerbate our fears, following the dictum "if it bleeds, it leads." Politicians also profit off our anxieties, laying the risks of contemporary life at the feet of their political adversaries and promising to offer us a "tough" response.

How can restorative justice counter this cultural atmosphere of fear and put minds at ease? In part, restorative justice attempts to alter the climate of fear by providing opportunities for victims and community members to meet with offenders and to recognize their common humanity. However, restorative justice needs to find opportunities to broaden its efforts toward cultural change. This attempt is already occurring through charismatic speakers, documentary, media stories, emotional engagement in actual restorative justice sessions, and other venues through which public awareness of restorative justice is generated. However, efforts need to be expanded and linked to broader movements for peace and social justice that are seeking to sponsor a more tolerant cultural world.

Restorative Justice and the Public Sphere

A final context for restorative justice is within the broader framework of democratic societies. Trends toward democratization at the local level have created opportunities for restorative justice to play a part in increasing public access to democratic participation. Notions of democracy, such as those espoused by proponents of "deliberative democracy" (Parkinson and Roche 2004; Dzur and Olson 2004), as discussed in Chapter 3, seek to open democratic processes to greater public involvement and to revitalize the "public sphere." Habermas (1989) derives the notion of the public sphere from his study of eighteenth-century public debates in which reasoned discussion took priority over brute force. For Habermas, this public sphere has the potential to serve as a model for public reflection, allowing citizens to deliberate and discuss the most pressing issues of the day. Subsequent authors have gone on to speak of micro-publics, or multiple publics, in which very specific matters might be addressed (Fraser 1992). Attaching itself to this development in democratic thinking, restorative justice may find for itself a space emerging for justifying restorative practices, not solely based upon a spiritual ideal, but, instead, as offering important micro-publics in which citizens can discuss matters related to local injustices.

This deliberative aspect can already be witnessed in specific applications of restorative justice. For example, the Centre for Community and Neighbourhoods (CCAN) in Burlington, Vermont, operates a Community Justice Centre through which many programs typical of restorative justice are administered: such as, victim offender mediations, reparation for victims, and offender reintegration services. However, CCAN also offers opportunities for citizens to discuss and problem solve with respect to issues of great concern to their communities. One recent example involved a case of three young people, ages fifteen to twenty-four, who were caught writing graffiti on downtown buildings. Through a broad-based effort, community members decided to create a "Community Art Space" to allow the legal display of graffiti art. As well, community groups cooperated in other city beautification projects with youth, investing them in city revitalization and beautification. CCAN has also brought community members together to discuss issues of racism, community safety, and community economic development, and their impact on life in Burlington (Ahladas and Sachs-Hamilton 2008).

Conclusion

There are, then, a number of contextual factors that must be taken into consideration when promoting and implementing restorative justice. Quantitative contextual factors, such as whether one is dealing with individuals or groups, have significant bearing on the methods used in and the outcomes expected from restorative justice. In contrast, an understanding of broader qualitative contextual factors makes one aware of the potential dangers of and challenges to restorative justice. The discussion of youth-based restorative justice was focused on demonstrating how restorative justice can be harnessed to the project of creating categories of governable subjects. It was argued that the designation "youth" is arbitrary in the sense that there is not a clear developmental stage captured by this age range. However, it does allow the force of law to be concentrated upon specific individuals who are perceived to be "risky." Likewise, the coincidence of the rise of restorative justice with the ascendancy of neoliberalism presents concerns that restorative justice may be turned toward achieving neoliberal goals, such as decentralization and responsibilization. In addition, the cultural context of restorative justice was presented to demonstrate the broad cultural change needed to advance restorative justice. In contrast, the expansion of participatory democracy may present opportunities for restorative justice to represent itself as an important addition to the public sphere, or as its own micro-public.

Chapter 7

Restorative Justice Criticisms

Restorative justice, despite its broad support, has received a great deal of critical attention over the years. In typical restorative justice fashion, restorativists have often embraced criticism and self-criticism as part of a necessary dialogue about how to improve justice in our communities. They even go so far as to invite some of their most avid critics to attend restorative justice conferences and to debate key concerns in writing. In this sense, restorative justice cannot be accused of being an insular movement afraid to look its critics square in the eye. However, it is also the case that some of the criticisms of restorative justice are more damning than others and require some deep rethinking rather than a mere tinkering with restorative justice concepts and procedures. There are, what have been here termed, both technical and substantive criticisms. The technical criticisms illustrate oversights and errors in restorative justice thinking that are correctable through minor adaptation and revision. In contrast, substantive criticisms attack the broader ethos of restorative justice, exposing contradictions and dangers at its very roots. To address these latter criticisms, restorative justice must engage in an intensive project of re-evaluation and re-invention.

In its initial stages, restorative justice was prone to defining itself through a series of stark oppositions. As seen in Howard Zehr's early work (see Chapter 3), listing the characteristics that distinguish restorative from retributive justice was a common practice for restorativists seeking to clarify the restorative vision of justice. This is certainly not an uncommon practice for any new movement, or for any process of identity formation, for that matter. We often strive toward an understanding of who we are through an exercise in establishing what we are not. How often, for example, do Canadians assert their national identity by portraying themselves as "not like Americans?"

This tendency in restorative justice thinking, however, has led to both technical and substantive critiques of restorative justice. Indeed, it speaks to the larger question of the degree to which restorative justice is, or should be, attached to the formal criminal justice system.

Technical Criticisms

Kathleen Daly's (2003; see also Walgrave 2004 and Roche 2007) criticisms of restorative justice can be viewed as "technical" rather than "substantive" because they are aimed at refining restorative justice thought rather than pointing out its irresolvable errors. Indeed, Daly's primary concern is to foster a more realistic understanding of restorative justice that avoids a stark and inaccurate differentiation from the formal criminal justice system. To begin, Daly notes that what often happens when restorative justice is compared to the formal criminal justice system is the ideal of restorative justice is set in contrast to the reality of retributive justice, so, for example, the punishment of imprisonment — with its tendency to institutionalize the offender and expose him or her to greater violence and pro-criminal attitudes — is cast against the ideal of community reintegration — where a caring community helps direct an offender onto the right path. Of course, the latter is an ideal vision of how restorative justice will work rather than an empirical comment on its current reality, where reintegration may prove to be an uneven and slow process, especially if community members do not step forward to offer their support.

Ideal visions of alternative justice forms often look very different when implemented. Indeed, when forced to operate within or alongside the criminal justice system, these visions are often prone to corruption; one need only recall that reform-oriented spiritual groups like the Quakers once supported imprisonment because they believed that, in its ideal form, prison would offer a quiet place for personal contemplation that would allow offenders the opportunity needed to foster personal change (Toews and Zehr 2004). In their wildest dreams, spiritual advocates of imprisonment could not have imagined these institutions would become massive warehouses for poor and minority groups in our societies (Stern 2006),

By focusing on the worst truths of the formal criminal justice system, the restorative portrayal of the criminal justice system also oversimplifies how the criminal justice system actually works. For example, it is erroneous to represent the criminal justice system as entirely formalistic and authoritative. As the example of plea-bargaining shows (see Chapter 2), lawyers and their clients can negotiate a settlement on the steps of the courthouse; therefore, the criminal justice system does offer opportunities for informal negotiation and compromise. As well, judges can deliver sanctions that involve punishments other than imprisonment, such as probationary or conditional sentences, that allow offenders to remain in their communities so long as they abide by the conditions of their sentences.

The wrongful portrayal of the criminal justice system, as well as the presentation of an overly idealized version of restorative justice, has in the long run, according to Daly (2003), done a disservice to the restorative justice movement. In actuality, restorative and retributive justices often work together. As has been demonstrated throughout this book, there are several points in the restorative justice process where assistance or input from representatives from the criminal justice system is required. From the gatekeeper referrals that initiate the process, to the funding that supports the agency that runs the program, to the judge who reviews the restorative agreement and decides whether or not it meets prevailing judicial standards, what we often witness is a partnership between the two justices rather than direct contestation. Indeed, much of restorative justice operates, to once again use Christine Harrington's (1985) terminology, "in the shadow of the law."

For instance, let's return to the example of the Community Holistic Circles of Healing (CHCH) program in Hollow Water, Manitoba (see Box 4.3). Hollow Water was a community beset with long running cycles of violence that were the residue of the harm wrought by Canadian residential schools. With generations of young people removed from their communities and raised in the cold and harsh environment of the residential schools, many Aboriginal children did not receive the socialization and cultural training they would have from living with their families, which would have better prepared them to be parents. As well, the lingering trauma of the residential school experience, combined with the broader impact of colonization (see Ross 1996), contributed to substance addictions within the community. To address the epidemic of sexual and family violence within the community, Hollow Water launched a circle program to help reintegrate "victimizers" back into the community, ensuring they would no longer be a danger to their loved ones or neighbours. The program involves first getting victimizers to take responsibility and admit to their actions. If they own up, or if the CHCH team believes they can convince them to own up, then the judge for their case will assign a probationary sentence that allows the victimizer to remain in the community for a combination of traditional Aboriginal and contemporary treatments. If, at any point, the victimizer fails to live up to their probation order, which mandates participation in CHCH, they are returned to the criminal justice system for formal processing (Lajeunesse 1996). Thus, throughout the process, the criminal justice system looms as means for coercing CHCH participation. In the National Film Board of Canada documentary, *Hollow Water*, we see the case of Richard Kennedy, who was assigned a probationary sentence within his community on the condition that he takes responsibility for his crime of sexually molesting his daughters and participates in CHCH programming. Kennedy only admits to his crimes after two years within the CHCH program, nearing the time when his probation period is about to end and he would likely be returned to the criminal justice system for further processing. Although one can recognize the difficulty an offender might have in coming to terms with his past and that this can be a lengthy process, one cannot discount the likelihood the threat of criminal justice played some role in swaying Richard Kennedy's decision to take responsibility. In addition, one should note in this case, the hybridic combination of formal and informal justice, with both community and state actors playing important roles.

For Daly, when restorative justice misrepresents itself and fails to adequately show its intersections and overlaps with the criminal justice system, this makes it very difficult to convince an already wary public of the merits of this new justice option. This is also the case when restorativists claim restorative justice is non-punitive. The reasonableness of this claim hinges upon what exactly we mean by "punishment" and "retribution." Is it, or is it not, a form of punishment to stand before one's community and admit to wrongdoing? It certainly causes discomfort and potential humiliation and embarrassment, so, if what we mean by punishment is an act that causes the wrongdoer a degree of discomfort, restorative justice is, in many cases, punitive. What differentiates restorative from retributive punishment in the minds of some restorativists is the fact the offender is given a say in what shape the sanction will take, whereas in the criminal justice system, penalties are imposed. This, however, does not take away from the fact that some form of inconvenience is decided upon and delivered to the offender, even if in a different form, such as a public apology or community work. If this were not the case, victims would be more likely to leave restorative meetings unsatisfied because of a sense that the wrongdoer has done nothing to atone for the harm caused.

R.A. Duff (2003) takes this point further to argue restorative justice can only be "properly" achieved through retributive punishment. For Duff, criminal wrongs upset normative relationships in our societies. Our shared values of "mutual trust, concern, and respect" are disrupted and challenged by the acts of the wrongdoer, and justice is an opportunity to recommit to these values. This can only occur if the offender recognizes the importance of these shared values through an apology that expresses his or her "repentant recognition and desire for reconciliation" (Duff 2003: 389). The severity of the breach of the normative order may also demand some other burdensome efforts on the part of the wrongdoer, such as participation in community work. In Duff's vision, then, restorative justice is not to be a "feel good" environment defined solely by positive cooperation amongst the stakeholders to a wrong. It is a space of moral censure in which the facilitator must take pains to communicate to the wrongdoer the grievous nature of his or her violation and to encourage remorse from this individual.

With both Duff (2003) and Daly (2003), we see criticisms designed not to evidence the sheer poverty of the idea of restorative justice but, rather, to make restorativists reconsider some of their grander claims. Only by redressing such overstatements, it is argued, will restorative justice be able to present an honest reflection of itself to the general public. Practitioners and proponents of restorative justice have, in many cases, taken this advice to heart. Indeed, a common refrain upon the introduction of any new restorative justice program is that it is not "soft" on crime. In saying this, the restorativist is communicating to the public that the offender will, in fact, experience discomfort through the restorative process and will have to bear a heavy burden of shame and responsibility. As well, fewer programs attempt to remain distant from the criminal justice system and instead have accepted there will be a certain amount of judicial oversight over their programs, especially with respect to judges having the final authority to accept or reject community-recommended sanctions. They also recognize they cannot operate without some level of cooperation from the state, especially if they want to continue to receive case referrals.

Other technical criticisms are aimed less at showing the connection between restorative and retributive justice and more at pointing out occasions where restorative justice has jettisoned elements of the criminal justice system that serve important purposes. For example, several scholars have worried about the loss of due process rights within restorative justice (e.g., Levrant et al. 1999; Skelton and Frank 2004). In particular, the maxim that one is "innocent until proven guilty" is sacrificed in restorative justice programs in which accused persons are asked to admit responsibility up front in order to guarantee their admission into the restorative process. This could present a grave problem if an accused person admits to charges he might otherwise be able to defend because he so fears the courts and is willing to sacrifice his rights to ensure participation in a more benign-seeming restorative justice program.

Other concerns include that restorative justice will lead to "net-widening" (Van Ness and Strong 2002; Umbreit and Zehr 1996; Wright 1991). Past diversion programs that sought to remove offenders from the criminal docket have been criticized for extending the reach of the state by processing through criminal justice programs harms that might otherwise have been dealt with informally (Cohen 1985). A contrast between my usually law-abiding siblings might help illustrate this point. When my older brother, then but a boy, was caught shoplifting at the local corner store, the police were called merely to scare him. The officer who came to the store gave him a stern lecture and then brought him home to my parents, who were told of the incident with the expectation they would take care of matters. Only a few years later, however, my sister was found shoplifting small items from a department store. The security guard called the police, and the arresting officer diverted her to a local anti-shoplifting program through which she performed some minimal community service tasks and met with other light-fingered girls to discuss the temptations of theft. Besides illustrating how well I have turned out in comparison to my reprobate siblings, this example shows that diversion, as a supposed "informal response" to wrongdoing, in fact resulted in a ramping up of the criminal justice response to petty crimes.

Restorative justice has presented the same danger in that it can be used as a less resource-dependent alternative for dealing with low-level crimes, widening the net of social control to capture graffiti scribblers, petty shoplifters, and even snowball throwers. This is not to say these individuals have not committed harms; rather, it is a question of whether the degree of harm they committed merits a state-supported response. One worry with mobilizing restorative justice for these infractions is that it will, despite its best intentions, stigmatize young individuals by offering an excessive response to minor forms of acting out, especially considering the aforementioned tendency of most youth to "drift" or age out of these sorts of activities (Matza 1990). All too frequently, overzealous responses to minor offences result in increased risk of the offender embracing a criminal identity, or simply becoming more likely to violate the conditions of their sentence, since the restorative process places them under greater surveillance and therefore greater risk of getting caught again (see Levrant et al. 1999).

A final technical criticism worth considering here is that restorative justice leads to disproportionate sentencing (Ashworth 2003). Since the interventions of the classical school of criminology, and in particular Cesare Beccaria's principle that the "punishment should fit the crime," we have an expectation there will be a relationship between the seriousness of the act committed and the sentence received. Moreover, we expect this relationship to hold true across the entirety of our society. Here, a hypothetical example might best illustrate the potential for controversy in terms of disproportionate sentencing in restorative justice. Imagine identical twins who have been raised in the exact same circumstances. At different points in time, approximately a year apart from one another, each twin embezzles $2000 from his employer to pay off gambling debts. In their separate trials, we would not expect one twin to receive time in prison while the other receives community work and counselling for his gambling addiction. Indeed, if there were a difference between the sentences, we would expect the second judge to provide a rationale for why her sentencing differed from that of her colleague who saw the previous case. Restorative justice, however, does not typically limit itself to sentencing guidelines or to past precedent. Its emphasis is instead on the collective efforts of the stakeholders to creatively resolve the particular harm (Sharpe 2007; Wright and Masters 2002), and creativity is not a recipe for ensuring regularity of sentencing. Thus, in the example of the twins, it is conceivable each twin would receive very different sanctions from his restorative justice conference.

None of these criticisms is intended as the final nail in the coffin of restorative justice. Instead, they point to oversights in restorative theorizing and practice that need to be addressed. The stark distinction between restorative and retributive justice can be resolved by a more nuanced understanding of the intersections between these two systems and by reconceptualizing what we mean by punishment. Greater attention to due process rights could be given by requiring that accused persons speak with a defence lawyer prior to entering the restorative program so they are fully apprised of their rights. Net-widening is addressed in some cases by programs restricting their clientele to only those clients who would receive prison time for their crimes, but in others by distancing the program from the state so it no longer gives the perception it is doing the state's "work." Finally, differential sentencing can be addressed by having judges review restorative justice sanctions, although in some cases, restorativists prefer to argue differential sentencing is a reflection of the very particular circumstances of each crime and should not be problematized (Braithwaite 1994).

This brief overview of potential restorative justice responses to technical criticisms serves primarily to reiterate that restorative justice and its guiding ethos are adaptable in the face of injustices, and criticisms, such as those discussed above, provide restorative justice the opportunity to improve its justice delivery and refine its practices. This is more difficult in the case of the substantive criticisms that are directed at the very heart of restorative justice.

Substantive Criticisms

Substantive criticisms challenge the "substance" or content of restorative justice. In this sense, such criticisms strike at the core presuppositions of restorative justice theory and practice, arguing these are unworkable or even dangerous offerings under current social circumstances. For example, expanding on the "net-widening" criticism discussed above, some scholars have wondered whether an expansion of state control is inevitable through restorative justice. The restorative justice process is viewed to be too thoroughly entrenched within the formal criminal justice system, as it is dependent on this system for referrals, funds, and even its terminology (e.g., terms like "victim," "offender," and "crime"). Moreover, the neoliberal conditions, described in the previous chapter, lead the state to seek out new ways to govern populations without relying solely upon the cumbersome machinery of the state, namely courts and prisons. Finally, these factors combine with the previously noted "quasi-market" conditions in which a rolled-back welfare state offers less funding for not-for-profit service providing agencies (see Chapter 6), requiring that surviving agencies struggle and compete for existing funds. Such conditions tend to provoke these agencies to make compromises in their programming and idealism so they might appeal to the needs and ideological leanings of people in power. For example, in research on restorative justice in British Columbia (see Woolford and Ratner 2003), R.S. Ratner and I came across one restorative justice agency that had attached itself to its local Great Canadian Superstore, acting as their preferred program for dealing with shoplifters. The agency was even considering taking the further step of allowing Superstore to advertise on agency pamphlets in order to ensure their continued relationship. This agency, like many others community justice groups in British Columbia, had begun its program with a small provincial government grant, but the challenges of sustaining their work was seen as difficult without increased government and corporate support. With these sort of pressures at play, the core principles and practices of restorative justice are likely to drift toward corruption, or to be wholly or partially co-opted by state agents (Levrant et al. 1999; Mika and Zehr 2003).

Others would suggest that, even prior to co-optation, restorative justice is complicit in a project of social control. Many such scholars are influenced by the work of Michel Foucault, the French philosopher and social historian, who, late in his career, developed the idea of "governmentality," which refers to "a way of problematizing life and seeking to act upon it" (Rose 1993: 288), to describe the sixteenth-century rise in arts of governance that were directed toward shaping the will and behaviour of individuals (Foucault 1991, 1994). Governmentality involves "any attempt to shape with some degree of deliberation aspects of our behaviour according to particular sets of norms and for a variety of ends" (Dean 1999: 10). Governance, according to Foucault, therefore, occurs not simply through the might of the state, but, rather, through the proliferation of ways of thinking that serve as background assumptions to guide our individual choices. That is, governance narrows the boundaries of what is thinkable so our individual decisions fit within a limited set of normative options. Thus, the logic of governmental rule takes shape within individual "mentalities" and circumscribes thought and action, thereby effecting a "responsibilisation corresponding to the new forms in which the governed are encouraged, freely and rationally, to conduct themselves" (Burchell, 1993: 276). For example, public education around issues of crime and risk prevention has been directed at preparing citizens to better safeguard their property and well-being. Through this education, it becomes a matter of common sense that a person should purchase a car alarm, a house alarm, and avoid certain areas of the city at specific times, alongside other acts of personal protection. Through this training, we become more responsible for governing our own self-management and safety and, more importantly, begin to think about our lives in terms of crime and risk prevention. We no longer ask the state to act as the guarantor of our safety; instead, this becomes the obligation of the self-governing citizen.

George Pavlich (2005) has described restorative justice as participating in several "governmentalities." The first restorative justice governmentality encourages participants in restorative justice meetings to examine and reshape their conduct in relation to their experiences of crime and justice. For example, offenders are asked to take responsibility for their actions, victims are asked to express how the crime has affected them and to present reasonable demands for repair, and community members are asked to participate in the reintegration of the offender and the healing of the victim. This governmentality works not only upon their behaviour in the actual meeting, but is also intended as a guide for their future behaviour. This goal of individual self-governance has additional benefits for the state, since individuals who accept and internalize restorative values and practices free the state of this responsibility, thereby lessening the costs and reducing the work of governance.

The second mode of restorative justice governmentality fashions a way of understanding the world (and crime in particular) that makes the pursuit of "restorative" justice appear more rational and understandable to those involved. If restorative justice is to govern our behaviour, it must first change how we think about crime and criminal justice. It does this by reframing or redefining core components of criminal justice. For Pavlich, this involves providing different answers to the questions:

1. What is governed? Unlike formal criminal justice, restorative justice claims to govern "harm" rather than "crime," since it is not the violations of the state's law but, rather, the harms suffered by individuals and communities that are of primary concern.
2. Who is governed? Those who are to be governed are all of those who have a stake in the crime and its effects — victim, offender, and community members — rather than just the offender.
3. Who governs? Whereas judges and lawyers are the individuals empowered through the practice of criminal justice, restorative justice seeks to give greater agency to victims, offenders, and community members.
4. What is appropriate governing? Instead of focusing on the past, restorative governance should be directed toward the future. It is therefore less a question of punishing a wrongdoer and more an issue of creating a dialogue among stakeholders so they can work out how to avoid repetition of the crime.

For Pavlich, the problem with these restorative justice governmentalities is they do not represent a true alternative to the criminal justice system. Instead, restorative justice is fundamentally dependent on the criminal justice system and criminal law. For Pavlich, this amounts to more than the problem that restorative justice tends to misrepresent both its relationship with and the workings of the criminal justice system, as was noted by Daly. More importantly, it means restorative justice is locked into the conceptual and practical tendencies of the criminal justice system and therefore fails to provide a true alternative to its dominance. For example, although restorative justice shifts our attention to the harm suffered by victims and community members, it nonetheless relies on criminal law to define the acts that are to be considered harmful. Therefore, it prevents itself from addressing harms that are not specified within criminal codes, as well as structural harms.

If restorative justice does not avoid the narrowing definitions of criminal law, it is likely to remain silent with respect to serious injustices that threaten to cause a great deal of harm. For instance, the Alberta Tar Sands have had a staggering effect on the Albertan and Canadian economies, but also on environmental conditions in northern Alberta. One of the most troubling cases of environmental damage has occurred in the village of Fort Chipewyan, 260 kilometres north of Fort McMurray, where doctors have confirmed the Aboriginal population suffers from a higher than expected rate of cancer, including rare bile-duct cancers. Fort Chipewyan rests on the shores of Lake Athabasca, which is fed by the Athabasca River and has been found to contain unsafe levels of arsenic, mercury, and polycyclic aromatic hydrocarbon. While there is not yet absolute proof the problems faced in this community are the result of the conversion of the Tar Sands' bitumen into crude oil, the processing of this crude does produce large amounts of contaminated water, all of which may not be properly contained. Does restorative justice not have a place in such a conflict? A restorative justice that sought to be a significant alternative to the formal criminal justice system, especially one geared toward transformative ends, would need to address such potentially disastrous injustices, given their terrible toll on human lives, even (or especially) if the law has not yet seen fit to criminalize them.

Likewise, restorative justice must be able to address structured inequalities that entail great levels of social harm. The continuing disparity between men's and women's wages, as well as the increasing feminization of poverty through the neoliberal rollback of social assistance, have left many mothers struggling to make ends meet and to support their children. When dealing with cases of fraud or other crimes committed by these desperately poor mothers, should restorative justice simply focus on the criminal act and ignore gendered disadvantages? Or, more ambitiously, can restorative justice not provide a space for discussion of and activism for state subsidized childcare, minimum incomes, and other policies that would assist lone parent families?

Pavlich (2001) also takes issue with restorative justice notions of "community" and "justice." For Pavlich, the restorative justice notion of community, even with the more nuanced concepts of "communities of care" or "micro-communities," has the potential to be exclusionary. This is because the term community suggests a bounded physical or symbolic space, whereby those not belonging to this space are placed beyond its boundaries, so even in the case of a "community of care" that is defined around familial and friendship relations, a limit is set with respect to which only a select few can claim inclusion. Ethically speaking, Pavlich finds this a problematic beginning for restorative justice, since it is still predicated on us/them thinking: *we* are members of this community of care and therefore share responsibilities to and for one another; *they* are not part of our community and therefore, we owe them no sense of obligation. Pavlich recommends, in contrast, a notion of "hospitality" instead of community. This is because the good host is one who welcomes and seeks to get to know his or her guest and therefore remains open to those who are different or unknown, an idea Pavlich (2001 and 2007) finds much more promising for relationship-building than the closed space of community.

Pavlich also alerts restorative justice advocates to the dangers of a justice alternative built upon compromised foundations. As noted above, he finds the restorative notion of justice too dependent on criminal justice reasoning, and he proposes instead that restorativists aspire toward a sense of justice that pushes beyond criminal justice's "conceptual horizons" and "calculates" justice in a manner free from criminal justice precepts (Pavlich 2005: 106, 116). In this sense, Pavlich's ambition is to provide critical deconstructive tools to help us truly think beyond the contemporary configuration of criminal justice. However, Pavlich does not, nor does he wish to, spell out what these new justice horizons might look like. Because Pavlich's critical project is directed toward removing limitations upon our thought and action, and toward opening our discussions to different justice possibilities, he is reluctant to prescribe exactly what the future justice should look like. Instead, in keeping with the spirit of Derrida's deconstruction, he proposes responses to injustice should take into account the specific and local circumstances of that injustice. If a person suffers an injustice at the hands of another, for example, in the form of a violent assault, we would not enter into this conflict with preconceived notions about who is the victim and who is the offender or what criminal code violation has occurred. Rather, an effort would be made to, like the good host, understand the particularity of each of these individuals and their situations. What initiated the violence? How did the two parties experience it? What are the cultural, economic, social, or political factors that contributed to this act of violence? Such questions are not entirely different from those that might be asked by restorative justice practitioners, but they are here removed from the discursive limits of the formal criminal justice system, which has the unfortunate tendency to shape the meanings drawn from and interpretations applied to specific cases of injustice.

Criticism and the Politics of Restorative Justice

Criticisms of restorative justice — only a handful of which have been considered here — are crucial to understanding and redirecting the politics of restorative justice. Not only do these criticisms help us to identify the current political barriers to effective restorative justice practice and the practical and technical oversights of existing restorative justice practice, they also encourage us to interrogate the foundational assumptions of restorative justice.

We learn, for example, from "net-widening" critics that restorative justice rests in a precarious political position that leaves it constantly at risk of co-optation. This is a technical criticism that demands a great deal of practitioner attention to the pressures faced in the day-to-day operations of a restorative justice agency, and to resist those that might corrupt or compromise the agency. However, when net-widening is expanded upon as a substantive criticism that identifies the structural tendencies toward co-optation, the matter is not so easily resolved through the good intentions of restorativists. What is then required is a broader social movement assault on the social and political conditions that prevent a fuller realization of restorative justice. Under current conditions, this means first and foremost an oppositional struggle against the policy tendencies of neoliberalism.

We also learn from critics of stark division between restorative and retributive justice that the representation of restorative justice as an alternative and polar opposite to the criminal justice system is disingenuous, at best. However, if we follow Pavlich's more substantive critique, the solution to this problem is more radical than simply being honest about the retributive debts of restorative justice. Instead, Pavlich's work demands a thorough re-imagining of justice that is not foreclosed by the limitations of the criminal justice system. We must think beyond criminal justice and hegemonic conceptualizations of victims and offenders, criminal law and practices, and the like, if restorative justice is to become transformative. Following Pavlich's lead, then, entails a rigorous critical opening up of restorative justice thinking — to the point where restorativists show a willingness to interrogate even the grounding assumptions of the restorative ethos.

Chapter 8

Transformation and the Politics of Restorative Justice

Taking the criticisms discussed in the previous chapter seriously, and responding to the neoliberal and retributive context in which restorative justice currently operates, the question is: how might restorative justice mobilize itself politically to combat the co-optation and full governmentalization of its justice philosophy and practices? Also, how might restorative justice participate in a broader transformative political project that works with and alongside other groups concerned with matters of social justice and the goal of overcoming injustices (e.g., anti-poverty groups, the labour movement, and anti-neoliberalism groups)?

While Sullivan and Tifft (2006: 5) present restorative justice as "subversive" and as an "insurgency" because it competes with the state over the question of how to approach issues of social harm, they also recognize this subversive quality can be dampened or diluted. Indeed, the aforementioned adaptability of restorative justice can lend it to application within a very conservative politics. Restorative justice can be, and is often, focused on street crime, on youth, and toward holding offenders accountable for crimes that are perceived to be solely the result of their individual choice. In this respect, it can serve the ideological purpose of individualizing criminal activity and victimization with little regard for the structural conditions that make crime possible (White 2008).

For some restorativists, the apolitical potential of restorative justice is one of its strengths. Van Ness and Strong (2002: 156) suggest that "restorative justice is neither a conservative nor a liberal agenda." Daly and Immarigeon (1998: 31) also note, "Restorative justice as a social movement can embrace both 'neo-liberalism,' with its focus on economic rationality, entrepreneurial activity, and concern to 'empower the consumer,' and grass-roots forms of democratic socialism." In fact, restorative justice has been frequently embraced by neoliberal nations concerned with fiscal conservatism and reducing the machinery of the state (Braithwaite 2003) but who still want to implement potent societal regulation strategies.

It could be argued, however, the political adaptability of restorative justice is a sign of weakness rather than strength. While one can appreciate the ways in which restorative justice can adjust to the very local circumstances of injustices and their causation, and thereby cater to the particular needs and challenges of an injustice context, political adaptability can be taken

146

as evidence that restorative justice lacks an adequate vision of social justice. It could be argued restorative justice can fit into any dominant political framework because it is little more than a palliative technique that softens the immediate harms of injustice and provides a less cumbersome means for dealing with minor offences, but offers no lasting vision of justice to which a society can aspire, and without an oppositional vision of justice, restorative justice is unlikely to do more than serve the dominant relations of ruling in our societies. Take, for example, the application of restorative justice principles through the Canadian 2003 *Youth Criminal Justice Act* (YCJA). Serge Charbonneau (2004) argues that although the YCJA recommends the restorative practice of conferencing, it also makes room for punitive responses to violent and repeat young offenders. This dualistic approach to youth justice results in the braiding of restorative and retributive sanctions, with conferencing serving as an initial response for minor offences and the court-based resources of the criminal justice system activated only for what are perceived to be more serious cases. In this way, restorative justice becomes a diluted and co-opted form of justice because it is limited to offences that might otherwise have been ignored by the criminal justice system. Thus, restorative justice supplements and supports the dominant criminal justice system, playing no more than a marginal role within this system by offering a more cost-effective approach for dealing with the "small stuff." From this marginal position, restorative justice has little power to call into question the gendered, class-based, or racialized dimensions of the criminal justice system.

For many restorativists, such a future for restorative justice would be anathema to their ambitions. They view restorative justice as part of a broader transformative movement toward making social conflicts more productive and positive. In an earlier work with R.S. Ratner, we referred to these restorativists as "communitarians" because of their commitment to a restorative justice that fosters transformative community change within and through social relationships (Woolford and Ratner 2003). For communitarians, creative and communicative relationships are the basis for transforming the social world, since we learn through problem-solving to confront head-on the obstacles and challenges to societal peace. In contrast, we designated as "governmental-ists" those restorativists who viewed restorative justice as merely another tool within the criminal justice toolbox and as a means to assist and support rather than transform the criminal justice system (Woolford and Ratner 2003). In the previous chapter, I mentioned the restorative justice program that affili-ated itself with the Great Canadian Superstore to act as its anti-shoplifting arm. This is one example of a governmentalist program. In other cases from our research, we came across restorative justice agencies that were content to deal only with minor crimes, or which used community accountability panels to moralize to young offenders. All of these groups were designated "governmentalist," since they appeared intent on advancing an uncritical "governmentality" among offenders, directing them on how to regulate their own behaviour in a more conciliatory and non-disruptive manner, but these agencies showed little interest in exploring the broader context of power in which the offences took place, or in empowering victims and offenders in a way that would enable them to question social injustices.

John Braithwaite (2002) has similarly distinguished between "social justice" and "administrative" practitioners, also capturing this contrast between the desired ends forwarded in different segments of the restorative justice movement (see also the "continuum of restorative possibilities" suggested by Mika and Zehr 2003: 138–9, as well as Van Ness 2002 and Sharpe 2004). Therefore, this division in the world of restorative justice is not just a Canadian phenomenon but, rather, one that is played out globally in existing and emerging restorative justice programs.

How can one advance a vision of social justice within the restorative movement without foreclosing the conversation about what exactly justice is? Pavlich (2007) has rightfully critiqued the tendency toward developing "universal" principles of restorative justice that are intended to apply in all restorative contexts. Such fixed notions of what are the "correct" values guiding restorative justice only serve to straightjacket and limit our approach to specific instances of injustice, and, as has been argued in this book, it is the flexibility and attention to situational specificity that are two of the most attractive features of restorative justice. Even worse, the establishment of unchanging principles of restorative justice encourages sedimentation of restorative justice thinking, which could lead the movement to fail to adequately reflect upon and critique its own principles and practice. The preference in this book has been for a restorative justice that is a "work in progress," which is always in the process of forming and reforming itself. A similar embrace of a restorative justice in flux can be found in the work of Zernova and Wright (2007: 104), who support a "politics of difference" with respect to the existing divisions in restorative justice. They contend:

> Maybe it could be beneficial for restorative justice advocates to focus not on developing unified visions and eliminating diversity but on learning to live and struggle with differences. Some may feel that their task is to develop restorative justice as an improvement on criminal justice; others may believe that restorative justice should pursue the larger aim of building a fairer society.

The question remains, however: How can restorative justice be "transformative" if it is defined by differences, and if it is in a constant state of identity formation? The lessons of transformation handed down from earlier periods of revolution suggest such change is brought by a vanguard steeped in revolutionary ideology. How, some might ask, can restorative justice bring about transformative change unless it follows a similar script? But in these "post-Socialist times" (Fraser 1997), we do not have at our disposal a unifying ideology to direct change. What we have instead are a diverse array of actors who are similarly troubled by the meanness and callous disregard of the neoliberal era. The task for these individuals and groups is to find a means to negotiate their differences while working with a common purpose, and this is not likely to occur through ideological closure, which risks excluding some concerns while privileging others (e.g., highlighting class oppression while overlooking gendered inequalities). With increasing global turmoil, such as market recession and environmental destruction, resulting from a lengthy period of neoliberal deregulation, the time has perhaps never been riper for restorativists to join the multitude of dissatisfied voices in pressing for social change.

Restorativists, however, cannot simply pursue a radical vision of transformation and ignore immediate needs within the criminal justice system that must be addressed. Indeed, even a restorative justice program that aspires toward transformation must engage in the present world and provide services that are of clear benefit to existing clients. Therefore, the project of transformation need not be divorced from everyday attempts to reform criminal justice. The goal may be one of broader transformation, but ex-offenders still require assistance in reintegrating into their communities (e.g., help with job and apartment seeking), victims still need support in overcoming the harmful effects of crime (e.g., therapeutic services), and communities still function better when they are less fearful. Criminal justice improvements are also part of a broader conversation about our vision for a future world, although they cannot be permitted to narrow or rigidly define our thinking about what is possible.

Transformative Justice

To maintain the balance between immediate needs and the goal of transformation, as well as to navigate the seeming contradiction of expressing transformation as a "goal" and yet wanting to keep the future of restorative justice open and indeterminate, the terms "social justice" and "transformation" must be refined. My emphasis will be upon what I refer to as "transformative justice" rather than social justice or transformation, since it better captures the active nature of justice as an ongoing project rather than as a fully imaginable or realizable end. That is to say, one cannot fully prescribe what the future justice will look like, and a crucial lesson of world history is that attempts to socially engineer a totalized vision of a just world too often end in corruption, authoritarianism, and disaster. Nazism and Stalinism are but two examples of visions of justice taken as prescribed ends for which any means were justified. Thus, like Pavlich, my notion of "transformative justice" does not come with a fully articulated definition of what the future world should look like. However, we know enough about the nature of injustice that some basic guidelines can be devised to help us in our pursuit of transformative justice. These guidelines, or signposts, are not envisioned here as a full and final end goal for the restorative justice movement, but, rather, as categories of injustice and remedy to guide thought and action without severely restricting our creativity.

A provisional understanding of transformation was offered in Chapter 1, where it was suggested that restorative justice offers opportunities for personal and social change. Restorative justice offers the potential for collective discussion of problems in our society, and through this discussion, we can learn about ourselves, and concentrate our efforts on changing ourselves, but also obtain a deeper understanding of our societies and what might require changing therein for a better world to arise. In this sense, the transformative potential of restorative justice rests within its process, which allows people to reflect deeply upon the many causes of injustice. However, it would be naïve to expect restorative justice meetings will necessarily gravitate toward anti-oppressive criticisms of self and world. What is to prevent a meeting from simply rationalizing existing relations of domination? For example, a community that finds patriarchal domination to be beneficial to community life may not use a restorative justice meeting dealing with spousal abuse to address the more widespread domination of women within the community. Instead, they may place pressure on the female complainant in the case to simply accept her role and to stop stirring up trouble (Acorn 2004). In this regard, restorative justice possesses no necessary critical political content, making some transformative guidelines necessary.

Recognition, Redistribution, and Representation

Nancy Fraser's (1997, 2000) three-dimension theory of justice provides at least a starting point for some transformative guidelines. For Fraser, injustices typically demand one or more of the following responses: recognition, redistribution, and representation. *Recognition* is needed in response to injustice of a cultural-symbolic nature. When someone misrecognizes you, they may impute upon you a wrong identity (e.g., calling a Cree person an "Indian") and/or devalue your social status based upon this imputed identity (e.g., as in racist discourse). Cultural-symbolic injustices can result in social exclusion, forced assimilation, or even attempts at extermination. With respect to injustices of a criminal nature, in many instances, there is a form of misrecognition at play, since crime disempowers an individual and deprives him or her of their sense of personal "dominion," to borrow the language of Braithwaite and

Petit (1990). When misrecognition occurs, recognition is due. If a person is assaulted (sexual or non-sexual), for example, a just response must involve recognition of his or her bodily integrity and rights to physical safety. Or, if a person is the victim of a racist hate crime, she, at minimum, requires recognition of her equal human worth.

However, Fraser notes recognition can be either affirmative or transformative in its response to cultural-symbolic injustices. Affirmative recognition tends to be superficial; it does not address the patterned cultural-symbolic injustices that are at the root of misrecognition. Affirmative repair in response to racism, for example, may provide public recognition of the equality of a targeted person or group, but does little to challenge our misguided patterns of racial thinking through which we imagine something as contentious as "race" to actually exist. In such a case, a member of an ethnic minority who comes to school only to find a racist epithet has been scrawled upon his locker, would receive affirmative repair when the perpetrator of this deed is caught, required to clean the locker, apologize, and write a research essay on the harms of racism. Here, the emphasis has been placed upon modifying individual behaviour without attempting to address broader processes of racism at the school or in society. In contrast, a transformative approach would seek to challenge structures of symbolic domination by interrogating the roots of cultural injustice. Therefore, if it were to be transformative, a restorative justice session dealing with the same case would want to do more than procure an apology and an essay from the person who vandalized school property with racist graffiti — it would need to examine more broadly the racial tensions at the school and in the community to understand their source and to inspire students to think critically toward the category of race. Such a project would seek to educate students and community members about the structural dimensions of racism, its roots, and its human consequences. Say, for example, the graffiti had targeted an Aboriginal student. This would present the opportunity for discussion of colonialism and the ways in which it disadvantaged and devalued Aboriginal communities, but also for education on the continued resistance and pride of Aboriginal peoples in the face of these demoralizing and racist assaults on their communities. The goal of these efforts, in short, would be to destabilize operative systems of racialized valuation.

Redistribution is needed for violations of a socio-economic nature. Socioeconomic injustices include the harms of economic exploitation (e.g., low wages that do not reflect one's contribution to economic production), marginalization from economic rewards (e.g., the exclusion of ethnic, gender, or racial groups from certain occupations, or the way in which men are more likely to be promoted than their female co-workers), and material deprivation in relation to other groups (e.g., the fact women tend to be paid less than men for similar work) (Fraser 1997: 13). Criminal injustices also tend to involve wrongs of a socio-economic nature, both in motivating circumstances for a crime (e.g., an offender may feel marginalized from the system of economic rewards because she is unable to find a job with adequate pay) and in its results (e.g., a victim may feel materially deprived as a result of the offence). As with responses to cultural-symbolic injustices, the forms of redistributive remedy offered in the aftermath of socio-economic injustice can be affirmative or transformative. Affirmative forms of redistribution offer only a minor surface redistribution of resources, such as in the form of small compensatory payments or community work in lieu of such a payment, but a transformative form of redistribution would aspire toward a deeper restructuring of societal relations of production. Such an approach would need to redress the broader system of inequality in our society, which is itself the criminogenic seedbed of a great deal of social injustice. For a restorative approach to be transformative, more must occur than the simple redistribution of money or services from offender to victim. Instead, consideration needs to be given to the social conditions that made the injustice possible. At the root of crime are issues like poverty, social disorganization, and economic marginalization, and unless these are addressed, a community is unlikely to create for itself conditions amenable to peaceful co-existence. Thus, a transformative restorative justice program would, for example, have a clear interest in working alongside anti-poverty groups to tackle issues of community poverty and to advocate for living wages for all of community members. A transformative restorative approach cannot simply stop at an agreement on compensation; it must move toward challenging the structured patterns of exclusion from fair economic participation.

The final remedy, *representation*, is offered in response to political injustices that deny individuals and groups a sense of social belonging and of inclusion in processes of decision-making and political framing. When groups or individuals are denied a voice in political matters, or denied political membership, they are deprived of fundamental rights within a democratic society. The response to this injustice can once again be affirmative or transformative. Affirmative representation provides only a token voice so the participation of the formerly excluded individual or group does not prove too disruptive to the system. This is the remedy offered through tools like victim impact statements, which are intended to correct the exclusion of victims from court proceedings, but do so by only providing the merely consultative inclusion of the victim's point of view, and thereby also serve to bolster the legitimacy of national criminal justice frameworks. In contrast, a transformative approach would seek to critique systems of representation that deny participation to certain groups and individuals in our societies. In this sense, restorative justice has already built into it a more transformative approach to participatory injustices, since it allows for the active participation of victims, offenders, and community members in justice decision-making. This is not to suggest, however, that restorative justice could not be more transformative in this regard, and its efforts could be directed toward fostering even broader forms of public participation in justice decision-making. For instance, transformative restorative justice programs in Aboriginal communities could press for broader powers of representation in the form of self-determination for Aboriginal peoples. While contemporary practices of circle sentencing offer affirmative representation of Aboriginal voices in local justice processes, transformative representation in these circumstances would involve greater community control over political and legal matters within community life. Such powers would enable communities, if they so chose, to pursue remedy for the many injustices in their midst, such as housing, addiction, violence, and the continuing legacy of residential schools.

These analytical guideposts offer direction for a transformative restorative justice. In each case — in terms of recognition, redistribution, and representation — the distinction between affirmative and transformative remedies allows us a model through which we can gauge the adequacy of a given response to injustice. Moreover, it offers us a transformative ideal that demands a thorough interrogation of existing conditions of domination rather than just a facile response to immediate harms. Anything less than a transformative approach to injustice tends to only scratch the surface of the problem, ignoring its deeper cultural, structural, and political roots.

It is also the case that injustices of misrecognition, maldistribution, or misrepresentation intersect. Therefore, the respective remedial strategies selected will have an impact on one another. Along these lines, Fraser (1997) makes the argument that transformative strategies of recognition, redistribution, and representation tend to align most favourably, as a combination of affirmative and transformative strategies can lead to contradictions and the canceling out of the transformative effort by the logic of the corresponding affirmative approach. In other words, if a restorative justice program were to support a more transformative redistributive strategy that sought to address more broadly the problem of Aboriginal poverty but took an affirmative strategy toward recognizing Aboriginal "identity" as a "racialized category," the net effect could be to essentialize Aboriginal peoples in a manner that makes the transformative redistributive strategy appear a special dispensation to a particular ethnic group rather than the just dues of original peoples wrongly dispossessed of their lands.

The Politics of Transformation

With this framework in mind, the challenge for restorative justice is that, as it gains greater political appeal, stronger efforts are made to use restorative justice as a tool of political domination and governance, and therefore to accentuate its affirmative potential while the project of transformation slips by the wayside. To strategize how we might combat this tendency, it is useful to return to the three senses of "politics" upon which this book is based: the political context of restorative justice; the politics of governance inherent in restorative justice; and restorative justice as a form of strategic political action. Through consideration of these three elements of restorative justice, some guidance can be offered to those who wish to maintain a restorative course toward a relentlessly transformative justice.

The Political Context of Restorative Justice

As has been stressed throughout this book, restorative justice operates in a political context. Understanding this context is therefore essential to implementing a transformative restorative justice, since this context shapes the structural and cultural conditions that a transformative approach would need to address. For example, in the current neoliberal context of criminal justice, one can observe the flexibility of neoliberal governments in their willingness to consider affirmative forms of recognition, redistribution, and representation. Indeed, it is within the neoliberal era that one can witness a greater recognition of victims, the development of restitution and compensation programs to redistribute funds to victims, and the more widespread use of victim impact statements as a form of victim representation (Woolford and Ratner 2008a). None of these efforts threatens the neoliberal social order. In fact, they achieve quite the opposite result. All of these remedies for victims of crime help construct a notion of victimhood that complements a neoliberal view of the world. The victim is represented as an isolated individual who was wronged for no other reason but the depravity of the offender. This harm is perceived to require remedy in the form of individual compensation and some limited venting through the victim impact statement, but the victim is largely restricted from any other performance of victimhood (e.g., there is little room for a forgiving and non-vindictive victim under this model). The contemporary approach to victims, then, although an improvement over previous times when the victim was simply ignored, is still largely affirmative since it serves to reproduce a worldview in which the victim is an isolated sufferer and his or her experience is in no way held to be symptomatic of broader social structural problems.

Restorative justice is suited for co-optation by neoliberal regimes because it can be used for these sorts of affirmative purposes. Restorative justice can siphon off criticisms of and anxieties toward the courts. It can provide a less costly venue for dealing with minor crimes so the retributive system can direct its energies and punitive resources toward what neoliberals consider more serious criminal violations. Thus, restorative justice does not replace the punitive violence of the state; instead, it serves to supplement and help focus this violence on those cases deemed most deserving. In this sense, restorative justice can be useful in helping neoliberal governments contend with a potential contradiction in their strategies of governance. Neoliberal governments need to maintain a sense of being tough on crime, but criminal justice systems are incredibly costly and cumbersome to administer. Restorative justice, therefore, allows these governments to divert less controversial crimes away from the system, while focusing their resources on those that represent, in their view, the greatest public "dangers." In this sense, it allows the neoliberal state to rule some offenders with its "left hand," using more cooperative restorative justice processes, while reserving the punitive might of its "right hand" for "risky" others (Wacquant 2001; Bourdieu 1998).

An affirmative restorative justice also fails to disrupt dominant patterns for designating risk in our society. The punishing "right hand" of the state is directed predominantly toward working class and marginalized youth, who are perceived to be "risky" because of their actual or potential involvement in street crimes. Meanwhile, the unacceptable loss of life and large public and personal expense caused by corporate crime is given less criminal justice attention. Turning again to the example of Maple Leaf Foods, Michael McCain has been afforded public acceptance because of his act of condolence and settlement payments to the victims of the listeriosis outbreak. However, he is not subject to the punitive arm of the state, despite what some would perceive as "risky" behaviour, especially since his company is one of the many that has lobbied the Conservative government to place responsibility for food inspection more directly in the hands of the food industry. Consistent with their neoliberal ideological leanings, the Conservatives are considering allowing the food industry to police itself, saving government and private dollars, but placing the public at greater risk of future food-related disease outbreaks (Canadian Press 2008). For these reasons and others, restorativists must be critically aware of the neoliberal discourses that shape the logic of governance in their jurisdictions and must seek to devise strategies to avoid their restorative justice programs being swept away in the sea of neoliberalism and contributing to this growing imbalance.

One problem with my portrayal of neoliberalism thus far, however, is that, as mentioned in Chapter 6, neoliberalism is not a unitary philosophy of governance. Neoliberalism is an adaptable logic that forms itself to its specific context. For this reason, scholars and students can play a role in educating restorativists by conducting detailed studies of the local contours of neoliberalism within specific regions and jurisdictions. For instance, the Alberta and Manitoba variants of neoliberalism are very different, with the former adapted to fit its context of oil wealth and social conservatism, while the latter blends neoliberal economic principles with Tony Blair-inspired Third Way social democracy. For each case, there are likely to be clear applications of neoliberal logic, but also exceptions to this logic, and these exceptions may offer opportunities for strategic action to advance a transformative rather than merely affirmative restorative justice.

Restorative Justice as Governance

A related concern is that restorative justice is, in its own right, a modality of governance. Restorative justice provides insights and tools that allow individuals to better govern themselves. This is not, in and of itself, a bad thing. What Foucault (1994) refers to as the "care of the self" can be a reflexive sense of who we are that allows us to disrupt the ways in which power operates upon our minds and bodies. However, the internalized self-governance promoted by restorative justice can also be an imposition of onerous social control if it asks people to become passive and non-confrontational. Indeed, the fact that conflict resolution techniques can be used to appease and pacify rather than to transform has been noted by several critical scholars (Dyck 2006; Pavlich 1996; Woolford 2005). For example, a university ombudsperson schooled in restorative justice techniques might function as a sort of mediator for student-professor conflicts. If a professor has been accused of sexual harassment of female students, the ombudsperson can convene a confidential mediation session that allows the parties to resolve the problem. The professor may come to understand his actions make the female students uncomfortable, and students may regain a modicum of trust that he will no longer act in this inappropriate manner. However, what has occurred here is remarkably convenient for preserving that status quo state of affairs on the university campus. The issues of professorial power, of "chilly climates," and of sexual harassment have all been buried with the resolution of the interpersonal conflict. Likewise, an Aboriginal group dealing with widespread sexual violence and addiction within their community may be well aware that the histories of Canadian colonialism and residential schooling have played a significant role in provoking these conditions, but may nonetheless be required or encouraged by the state gatekeepers to the circle sentencing process to concentrate their efforts on dealing with the immediate concerns of healing individuals and family from violence and substance abuse, and to leave aside their broader and more time-consuming critique of Canadian colonialism. It seems, therefore, that at every step, the transformative power of restorative justice is reduced and exchanged for the (albeit very understandable) pragmatics of resolving the immediate problem.

Put in everyday terms, there is nothing inherently wrong with restorative justice promoting that people learn how to communicate effectively and resolve conflicts on their own, unless this is encouraged in a manner where the person does not reflect on the nature of the conflict and seeks instead to automatically resolve conflict, regardless of whether the conflict might serve a productive purpose.

For these reasons, restorative justice must acknowledge it does offer governance, and it must seek to govern well. Gil (2006: 509) discusses this issue in the following terms:

> Expanding critical consciousness in everyday social encounters, as well as in professional service settings, involves political discourse. When people interact socially and professionally, their actions and communications can either conform to, or challenge, the social status quo and prevailing patterns of human relations. When people speak and act in accordance with "normal" expectations, they reinforce, by implication, the existing social order and its "common sense" consciousness.

Thus, according to Gil, restorative justice needs to create opportunities for the "emergence of critical consciousness." Such a consciousness would not simply reproduce the normative relations of our social and political worlds; it would instead be inspired to question these worlds and to look toward alternative possibilities. If restorative justice is to govern well, it can only do so by encouraging its participants to be critical agents capable of challenging unfair norms and practices within their everyday lives. It can only do so by moving conflict resolution beyond the limits of affirmative repair. It can only do so by helping people become more than just automatic repressors of conflict — they must become agents capable of assessing their internalized habits and assumptions about the world, allowing them to disrupt patterns of domination that are embedded in their day-to-day worlds.

Restorative Justice and Strategic Political Action

Restorative justice theorists often place a great deal of emphasis on ideational change — that is, on the need for a new lens or paradigm (Zehr 1990; Redekop 2007). As noted above, ideational change, such as a newfound "critical consciousness," is important for counter-hegemonic action, since we need to open space for new views of the world to take hold if we want to sponsor transformative justice. However, a political strategy for promoting social change is also necessary. It is on this level that it is most crucial that restorative justice act as a "social movement," with elements within that movement dedicated to networked disruptions of structural violence. The following are a series of strategic "slogans" that might be useful to those pursuing transformative restorative justice:

1. *Play to Restorative Strengths*: The practice that most clearly distinguishes

restorative justice from other justice processes is its emphasis on open-ended, multi-party communication. In its attempt to create forums in which citizens can communicate their thoughts and feelings on specific matters of injustice, as well as on broader issues of criminal and social justice, restorative justice also overlaps with theories of deliberative democracy that seek to increase citizen input into governance (see Parkinson and Roche 2004; Dzur and Olson 2004; and Braithwaite and Petit 1990 for related ideas; see also Chapters 3 and 6). Parkinson and Roche (2004) view restorative justice as "a vibrant, grassroots example of deliberation in practice" (Parkinson and Roche, 2004: 506); however, they do not feel restorative justice has yet fully met the deliberative standards of inclusiveness, equality between participants, transformative power, scope and decisiveness, and accountability. Thus, an engagement with theories of deliberative democracy provides restorative justice with evaluative tools through which it can assess the democratic adequacy of its practices: Has restorative justice done enough to include all potential participants? Does it institute sufficient measures to ensure equality between participants? Does it provide participants with meaningful transformative power in the sense that they can bring change to their lives and worlds? Does it extend the democratic scope of decision-making across all populations? Does it create channels for ensuring democratic accountability so we are collectively responsible for our democratic decisions? Restorative justice, in many of its forms, strives toward positive answers to all of these questions, but these deliberative ideals could still be realized to a greater degree. It should, however, also be noted this strategic slogan is about more than just the internal evaluation of restorative justice; it also has significant bearing on how restorative justice represents itself publicly. If restorative justice is part of a larger movement to extend and invigorate democracy, it will find itself partnered with other groups seeking to transform our democratic institutions. Restorative justice should, therefore, attach itself to this broader public discussion on what it means to be a participatory and deliberative democracy. Thus, a restorative justice agency in a poor neighbourhood cannot just commit itself to handling the "crime" component of community life, while matters of racism and ethnic tension, gendered poverty, community economic development, and other such issues are left to likewise isolated agencies. If what restorative justice does well is to foster discussion and deliberation, and if the issues dealt with by these agencies are directly connected to the criminal problems addressed through restorative justice, then broader deliberative processes must be established to together tackle the interlinking problems of poverty, race and gender inequality, and crime.

2. *Ideas Are Not Enough*: There is occasionally the sense in the restorative

justice literature that if our ideas are sufficiently appealing and firmly rooted to our moral systems of thought (spiritual and otherwise), we will inevitably convert the non-believers and bring them to see the light of restorative justice. Unfortunately, ideas alone are rarely enough to shift hegemonic patterns of thought and behaviour. Even when verbal agreement is achieved and someone concedes restorative justice seems like a good idea, there still exists a bulwark of deeply habituated and institutionalized practice that must be addressed. Restorative justice must, therefore, strive to change not only thoughts, but also deeply embedded habits. Efforts should therefore be made to encourage participatory and deliberative practices in day-to-day life. This means restorative justice must be about more than simply holding victim-offender mediations when specific instances of crime occur. It also entails support for town hall meetings, public forums, local consultations, and other exercises in local decision-making and problem-solving. Democratic participation, however, does not only mean engagement in public discussion. At times, more radical intervention is required to expand the terrain of public debate. In instances where specific concerns cannot gain any traction on the public agenda, civil disobedience, protest, and legal challenges may be necessary. This sort of confrontational behaviour may seem contrary to the restorative worldview, but we sometimes come up against social and historical circumstances that prevent full discussion of our concerns. Rosa Parks' decision to take a seat reserved for white customers was an act of civil disobedience that sparked larger protests. These protests, although certainly not restorative in any direct sense, helped to pry open a political order that was reluctant to discuss matters of racial equality. In this sense, there are times when confrontational action is necessary to create the conditions for cooperation and to help re-pattern human behaviour. Could victims and ex-offenders together march upon city hall to demand that the brutal poverty of their neighbourhoods be addressed? Could restorative practitioners band with like-minded agencies to lobby for better social services in their communities? Efforts such as these must be made to achieve tangible benefits to everyday people and to attack the roots of crime and injustice.

3. *There Are Opponents*: Following from the previous slogan, it would be nice to think restorative justice is in everyone's interests. The unfortunate truth is, however, some people are deeply invested in the existing criminal justice system. The current system provides them with status, authority, legitimacy, and wealth. This is even true of "governmentalist" restorative justice programs that offer their compromised and diluted versions of restorative justice. Others are emotionally attached to the idea of retribution and will not be easily swayed to let it go. Indeed, in multicultural

societies, we must admit there are cultural sectors of these societies for whom retribution is deeply ingrained. A more restorative system is therefore likely to be experienced by many as a form of rupture in that it breaks down, for some, material benefits, as well as sensibilities they have long used to understand their world. There is, therefore, no painless transformation toward restorative justice, and restorativists must work to make all of these invested groups part of the conversation. Weaning individuals from emotional and cultural attachments to punitive justice may well be a long-term project that requires intergenerational efforts to open people to non-punitive justice ideals. In contrast, those with deeply vested economic and political interests in the current criminal justice system — those whose jobs and incomes depend on our extensive prison system, for example, or those neoliberal politicians who gain political capital by grandstanding on "law and order" issues — will be unlikely to allow anything but an affirmative form of restorative justice to take hold. The reality is, then, that there may come a time when more protest and direct action is needed to force these gatekeepers from their entrenched positions.

4. *Seek Popular Rather than Professional Legitimacy:* Professionalization is increasingly becoming the norm in conflict resolution circles. The long debate over whether it is better to have local laypersons facilitating restorative justice, or whether specific training is required to ensure appropriate restorative practice, appears to have been won by the latter group. And no one can deny training and professional standards are useful in many circumstances. Conflicts are complex phenomena, and people should be as well-prepared as they can be to facilitate them rather than blindly feeling their way through. However, this does not mean the assessed quality of a facilitator should be based upon his or her professional status. A certificate in hand should not be enough to establish facilitator credentials; instead, more should depend on the perspectives of the participants in restorative justice. Did this person empower the participants? Were participants satisfied with the process? Did the facilitator open the discussion to consideration of broader structural injustices? Such questions should be central when determining the legitimacy of facilitators. Moreover, facilitator training should be directed toward standards other than those typical of lawyers and other conflict resolution professionals. For example, Dyck (2006: 530) notes, "One of the key reasons why the structural dimension is often ignored is that many restorative justice programs focus their training almost exclusively on the development of interpersonal communications skills." Facilitators simply are not trained to identify and address structural imbalances. They are also not trained in linking specific individual troubles to broader

social injustices. Nor do they receive advice on assessing the nature of government and how to navigate governing ideological presuppositions. In sum, it is not inevitable that professional involvement in restorative justice result in the co-optation or dilution of transformative justice. For Olson and Dzur (2004: 151), "Democratic professionals seek to open up their domains of authority to lay participants, to share tasks, and to share in the construction of norms that constrain and direct professional action" (see Shapland et al. 2006 for evidence of professional acceptance of restorative justice principles). In this sense, the professional status of a restorative justice practitioner is not a badge of authority to be worn to better regulate restorative sessions, but a means for facilitating more productive discussion.

5. *Link Up and Network*: To quote Dyck (2006: 542) once again, "A transformative practice would see restorative justice agencies investing time and energy in developing accountable relationships with advocacy and social action groups in our communities." By recognizing the ways in which our work is related to these groups, we would become less inclined to work in isolation or, as is sometimes the case, against them. This encapsulates well the slogan "Link up and network." There are a multitude of social actors and groups working toward a similar set of goals. The affirmative practice of restorative justice isolates injustices from their broader social conditions. In contrast, a transformative practice understands these injustices as part of a bigger picture, which is difficult to address from an isolated spot in the vast arrangement of society. Therefore, restorative justice groups must network beyond the realm of criminal justice, taking into consideration their common goals with community economic development, anti-poverty, anti-racism, feminist, and other such groups. By linking their activities, these groups can exert pressure upon the state and civil society from multiple positions, creating a more broad-based effort to shift dominant patterns of thought and action.

6. *Keep Going*: Restorative justice should not allow itself the luxury of completion. It is an ideal that can always be improved upon, that can always be further advanced. To think otherwise is to allow stasis to set in and to get too comfortable. For this reason, transformative justice does not end with the full realization of economic redistribution, cultural recognition, and social representation. Each of these projects will have its unintended consequences, and new injustices will arise in the pursuit of a better world. A transformative justice that is not sensitized to these possibilities risks falling into the traps of dogmatism or totalization, through which an idealized vision is held desperately onto no matter what contradictory evidence has arisen to suggest that problems within the vision exist. No matter what successes we achieve in terms of gain-

ing new resources for our communities, we must continue to critically evaluate these achievements and press them further. Therefore, for example, a new community program that offers micro-loans and other funding incentives to marginalized community members may be a success achieved by a restorative justice agency in concert with other local groups, but that agency must still examine closely how these loans are distributed: Are they equally available to all community members? Are there any groups who are excluded from the program?

7. *Commit to Reflexivity*: There is no restorative core that must be protected from all criticism. A reflexive engagement means we must be willing to challenge all elements of our thought, including the guiding presuppositions of the restorative justice ethos. The goal is to uncover the subterranean politics lurking within these assumptions and to devise new understandings of restorativeness when the old ones fail. Thus, even the restorative ethos should remain open to critique, since a blind faith in the power of communication to heal social rifts can sometimes mask structural inequalities that are at the base of those rifts — as if to say, "Talk it out, but don't probe too deeply into structurally embedded forms of social injustice."

Final Thought

This book has sought to navigate two conceptions of the world: a world of process that is open and indeterminate, and a world of regularity in which structured patterns of domination maintain an overarching system of power. Although these may seem, upon first glance, contradictory, the truth is things remain in movement, even though general patterns can be discerned. Restorative justice must embrace this unsettled state, allow for a degree of uncertainty, and yet commit to a notion that patterns can change for the better.

In the end, restorative justice is a movement with many competing parts. Those that affirm the present social order appear, for the moment, to be winning out, and this, in my view, is unfortunate. The potential of restorative justice is to be part of something bigger. Through an enabling politics networked with other social justice movements, restorative justice can aspire toward transformative justice.

References

Abel, Richard L. 1982. "The Contradictions of Informal Justice." In R. Abel (ed.) *The Politics of Informal Justice: The American Experience* Volume 1. New York: Academic Press.

Achilles, Mary, and Lorraine Stutzman-Amstutz. 2006. "Responding to the Needs of Victims: What Was Promised, What Has Been Delivered." In D. Sullivan and L. Tifft (eds.), *Handbook of Restorative Justice: A Global Perspective*. London and New York: Routledge.

Acker, James R. 2006. "Hearing the Victim's Voice Amidst the Cry for Capital Punishment." In D. Sullivan and L. Tifft (eds.), *Handbook of Restorative Justice: A Global Perspective*. London and New York: Routledge.

Acorn, Annalise E. 2004. *Compulsory Compassion: A Critique of Restorative Justice*. Vancouver: UBC Press.

Adam, Heribert. 2001. "Divided Memories: Confronting the Crimes of Previous Regimes." *Telos* 118: 87–109.

Agamban, Giorgio. 1993. *The Coming Community*. Minneapolis: University of Minnesota Press.

Aggestam, K. 1995. "Reframing International Conflicts: 'Ripeness' in International Mediation." *Paradigms* 9 (2): 86–106.

Ahladas, Yiota, and Ben Sachs-Hamilton. 2008. "Community Is No Cliché: It Works… the Burlington Way." *Yes Magazine*. <http://yesmagazine.org/article.asp?ID=2538>

Alcoff, Linda, and Laura Gray. 1993. "Survivor Discourse: Transgression or Recuperation?" *Signs: Journal of Women in Culture and Society* 18, 260–90.

Alexander, Jeffrey C. 2004. "On the Social Construction of Moral Universals: The 'Holocaust' from War Crime to Trauma Drama." In J. Alexander, R. Eyerman, B. Giesen, N.J. Smelser and P. Sztompka (eds.), *Cultural Trauma and Collective Identity*. Berkeley: University of California Press.

Anderson, Elijah. 1999. *The Code of the Street: Decency, Violence and the Moral Life of the Inner City*. New York and London: W.W. Norton.

Ashworth, Andrew. 2003. "Responsibilities, Rights and Restorative Justice." In G. Johnstone (ed.), *A Restorative Justice Reader: Texts, Sources, Context*. Cullompton, UK: Willan Publishing.

Barnett, Randy. 1977. "Restitution: A New Paradigm of Criminal Justice." *Ethics* 87, 4: 279–301.

Bartlett, W., and J. Le Grand. 1993. *Quasi-markets and Social Policy*. Basingstoke: Palgrave Macmillan.

Bauman, Zygmunt. 2001. *Community: Seeking Safety in an Insecure World*. Cambridge: Polity Press.

Benhabib, Seyla. 1992. *Situating the Self: Gender, Community and Postmodernism in Contemporary Ethics*. New York: Routledge.

_____. 1996. "Toward a Deliberative Model of Democratic Legitimacy." In S.

Benhabib (ed.), *Democracy and Difference: Contesting the Boundaries of the Political.* Princeton, NJ: Princeton University Press.

Bonta, James, Jennifer Rooney, and Suzanne Wallace-Capretta. 1998. *Restorative Justice: An Evaluation of the Restorative Resolutions Project.* Ottawa: Solicitor General of Canada.

Bottoms, A.E. 1995. "The Philosophy and Politics of Punishment and Sentencing." In C. Clarkson and R. Morgan (eds.), *The Politics of Sentencing Reform.* Oxford: Clarendon Press.

_____. 2003. "Some Sociological Reflections on Restorative Justice." In A. von Hirsch, J. Roberts, A.E. Bottoms, K. Roach, and M. Schiff (eds.), *Restorative Justice and Criminal Justice: Competing or Reconcilable Paradigms?* Oxford, UK: Hart Publishing.

Bourdieu, Pierre. 1987. "The Force of Law: Toward a Sociology of the Jurdical Field." *Hastings Law Journal* 38: 805–53.

_____. 1998. *Acts of Resistance: Against the Tyranny of the Market.* New York: New Press.

_____. 1990. *The Logic of Practice.* Cambridge: Polity Press.

Braihwaite, John. 1989. *Crime, Shame and Reintegration.* Cambridge, UK: Cambridge University Press.

_____. 1994. "Thinking Harder About Democratizing Social Control." In J. Alder and J. Wundersitz (eds.), *Family Conferencing and Juvenile Justice: The Way Forward of Misplaced Optimism?* Canberra: Australian Institute of Criminology.

_____. 1999. "Restorative Justice: Assessing Optimistic and Pessimistic Accounts." *Crime and Justice: A Review of Research* 25: 1–127.

_____. 2002. *Restorative Justice and Responsive Regulation.* New York: Oxford University Press.

_____. 2003. "Restorative Justice and a Better Future." In G. Johnstone (ed.), *A Restorative Justice Reader: Texts, Sources, Context.* Cullompton, UK: Willan Publishing.

Braithwaite, John, and Kathleen Daly. 1994. "Masculinities, Violence and Communitarian Control." In T. Newburn and E. Stanko (eds.), *Just Boys Doing Business? Men, Masculinities and Crime.* London: Routledge.

Braithwaite, John, and Stephen Mugford. 1994. "Conditions of Successful Reintegration Ceremonies: Dealing with Juvenile Offenders." *British Journal of Criminology* 34, 2: 139–71.

Braithwaite, John, and Philip Petit. 1990. *Not Just Desserts: A Republican Theory of Criminal Justice.* Oxford: Clarendon Press.

Brooks, Roy L, 2003, "Reflections on Reparations." In J. Torpey (ed.), *Politics and the Past: On Repairing Historical Injustices.* Lanham, NJ: Rowman and Littlefield.

Browning, Christopher R. 2004. *The Origins of the Final Solution: The Evolution of Nazi Jewish Policy, September 1939–March 1942.* With contributions by Jürgen Matthäus. Lincoln, Nebraska: University of Nebraska Press and Yad Vashem, Jerusalem.

Burchell, Graham. 1993. "Liberal Government and Techniques of the Self." *Economy and Society*, 22, 3 (August): 267–82.

Burger, Chief Justice Warren. 1979. "Address Before the National Conference on the Causes of Popular Dissatisfaction with the Administration of Justice, April 7–9, 1976." Reprinted in A.L. Levin and R.R. Wheeler (eds.), *The Pound Conference: Perspectives on Justice in the Future.* St Paul, MN: West Publishing.

Canadian Press. 2008. "Deregulating Food Inspection Too Risky: Union." *CTV News*, November 8. <http://www.ctv.ca/servlet/ArticleNews/story/CTVNews/20081103/food_inspection_081103?s_name=&no_ads=>

References

CBC News. 2009. "Manitoba Métis Win Hunting Rights Case." CBC News January 8. <http://www.cbc.ca/canada/manitoba/story/2009/01/08/metis-hunting. html>

Charbonneau, Serge. 2004. "The Canadian Youth Criminal Justice Act 2003: A Step Forward for Advocates of Restorative Justice?" In E. Elliott and R.M. Gordon (eds.), *New Directions in Restorative Justice: Issues, Practice, Evaluation.* Cullompton, UK: Willan.

Christie, Nils. 1977. "Conflicts as Property." *British Journal of Criminology* 17, 1: 1–15.

_____. 1986. "The Ideal Victim." In E. A. Fattah (ed.), *From Crime Policy to Victim Policy.* London: MacMillan.

Christodoulidis, Emilios A. 2000. "'Truth and Reconciliation' as Risks." *Social & Legal Studies* 9, 2: 179–204.

Clifford, James. 1988. *The Predicament of Culture: Twentieth-Century Ethnography, Literature, and Art.* Cambridge, MA: Harvard University Press.

Cohen, Albert K. 1965. "The Sociology of the Deviant Act." *American Sociological Review* 30: 5–14.

Cohen, Stanley. 1985. *Visions of Social Control: Crime, Punishment, and Classification.* Oxford: Polity Press.

Cole, Tim. 1999. *Selling the Holocaust: From Auschwitz to Schindler, How History is Bought, Packaged, and Sold.* New York: Routledge.

Comack, Elizabeth, and Gillian Balfour. 2004. *The Power to Criminalize: Violence, Inequality, and Law.* Halifax, NS: Fernwood Publishing.

Consedine, Jim. 1995. *Restorative Justice: Healing the Effects of Crime.* Lyttleton, NZ: Ploughshares.

_____. 2003. "The Maori Restorative Tradition." In Gerry Johnstone (ed.), *A Restorative Justice Reader: Texts, Sources, Context.* Cullompton, UK: Willan Publishing.

Cote, Jim, and Anton Allahar. 1995. *Generation on Hold: Coming of Age in the Late Twentieth Century.* New York: NYU Press.

Coy, Patrick G., and Timothy Hedeen. 2005. "A Stage Model of Social Movement Co-optation: Community Mediation in the United States." *The Sociological Quarterly* 26: 405–35.

Crawford, Adam. 2003. "The Prospects for Restorative Youth Justice in England and Wales: A Tale of Two Acts." In K. McEvoy and T. Newburn (eds.), *Criminology, Conflict Resolution and Restorative Justice.* Houndsmills, Basingstoke, Hampshire: Palgrave Macmillan.

Crawford, Adam, and Tim Newburn. 2002. "Recent Developments in Restorative Justice for Young People in England and Wales: Community Participation and Representation." *British Journal of Criminology* 42: 476–85.

Cunneen, Chris. _____. 1997. "Community Conferencing and the Fiction of Indigenous Control." *Australian and New Zealand Journal of Criminology* 30: 292–311.

_____. 2002. "Restorative Justice and the Politics of Decolonisation." In E. Weitkamp and H. Kerner (eds.), *Restorative Justice: Theoretical Foundations.* Cullompton, UK: Willan Publishing.

_____. 2006. "Exploring the Relationship Between Reparations, the Gross violation of Human Rights, and Restorative Justice." In D. Sullivan and L. Tifft (eds.), *Handbook of Restorative Justice: A Global Perspective.* London and New York: Routledge.

_____. 2007. "Reviving Restorative Justice Traditions." In G. Johnstone and D.W. Van Ness (eds.), *Handbook of Restorative Justice.* Cullompton, UK: Willan Publishing.

Daly, Kathleen. 2006. "The Limits of Restorative Justice." In D. Sullivan and L. Tifft (eds.), *Handbook of Restorative Justice: A Global Perspective*. London and New York: Routledge.

_____. 2003. "Restorative Justice: The Real Story." In Gerry Johnstone (ed.), *A Restorative Justice Reader: Texts, Sources, Context*. Cullompton, UK: Willan Publishing.

Daly, Kathleen, and Russ Immarigeon. 1998. "The Past, Present, and Future of Restorative Justice: Some Critical Reflections." *Contemporary Justice Review* 1: 21–45.

Dean, Mitchell. 1999. *Governmentality: Power and Rule in Modern Society*. London: Sage.

Delbo, Charlotte. 1995. *Auschwitz and After*. New Haven, CT: Yale University Press.

Derrida, Jacques. 1992. "Force of Law: The 'Mystical Foundation of Authority.'" In D. Cornell, M. Rosenfeld, and D.G. Carlson (eds.), *Deconstruction and the Possibility of Justice*. London: Routledge.

Deutsch, M. 1973. *The Resolution of Conflict: Constructive and Destructive Processes*. New Haven, CT: Yale University Press.

Diani, Mario. 1992. "The Concept of Social Movement." *The Sociological Review* 40, 1: 1–25.

Dignan, James, Anne Atkinson, Helen Atkinson, Marie Howes, Jennifer Johnstone, Gwen Robinson, Joanna Shapland, and Angela Sorsby. 2007. "Staging Restorative Justice Encounters Against a Criminal Justice Backdrop: A Dramaturgical Analysis." *Criminology & Criminal Justice* 7, 1: 5–32.

Dryzek, J. S. 2000. *Deliberative Democracy and Beyond*. Oxford: Oxford University Press.

Duff, R.A. 2003. "Restorative Punishment and Punitive Restoration." In Gerry Johnstone (ed.), *A Restorative Justice Reader: Texts, Sources, Context*. Cullompton, UK: Willan Publishing.

Duguid, S. 2000. *Can Prisons Work? The Prisoner as Object and Subject in Modern Corrections*. Toronto, ON: University of Toronto Press.

Durkheim, Emile. 1984 [c1933]. *The Division of Labour in Society*. New York: Free Press.

Dyck, David. 2006. "Reaching Toward a Structurally Responsive Training and Practice of Restorative Justice." In D. Sullivan and L. Tifft (eds.), *Handbook of Restorative Justice: A Global Perspective*. London and New York: Routledge.

Dzur, Albert W., and Susan M. Olson. 2004. "The Value of Community Participation in Restorative Justice." *Journal of Social Philosophy* XXXV, 1 (Spring): 91–107.

Elias, Robert. 1986. *The Politics of Victimization: Victims, Victimology and Human Rights*. Oxford: Oxford University Press.

Elliott, Elizabeth, and Robert M. Gordon (eds.). 2005. *New Directions in Restorative Justice: Issues, Practice, Evaluation*. Cullompton, UK: Willan Publishing.

Ewick, P., and S.S. Silbey. 1998. *The Common Place of Law: Stories of Popular Legal Consciousness*. Chicago: University of Chicago Press.

Fattah, Ezzat A. (ed.). 1992. *Towards a Critical Victimology*. New York: St. Martin's Press.

Fein, Helen. 1993. *Genocide: A Sociological Perspective*. London: Sage Publications.

Fisher, R., and W. Ury. 1991. *Getting to Yes: Negotiating Agreement Without Giving In*. Second edition. New York: Penguin Books.

Fishkin, J.S. 1991. *Democracy and Deliberation: New Directions for Democratic Reform*. New Haven, CT: Yale University Press.

Fisk, Milton. 1993. "Introduction: The Problem of Justice." In M. Fisk (ed.), *Key Concepts in Critical Theory: Justice*. New Jersey: Humanities Press.

Fitzpatrick, Peter. 1995. "The Impossibility of Popular Justice." In S. Engle Merry and N. Milner (eds.), *The Possibility of Popular Justice: A Case Study of Community Mediation in the United States*. Ann Arbor: The University of Michigan Press.

Foucault, Michel. 1977. *Discipline and Punish: The Birth of the Prison*. New York: Pantheon Books.

_____. 1991. "Governmentality." In G. Burchell, C. Gordon and P. Miller (eds.), *The Foucault Effect: Studies in Governmentality with Two Lectures by and an Interview with Michel Foucault*. Chicago: University of Chicago Press.

_____. 1994. *Ethics, Subjectivity and Truth*. New York: The New Press.

Frank, Anne. 1995 [1947]. *The Diary of a Young Girl*. New York: Doubleday.

Fraser, Nancy. 1992. "Rethinking the Public Sphere: A Contribution to the Critique of Actually Existing Democracy." In Craig Calhoun (ed.), *Habermas and the Public Sphere*. Cambridge, MA: MIT Press.

_____. 1997. *Justice Interruptus: Critical Reflections on the "Postsocialist Condition."* New York: Routledge.

_____. 2000. "Rethinking Recognition." *New Left Review* 3, May–June: 107–20.

_____. 2003. "From Discipline to Flexibilization? Rereading Foucault in the Shadow of Globalization." *Constellations* 10, 2: 160–71.

Galaway, B., and J. Hudson (eds.). 1996. *Restorative Justice: International Perspectives*. Monsey, NY: Criminal Justice Press.

Garfinkel, Harold. 1956. "Conditions of Successful Degradation Ceremonies." *American Journal of Sociology*, 61: 420–24.

Garland, David. 2001. *The Culture of Control: Crime and Social Order in Contemporary Society*. Chicago: University of Chicago Press.

Gavrielides, Theo. 2007. *Restorative Justice Theory and Practice: Addressing the Discrepancy*. Helsinki: European Institute for Crime Prevention and Control.

Giddens, Anthony. 1991. *Modernity and Self-Identity: Self and Society in the Late Modern Age*. Stanford, CA: Stanford University Press.

Gil, David G. 2006. "Toward a 'Radical' Paradigm of Restorative Justice." In D. Sullivan and L. Tifft (eds.), *Handbook of Restorative Justice: A Global Perspective*. London and New York: Routledge.

Goldschmidt, Siegfried. 1945. *Legal Claims Against Germany*. New York: Dryden Press.

Goschler, Constantin. 1991. "The United States and *Wiedergutmachung* for Victims of Nazi Persecution: From Leadership to Disengagement." In A. Frohn (ed.), *Holocaust and Shilumim: The Policy of Wiedergutmachung in the Early 1950s*. Washington, DC: German Historical Institute.

_____. 2004. "German Compensation to Jewish Nazi Victims." In J. M. Diefendorf (ed.), *Lessons and Legacies IV: New Currents in Holocaust Research*. Evanston, IL: Northwestern University Press.

Gramsci, Antonio. 1971. *Selections from the Prison Notebooks (Selections)*. New York: International Publishers.

Habermas, Jürgen. 1984. *The Theory of Communicative Action: Reason and the Rationalization of Society*. Volume 1. Boston: Beacon Press.

_____. 1989. *The Structural Transformation of the Public Sphere*. Cambridge, MA: Polity Press.

_____. 1990. *Moral Consciousness and Communicative Action*. Cambridge, MA: MIT Press.

_____. 1999. *Between Facts And Norms: Contributions to a Discourse Theory of Law and Democracy*. Cambridge, MA: MIT Press.

Haig-Brown, Celia. 1988. *Resistance and Renewal: Surviving the Indian Residential School*, Vancouver: Tillacum Library.

Hampton, Jean. 1998. "Punishment, Feminism, and Political Identity: A Case Study in the Expressive Meaning of Law." *Canadian Journal of Law and Jurisprudence* 11, 1: 23–45.

Hannah-Moffat, Kelly, and Margaret Shaw. 2001. *Taking Risks: Incorporating Gender and Culture into the Classification and Assessment of Federally Sentenced Women in Canada.* Ottawa: Status of Women.

Hardt, Michael, and Antonio Negri. 2000. *Empire.* Cambridge, MA: Harvard University Press.

_____. 2004. *Multitude: War and Democracy in the Age of Empire.* New York: Penguin.

Harrington, Christina B. 1985. *Shadow Justice: The Ideology and Institutionalization of Alternatives to Court.* Westport, CT: Greenwood Press.

Hart-Landsberg, Martin. 2006. "Neoliberalism: Myths and reality." *Monthly Review* 57, 11. <http://www.monthlyreview.org/0406hart-landsberg.htm>

Hartman, Yvonne. 2005. "In Bed with the Enemy: Some Ideas on the Connections between Neoliberalism and the Welfare State." *Current Sociology* 53, 1: 57–73.

Hay, Colin. 2006. "Political Ontology." In R.E. Goodin and C. Tilly (eds.), *The Oxford Handbook of Contextual Political Analysis.* Oxford: Oxford University Press.

Hayner, Priscilla B. 2002. *Unspeakable Truths: Facing the Challenge of Truth Commissions.* New York and London: Routledge.

Herf, Jeffrey. 1997. *Divided Memory: The Nazi Past in the Two Germanys.* Cambridge, MA: Harvard University Press.

Heritage Community Foundation. 2002. "Great Alberta Law Cases" Inside the Courtroom." *Alberta Online Encyclopedia.* <http://www.albertasource.ca/lawcases/civil/murdoch/murdoch_trial_courtroom.htm>

Herman, Susan. 2004. "Is Restorative Justice Possible Without a Parallel System for Victims?" In H. Zehr and B. Toews (eds.), *Critical Issues in Restorative Justice.* Monsey, New York and Cullompton, UK: Criminal Justice Press and Willan Publishing.

Hofrichter, Richard. 1982. "Neighborhood Justice and the Social Control Problems of American Capitalism: A Perspective." In Richard Abel (ed.), *The Politics of Informal Justice: The American Experience.* Volume 1. New York: Academic Press.

_____. 1987. *Neighborhood Justice in Capitalist Society: The Expansion of the Informal State.* New York: Greenwood.

Hogarth, John. 1971. *Sentencing as a Human Process.* Toronto: University of Toronto Press.

Hogeveen, Bryan. 2006. "Unsettling Youth Justice and Cultural Norms: The Youth Restorative Action Project." *Journal of Youth Studies* 9, 1: 47–66.

Hogeveen, Bryan, and Joanne Minaker. 2008. *Youth, Crime and Justice: Issues of Power and Justice.* Toronto: Pearson.

Hogeveen, Bryan, and Andrew Woolford. 2006. "Critical Criminology and Possibility in the Neoliberal Ethos." *Canadian Journal of Criminology and Criminal Justice* 48, 5: 681–702.

Hudson, Barbara. 2003. *Justice in the Risk Society.* London: Sage.

Hunt, Ronald. 2000. "Conferencing a Serious Arson Case." <http://iirp.org/library/t2000/t2000_rhunt.html>

Illich, Ivan. 1977. *Towards a History of Needs.* New York: Pantheon Books.

Illich, Ivan, Irving Zola, John McKnight, and Harley Shaiken. 1977. *Disabling Professions.* London: Marion Boyars.

Jameson, Frederic. 1991. *Postmodernism, or, the Cultural Logic of Late Capitalism.* Durham, NC: Duke University Press.

References

Jelinek, Yeshayahu A. 1990. "Political Acumen, Altruism, Foreign Pressure or Moral Debt: Konrad Adenauer and the 'Shilumim.'" *Tel Aviver Jahrbuch für Deutsche Geschichte* 19: 77–102.

Jessop, Bob. 2002. "Liberalism, Neoliberalism, and Urban Governance: A State-Theoretical Perspective." *Antipode* 34, 3: 452–72.

Johnstone, Gerry. 2002. *Restorative Justice: Ideas, Values, Debates*. Devon, UK: Willan Publishing.

_____. 2004. "How, and in What Terms, Should Restorative Justice Be Conceived?" In H. Zehr and B. Toews (eds.), *Critical Issues in Restorative Justice*. Cullompton, UK: Willan Publishing.

Johnstone, Gerry, and Daniel Van Ness. 2007. "The Meaning of Restorative Justice." In G. Johnstone and D.W. Van Ness (eds.), *Handbook of Restorative Justice*. Cullompton, UK: Willan Publishing.

Kant, Immanuel 1873. *Fundamental Principles of the Metaphysics of Morals*. London: Longmans, Green, & Co.

Kay, Judith W. 2006. "Murder Victims' Families for Reconciliation: Story-Telling for Healing, as Witness, and in Public Policy." In D. Sullivan and L. Tifft (eds.), *Handbook of Restorative Justice: A Global Perspective*. London and New York: Routledge.

Kim, Hubert. 1999. "German Reparations: Institutionalized Insufficiency." In Roy L. Brooks (ed.), *When Sorry Isn't Enough: The Controversy over Apologies and Reparations for Human Injustice*. New York: New York University Press.

Koontz, Claudia. 2003. *The Nazi Conscience*. Cambridge, MA: Belknap Press.

Kriesberg, Louis. 2008. "Waging Conflicts Constructively." In S. Byrne, J. Senehi, D. Sandole, and I. Staroste-Sandole (eds.), *Conflict Resolution: Core Concepts, Theories, Approaches and Practices*. London: Routledge.

Kritz, Neil J. 1995. *Transitional Justice: How Emerging Democracies Reckon with Former Regimes*. Washington, DC: United States Institute of Peace Press.

Krog, Antjie. 1998. *Country of My Skull: Guilt, Sorrow, and the Limits of Forgiveness in the New South Africa*. New York: Three Rivers Press.

Kueneman, Rodney. 2008. "The Origins and Role of Law in Society." In Rick Linden (ed.), *Criminology: A Canadian Perspective*. Volume 5. Toronto: Thomson-Nelson.

Kurki, L. 2000. "Restorative Justice and Community Justice in the United States." *Crime and Justice* 27: 235–303.

Lajeunesse, Therese. 1996. *Evaluation of Community Holistic Circle Healing. Hollow Water First Nation. Volume 1: Final Report*. Manitoba: Thérèse Lajeunesse & Associates Ltd.

Laroque, Emma. 1997. "Re-Examining Culturally Appropriate Models in Criminal Justice Applications." In Michael Asch (ed.), *Aboriginal and Treaty Rights in Canada: Essays on Laws, Equality, and Respect for Difference*. Vancouver: UBC Press.

Latimer, J., C. Dowden, and D. Muise. 2001. *The Effectiveness of Restorative Justice Practices: A Meta-Analysis*. Ottawa: Department of Justice, Canada.

Levi, Primo. 1989. *The Drowned and the Saved*. New York: Vintage International.

Levrant, S., F.T. Cullen, B. Fulton, and J.F. Wozniak. 1999. "Reconsidering Restorative Justice: The Corruption of Benevolence Revisited?" *Crime and Delinquency* 45: 3–27.

Llewellyn, Jennifer. 2007. "Truth Commissions and Restorative Justice." In G. Johnstone and D.W. Van Ness (eds.), *Handbook of Restorative Justice*. Cullompton, UK: Willan Publishing.

Llewellyn, Jennifer, and Robert Howse. 1998. *Restorative Justice: A Conceptual Framework*. Ottawa: Law Commission of Canada.

Maier, Charles S. 1988. *The Unmasterable Past: History, Holocaust, and German National Identity*. Cambridge, MA: Harvard University Press.

Mamdani, Mahmood. 2000. "The Truth According to the TRC." In I. Amadiume and A. An-Na'im (eds.), *The Politics of Memory: Truth, Healing & Social Justice*. London: Zed Books.

_____. 2001. *When Victims Become Killers: Colonialism, Nativism, and the Genocide in Rwanda*. Princeton, NJ: Princeton University Press.

Marchak, Patricia. 2008. *No Easy Fix: Global Responses to Internal Wars and Crimes against Humanity*. Montreal and Kingston: McGill-Queen's University Press.

Marshall, Tony F. 1999. *Restorative Justice: An Overview*. London: Home Office, Research Development and Statistics Directorate.

Martinson, R. 1974. "What Works? Questions and Answers about Prison Reform." *The Public Interest* Spring: 22–54.

Matthews, Roger (ed.). 1988. *Informal Justice?* London: Sage.

Matza, David. 1990. *Delinquency and Drift*. New Brunswick, NJ: Transaction.

Maxwell, Gabrielle, and Allison Morris. 1993. *Family, Victims and Culture: Youth Justice in New Zealand*. Wellington: Special Policy Agency and Institute of Criminology, Victoria University of Wellington.

Maxwell, Gabrielle, Allison Morris, and Hennesey Hayes. 2006. "Conferencing and Restorative Justice." In D. Sullivan and L. Tifft (eds.), *Handbook of Restorative Justice: A Global Perspective*. London and New York: Routledge.

McCold, Paul. 2006. "The Recent History of Restorative Justice, Mediation, Circles, and Conferencing." In D. Sullivan and L. Tifft (eds.), *Handbook of Restorative Justice: A Global Perspective*. London: Routledge.

McCold, Paul, and Benjamin Wachtel. 1998. "Restorative Policing Experiment: The Bethlehem Pennsylvania Police Family Group Conferencing Project." Pipersville, Pennsylvania: Community Service Foundation.

McCold, Paul, and Ted Wachtel. 1998. "Community is Not a Place: A New Look at Community Justice Initiatives." *Contemporary Justice Review*, 1, 1: 71–85.

_____. 2002. "Restorative Justice Theory Validation." In E. Weitkamp and H. Kerner (eds.), *Restorative Justice: Theoretical Foundations*. Cullompton, UK: Willan Publishing.

McEvoy, Kieran, and Anna Ecksson. 2006. "Restorative Justice in Transition: Ownership, Leadership, and 'Bottom-Up' Human Rights." In D. Sullivan and L. Tifft (eds.), *Handbook of Restorative Justice: A Global Perspective*. London and New York: Routledge.

McEvoy, Kieran, and Tim Newburn. 2003. "Criminology, Conflict Resolution and Restorative Justice." In K. McEvoy and T. Newburn (eds.), *Criminology, Conflict Resolution and Restorative Justice*. Houndsmills, Basingstoke, Hampshire: Palgrave Macmillan.

McLachlin, Beverly. 2004. "Judging in a Democratic Society." Sixth Templeton Lecture on Democracy, University of Manitoba, June 3.

Meierhenrich, Jens. 2008. *The Legacies of Law: Long-Run Consequences of Legal Development in South Africa, 1652–2000*. Cambridge, MA: Cambridge University Press.

Miers, David. 1989. "Positivist Criminology: A Critique." *International Review of Victimology* 1: 3–22.

Mika, Harry, and Howard Zehr. 2003. "A Restorative Framework for Community

References

Justice Practice." In K. McEvoy and T. Newburn (eds.), *Criminology, Conflict Resolution and Restorative Justice.* Houndsmills, Basingstoke, Hampshire: Palgrave Macmillan.

Mill, John Stuart. 1993 [c1861]. "On the Connection Between Justice and Utility." In M. Fisk (ed.), *Key Concepts in Critical Theory: Justice.* New Jersey: Humanities Press.

Milloy, John S. 1999. *A National Crime: The Canadian Government and the Residential School System, 1879 to 1986.* Winnipeg, Manitoba: University of Manitoba Press.

Mills, C. Wright. 1959. *The Sociological Imagination.* New York: Oxford University press.

Minow, Martha. 1999. *Between Vengeance and Forgiveness: Facing Genocide and Mass Violence.* Boston: Beacon Press.

Monture-Angus, Patricia. 1999. *Journeying Forward: Dreaming First Nations' Independence.* Halifax, NS: Fernwood Publishing.

Moore, D.B., and T.A. O'Connell. 2003. "Family Conferencing in Wagga Wagga: A Communitarian Model." In G. Johnstone (ed.), *A Restorative Justice Reader: Texts, Sources, Context.* Cullompton, UK: Willan Publishing.

Morris, Ruth. 1994. *A Practical Path Toward Transformative Justice.* Toronto: Rittenhouse.

Morrison, Brenda. 2007. "Schools and Restorative Justice." In G. Johnstone and D.W. Van Ness (eds.), *Handbook of Restorative Justice.* Cullompton, UK: Willan Publishing.

Moses, Siegfried. 1944. *Jewish Post-War Claims.* Tel Aviv: Irgun Olej Merkaz Europa.

Murphy, Jeffrie G., and Jean Hampton. 1988. *Forgiveness and Mercy.* Cambridge, UK: Cambridge University Press.

Nader, Laura. 1990. *Harmony Ideology: Justice and Control in a Mountain Zapotec Village.* Stanford, California: Stanford University Press.

Nancy, Jean-Luc. 1991. *The Inoperative Community.* Minneapolis: University of Minnesota Press.

Napoleon, Val. 2004. "By Whom, and by What Processes, is Restorative Justice Defined?" In H. Zehr and B. Toews (eds.), *Critical Issues in Restorative Justice.* Cullompton, UK: Willan Publishing.

Niven, Bill. 2002. *Facing the Nazi Past: United Germany and the Legacy of the Third Reich.* London and New York: Routledge.

Novick, Peter. 1999. *The Holocaust in American Life.* Boston: Mariner Books.

Offe, Claus. 1997. *Varieties of Transition: The East European and East German Experience.* Cambridge, MA: MIT Press.

Olson, Susan M and Albert W. Dzur. 2004. "Revisiting Informal Justice: Restorative Justice and Democratic Professionalism." *Law & Society Review* 38, 1: 139–76.

Osiel, Mark. 1999. *Mass Atrocity, Collective Memory and the Law.* New Brunswick, NJ: Transaction.

Parkinson, John, and Declan Roche. 2004. "Restorative Justice: Deliberative Democracy in Action?" *Australian Journal of Political Science,* 39, 3: 505–18.

Pavlich, George. 1996a. *Justice Fragmented: Mediating Community Disputes Under Postmodern Conditions.* London: Routledge.

_____. 1996b. "The Power of Community Mediation: Government and Formation of Self." *Law and Society Review* 30: 101–27.

_____. 2001. "The Force of Community." In H. Strang and J. Braithwaite (eds.), *Restorative Justice and Civil Society.* Cambridge: Cambridge University Press.

_____. 2005. *Governing Paradoxes of Restorative Justice.* London: GlassHouse Press.

_____. 2007. Ethics, Universal Principles, and Restorative Justice." In G. Johnstone and D.W. Van Ness (eds.), *Handbook of Restorative Justice.* Cullompton, UK: Willan Publishing.

Peachey, Dean E. 2003. "The Kitchener Experiment." In G. Johnstone (ed.), *A Restorative Justice Reader: Texts, Sources, Context*. Cullompton, UK: Willan Publishing.

Pennell, Joan, and Gale Burford. 2002. "Feminist Praxis: Making Family Group Conferencing Work." In H. Strang and J. Braithwaite (eds.), *Restorative Justice and Family Violence*. Cambridge, UK: Cambridge University Press.

Pepinsky, Harold E., and Richard Quinney (eds.). 1990. *Criminology as Peacemaking*. Bloomington, IN: Indiana University Press.

Picard, Cheryl A. 1998. *Mediating Interpersonal and Small Group Conflict*. Ottawa: Golden Dog Press.

Pollard, Sir Charles. 2001. "'If Your Only Tool Is a Hammer, All Your Problems Will Look Like Nails.'" In H. Strang and J. Braithwaite (eds.), *Restorative Justice and Civil Society*. Cambridge: Cambridge University Press.

Power, Samantha. 2002. *"A Problem From Hell": America and the Age of Genocide*. New York: Basic Books.

Pranis, Kay. 2005. *The Little Book of Circle Processes: A New/Old Approach to Peacemaking*. Intercourse, PA: Good Books.

Pross, Christian. 1998. *Paying for the Past: The Struggle over Reparations for Surviving Victims of the Nazi Terror*. Baltimore: Johns Hopkins University Press.

Putnam, Robert. 2000. *Bowling Alone: The Collapse and Revival of American Community*. New York: Touchstone.

Puxon, Grattan. 1981. "Gypsies Seek Reparations." *Patterns of Prejudice* 15: 21–25.

Rawls, John. 1971. *A Theory of Justice*. Cambridge, MA: Belknap Press of Harvard University.

_____. 1993. "Justice as Fairness: Political not Metaphysical." In M. Fisk (ed.) *Key Concepts in Critical Theory: Justice*. New Jersey: Humanities Press.

Raye, Barbara E., and Ann Warner Roberts. 2007. "Restorative Processes." In G. Johnstone and D.W. Van Ness (eds.), *Handbook of Restorative Justice*. Cullompton, UK: Willan Publishing.

Redekop, Paul. 2007. *Changing Paradigms: Punishment and Restorative Discipline*. Scottdale, Pennsylvania: Herald Press.

Robinson, Nehemiah. 1944. *Indemnification and Reparations — Jewish Aspects*. New York: Institute of Jewish Affairs.

Roche, Declan. 2007. "Restitution and Restorative Justice." In G. Johnstone and D.W. Van Ness (eds.), *Handbook of Restorative Justice*. Cullompton, UK: Willan Publishing.

Rose, Nikolas. 1993. "Government, Authority and Expertise in Advanced Liberalism." *Economy and Society* 22, 3 (August): 283–99.

_____. 1996. "Governing 'Advanced' Liberal Democracies." In A. Barry, T. Osborne and N. Rose (eds.), *Foucault and Political Reason: Liberalism, Neo-liberalism and Rationalities of Government*. UCL Press.

_____. 1999. *Powers of Freedom: Reframing Political Thought*. Cambridge, UK: Cambridge University Press.

Ross, Rupert. 1996. *Returning to the Teachings: Exploring Aboriginal Justice*. Toronto: Penguin Books.

Sagi, Nana. 1980. *German Reparations: A History of the Negotiations*. Jerusalem, Israel: Magnes Press, Hebrew University.

Schrafstetter, Susanna. 2003. "The Diplomacy of *Wiedergutmachung*: Memory, the Cold War, and the Western European Victims of Nazism, 1956–1964." *Holocaust and Genocide Studies* 17, Winter: 459–79.

References

Sebba, Leslie. 1980. "The Reparations Agreements: A New Perspective." *Annals of the American Academy of Political and Social* Science 450: 202–12.

Selva, L.H., and R.M. Böhm. 1987. "A Critical Examination of the Informalism Experiment in the Administration of Justice." *Crime and Social Justice* 29: 43–57.

Shapland, J., A. Atkinson, H. Atkinson, E. Colledge, J. Dignan, M. Howes, J. Johnstone, G. Robinson, and A. Sorsby. 2006. "Situating Restorative Justice Within Criminal Justice." *Theoretical Criminology* 10, 4: 505–32.

Sharpe, Susan. 2004. "How Large Should the Restorative Justice 'Tent' Be?" In H. Zehr and B. Toews (eds.), *Critical Issues in Restorative Justice.* Cullompton, UK: Willan Publishing.

_____. 2007. "The Idea of Reparation." In G. Johnstone and D.W. Van Ness (eds.), *Handbook of Restorative Justice.* Cullompton, UK: Willan Publishing.

Shonholtz, Raymond. 1984. "Neighborhood Justice Systems: Work, Structure and Guiding Principles." *Mediation Quarterly* 5: 3–30.

Simmel, Georg. 1908. *The Sociology of Georg Simmel.* (K. Wolff, ed.) New York: Free Press.

Skelton, Ann, and Cheryl Frank. 2004. "How Does Restorative Justice Address Human Rights and Due Process Issues?" In H. Zehr and B. Toews (eds.), *Critical Issues in Restorative Justice.* Cullompton. UK: Willan Publishing.

Stern, Vivian. 2006. *Creating Criminals: Prisons and People in a Market Society.* London: Zed Books.

Strang, Heather. 2001. *Victim Participation in a Restorative Justice Process.* Oxford: Oxford University Press.

Stuart, Barry. 1996. "Circle Sentencing: Turning Swords into Ploughshares." In B. Galaway and J. Hudson (eds.), *Restorative Justice: International Perspectives.* Monsey, NY: Criminal Justice Press.

Stuart, Barry, and Kay Pranis. 2006. "Peacemaking Circles: Reflections on Principal Features and Primary Outcomes." In D. Sullivan and L. Tifft (eds.), *Handbook of Restorative Justice: A Global Perspective.* London and New York: Routledge.

Sullivan, Dennis, and Larry Tifft. 2001. *Restorative Justice: Healing the Foundations of Our Everyday Lives.* Monsey, NY: Willow Tree.

_____. 2006. "Introduction: The Healing Dimension of Restorative Justice: A One-World body." In D. Sullivan and L. Tifft (eds.), *Handbook of Restorative Justice: A Global Perspective.* London and New York: Routledge.

Sykes, Gresham M., and David Matza. 1957. "Techniques of Neitralization: A Theory of Delinquency." *American Sociological Review* 22, 6: 664–70.

Tavuchis, Nicholas. 1991. *Mea Culpa: A Sociology of Apology and Reconciliation.* Stanford. CA: Stanford University Press.

Teitel, Ruti. 2000. *Transitional Justice.* New York: Oxford University Press.

Thom, Brian. 2006. "The Paradox of Boundaries in Coast Salish Territories." Paper presented at Indigenous Cartographies and Representational Politics; an International Conference. Ithaca, NY: Cornell University, March 3–5.

Tickell, A., and J.A. Peck. 1995. "Social Regulation After Fordism: Regulation Theory, Neoliberalism and the Global–Local Nexus." *Economy and Society* 24, 3, August: 357–86.

Toews, Barb, and Howard Zehr. 2004. "Preface." In H. Zehr and B. Toews (eds.), *Critical Issues in Restorative Justice.* Cullompton, UK: Willan Publishing.

Torpey, John. 2001. "'Making Whole What has been Smashed': Reflections on Reparations." *The Journal of Modern History* 73, June: 333–58.

_____. 2003. "Introduction." In J. Torpey (ed.), *Politics and the Past*. Oxford: Rowman and Littlefield Publishers.

_____. 2006. *Making Whole What has Been Smashed: On Reparations Politics*. Cambridge, MA: Harvard University Press.

Turk, Austin. 1969. *Criminality and Legal Order*. Chicago: Rand McNally.

Tutu, Desmond. 1999. *No Future Without Forgiveness*. New York: Image, Doubleday.

Umbreit, Mark, Robert B. Coates, and Betty Vos. 2006. "Victim Offender Mediation: An Evolving Evidence-Based Practice." In D. Sullivan and L. Tifft (eds.), *Handbook of Restorative Justice: A Global Perspective*. London and New York: Routledge.

Umbreit, Mark, and Howard Zehr. 1996. "Restorative Family Group Conferences: Differing Models and Guidelines for Practice." *Federal Probation* 60, 3: 24–9.

United Nations. 2007. *Handbook of Restorative Justice Programs*. New York: United Nations.

United Nations Economic and Social Council. 2000. *Basic Principles on the Use of Restorative Justice Programmes in Criminal Matters, Resolutions and Decisions*. Adopted by the Social Council and its Substantive Session of 2002/12. <http://www.library.dal.ca/law/Guides/RestPathfinder/ RestorativeDeclarationpdf.pdf>

Van Ness, Daniel. 1993. "New Wine in Old Wine Wineskins: Four Challenges of Restorative Justice." *Criminal Law Forum* 4, 2: 251–76.

Van Ness, Daniel, and Karen Heetderks Strong. 2002. *Restoring Justice*. Cincinnati: Anderson.

Villa-Vicencio, Charles. 2006. "Transitional Justice, Restoration, and Prosecution." In D. Sullivan and L. Tifft (eds.), *Handbook of Restorative Justice: A Global Perspective*. London and New York: Routledge.

Wacquant, Loïc. 2001. "The Penalization of Poverty and the Rise of Neoliberalism." *European Journal on Criminal Policy and Research* 9, 4 (Winter): 401–12.

_____. 2004. "Critical Thought as Solvent of Doxa." *Constellations* 11, 1 (Spring): 97–101.

Walgrave, Lode. 2002. "From Community to Domination: In Search of Social Values for Restorative Justice." In E. Weitekamp and H.J. Kerner (eds.), *Restorative Justice: Theoretical Foundations*. Cullompton, UK: Willan Publishing.

_____. 2004. "Has Restorative Justice Theory Appropriately Responded to Retribution Theory and Impulses?" In H. Zehr and B. Toews (eds.), *Critical Issues in Restorative Justice*. Cullompton, UK: Willan Publishing.

Walkate, Sandra. 1989. *Victimology: the Victim and the Criminal Justice Process*. London: Unwin Hyman.

_____. 2006. "Changing Boundaries of the 'Victim' in Restorative Justice: So Who is the Victim Now?" In D. Sullivan and L. Tifft (eds.), *Handbook of Restorative Justice: A Global Perspective*. London and New York: Routledge.

Weber, Max. 1946. *From Max Weber: Essays in Sociology*. (H.H. Gerth and C. Wright Mills eds.) New York: Oxford University Press.

Weisel, Elie. 2006 [1972]. *Night*. New York: Hill and Wang.

Weitekamp, Elmar. 2003. "The History of Restorative Justice." In G. Johnstone (ed.), *A Restorative Justice Reader*, Cullompton, UK: Willan.

White, Rob. 2008. "Restorative Justice, Inequality, and Social Change." In C. Brooks and B. Schissel (eds.), *Marginality & Condemnation: An Introduction to Criminology*. Second edition. Black Point, NS and Winnipeg, Manitoba: Fernwood Publishing.

Wiebe, Rudy, and Yvonne Johnson. 1999. *Stolen Life: The Journey of a Cree Woman*. Toronto: A.A. Knopf Canada.

References

Wilson, Richard. 2001. *The Politics of Truth and Reconciliation in South Africa: Legitimizing the Post-Apartheid State*. Cambridge, UK: Cambridge University Press.

Woolford, Andrew. 2005. *Between Justice and Certainty: Treaty-Making in British Columbia*. Vancouver: University of British Columbia Press.

Woolford, Andrew, and R.S. Ratner. 2003. "Nomadic Justice: Restorative Justice on the Margins of Law." *Social Justice* 30: 177–94.

_____. 2005. "Selling Mediation: The Marketing of Alternative Dispute Resolution." *Peace and Conflict Studies Journal* 12, 1: 1–21.

_____. 2008a. *Informal Reckonings: Conflict Resolution in Mediation, Restorative Justice and Reparation*. London: Routledge-Cavendish.

_____. 2008b. "Mediation Games: Justice Frames." In S. Byrne, J. Senehi, D. Sandole, and I. Staroste-Sandole (eds.), *Conflict Resolution: Core Concepts, Theories, Approaches and Practices*. London: Routledge.

Woolford, Andrew, and Stefan Wolejszo. 2006. "Collecting on Moral Debts: Reparations, The Holocaust, and the Porrajmos." *Law & Society Review* 40, 4: 871–902.

Wright, Martin. 1991. *Justice for Victims and Offenders: A Restorative Response to Crime*. Milton Keynes: Open UP.

Wright, Martin, and Guy Masters. 2002. "Justified Criticism, Misunderstanding, or Important Steps on the Road to Acceptance." In E. Weitkamp and H. Kerner (eds.), *Restorative Justice: Theoretical Foundations*. Cullompton, UK: Willan Publishing.

Yazzie, R., and J.W. Zion. 2003. "Navajo Restorative Justice: The Law of Equality and Justice." In G. Johnstone (ed.), *A Restorative Justice Reader: Texts, Sources, Context*. Cullompton, UK: Willan Publishing.

Zehr, Howard. 1990. *Changing Lenses: A New Focus for Crime and Justice*. Scottdale, PA: Herald.

_____. 1995. "Justice Paradigm Shift? Vales and Visions in the Reform Process." *Mediation Quarterly* 12, 3 (Spring): 207–16.

Zernova, Margarita, and Martin Wright. 2007. "Alternative Visions of Restorative Justice." In G. Johnstone and D.W. Van Ness (eds.), *Handbook of Restorative Justice*. Cullompton, UK: Willan Publishing.

Zweig, Ronald W. 1987. *German Reparations and the Jewish World: A History of the Claims Conference*. Boulder, CO: Westview Press.